POWER HUNGRY

POWER HUNGRY

STRATEGIC INVESTING IN TELECOMMUNICATIONS, UTILITIES, AND OTHER ESSENTIAL SERVICES

ROGER S. CONRAD

John Wiley & Sons, Inc.

Published by John Wiley & Sons, Inc.
Published simultaneously in Canada.

This publication is designed to provide accurate and authoritative
information in regard to the subject matter covered. It is sold with the
understanding that the publisher is not engaged in rendering professional
services. If professional advice or other expert assistance is required, the
services of a competent professional person should be sought.

Library of Congress Cataloging-in-Publication Data:

Conrad, Roger S.
    Power hungry : strategic investing in telecommunications, utilities &
other essential services / by Roger S. Conrad.
        p.   cm.
    Includes index.
    ISBN 0-471-44295-X (cloth : alk. paper)
        1. Stocks—Prices—United States.   2. Electric utilities—United States.
    3. Telecommunication—United States.   4. Investments—United States.
    I. Title.

HG4915 .C66 2002

332.63'22—dc21   2001045633

Printed in the United States of America.

10 9 8 7 6 5 4 3 2 1

To Sarah, Nate, and Annlouise

Contents

Contents

Acknowledgments

I would like to first thank my editor at John Wiley & Sons, Inc., Debby Englander; my agent Robert DiForio; and KCI publisher Walter Pearce for enabling this project to become a reality. I owe a major debt of gratitude to my KCI editor Gregg Early, who gave me the needed push to get started and whose careful reading and editing at every stage kept the book in focus. Thanks also to my artist Trae Turner for her help preparing the many charts and graphs and for keeping me on schedule, and to all those who graciously consented to be interviewed for the book and/or reviewed it. I literally couldn't have written it without you.

No list of acknowledgments for this book would be complete without a heartfelt thanks to Allie Ash, who gave me a start in the investment newsletter business, and to my friend Stephen Leeb, whose counsel has enabled me to grow into it. Last but not least, thanks to all my colleagues at KCI Communications, past and present.

Introduction

When I began writing my advisory *Utility Forecaster* in 1989, analyzing the utility industry for investors was easy. Dividend safety was my one and only priority. My research focused on the regulators who set utilities' rates, and whether the need for a rate increase posed a threat to dividends.

The average utility CEO's job was also uncomplicated. As long as regulators were friendly, companies could count on a payoff from virtually any investment they made. In fact, as one executive joked to me privately, it was the only business where he could boost profits by buying a new set of office furniture.

However, over the past decade or so, that world has been turned upside down. Convinced that America's electricity, gas, communications, and water could be provided more efficiently and cheaply in a competitive market, state and federal lawmakers have thrown out the rules put in place during the Great Depression of the 1930s. The unchallenged monopolies of more than 60 years have been broken, and new competitors have entered the market for the first time since the early 1900s.

The results have shocked the world. Far from falling apart and fading away, the former monopolies have become more powerful than ever. Companies that once grew revenue and earnings by 3 percent a year, or less, are now enjoying growth of 10 percent and up.

Instead of multiplying the ranks of would-be competitors, the need to get bigger to meet and beat the new competition has triggered a wave of more than 100 utility mergers. Industries once made up of protected local fiefdoms are now the battlegrounds of a handful of giants with global reach.

Since the mid-1990s, the seven Baby Bells, offspring of the 1984 breakup of AT&T, have merged into four. Competition and consolidation have winnowed the ranks of major U.S. cellular providers to a half dozen. And a flurry of deals has shrunk the number of major electric and gas companies by a full third.

The promise of lower rates was the key selling point of this deregulation. But even as monopoly-era "inefficiencies" have been squeezed out, consumers across the nation have seen their electric and gas bills multiply. The average American's heating bill, for example, virtually doubled during the winter of 2000–2001, as tight natural gas supplies pushed rates sharply higher.

For electricity, citizens of San Diego, the first American city to be fully deregulated, saw their rates triple over the summer of 2000 (see Figure I.1). Like citizens of a third-world nation, Californians statewide now suffer rolling blackouts and face massive rate hikes and tax increases to keep their major utilities in business. Throughout the Northeast, electric rates have risen as higher gas prices and scarce power-generating capacity have driven wholesale costs into the stratosphere. In fact, wholesale power prices in eight of the eleven largest markets nationwide more than doubled between 1997 and 2000.

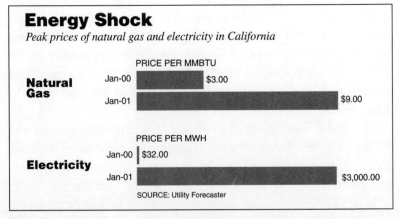

Figure I.1

The aftermath of the 1996 Telecommunications Act has seen the development of myriad new products and services, as the former monopolies have awakened to the profit motive, but the flurry of new entrants attracted by deregulation has dried up. Many fry have found they simply don't have the resources to compete, a fact driven home by the sharp decline in small telecoms' stock prices in 2000–2001. That's left the industry increasingly concentrated in the hands of the biggest players, the most successful of which have been the remaining Baby Bells.

As for new services, contrary to the promises of deregulation advocates, only a minority of Americans can afford the $400 or more in monthly bills needed to pay for cellular, Internet, cable television, call waiting, caller ID, and other popular services. In fact, most have shown little interest in the high-speed broadband services touted as the country's communications bridge to the twenty-first century.

New competitors were supposed to bring down the cost of basic local and long-distance service, but because they've focused on large users, millions of low-volume users have actually seen their phone bills rise over the past few years under deregulation. Subsidies that once held basic rates low in poor and rural areas have been abandoned or eliminated.

Moreover, as companies have focused on well-heeled customers who can afford to pay for advanced services, they've downsized, laying off thousands of workers. As a result, overall service quality has declined, as evidenced by the record number of complaints filed with now mostly toothless state regulatory agencies. With every vaunted advance in technology, increasing numbers of consumers are being left on the wrong side of a digital divide.

Investors have found the activity in utility stocks under deregulation just as unexpected. The doomsday scenario envisioned for the former monopolies hasn't happened. Instead, the best companies have become growth stocks (see Figure I.2) and the worst-run utilities are in a desperate race against time to merge with a more powerful competitor, or else face extinction.

The upshot: Picking utility stocks is more lucrative than at any time since the 1920s. It's a lot harder separating the wheat from the chaff, however. Those who simply buy the local utility without

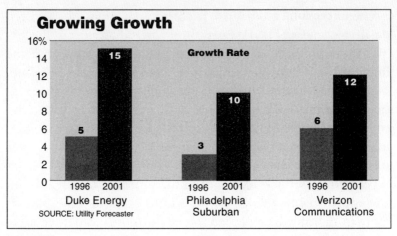

Figure I.2

thinking are more likely to pick up a dog. In fact, many companies
are no longer even locally owned, but are subsidiaries of budding
multinationals based in Atlanta, Houston, Charlotte, and London.

MISSING THE POINT

Deregulation's unexpected results have sparked a heated public
debate over who's to blame. Proponents of competition have
accused policymakers of not going far enough, changing only
parts of systems while leaving the basis of the old monopoly systems intact.

Consumer advocates have called flawed the entire concept of
opening regulated essential service industries to competition.
Others, particularly would-be competitors, have faulted the utilities themselves for thwarting needed changes. And utilities, in
turn, have blamed regulation for tying their hands and consumers for being unwilling to pay the true cost of service.

Not surprisingly, all of these critiques have some merit. But
proponents and detractors alike have missed the most important
point of utility deregulation: Opening markets doesn't automatically cut rates or improve service. It simply ensures money will
flow where it's needed most. It flows most easily through big,
powerful companies to meet the needs of heavy users of services.

Moving capital efficiently will ensure lower rates and better service in the long haul, but free markets are often bumpy, particularly when there's an imbalance between supply and demand.

Until the 1930s, there were few limits on how utilities conducted their business. Companies expanded rapidly through acquisitions to gain financial strength and greater economies of scale, allowing them to cut costs. Ultimately, virtually the nation's entire energy grid wound up in the hands of J.P. Morgan. Water became the province of giant, municipally owned monopolies. Communications became the domain of one of the most powerful companies in the history of the world, AT&T. The ride was rough, but in the process, America's utilities transformed society. Electric power, natural gas, telecommunications, and clean water became universal services, rather than the exclusive privilege of the wealthiest.

Landmark federal legislation passed during the 1930s created a check on utilities' growing power: regulation. Utilities remained monopolies, but state, local, and federal officials had new powers to ensure they operated in the public interest, and the prices of utility services were strictly controlled. In energy, the multinational empires dissolved into regional units.

Over the next 50 years, utilities continued to meet the needs of customers, but capital flows followed regulators' edicts rather than market forces, and inefficiencies crept in. By the 1980s, capital flow had all but dried up in energy, as well as in communications and water.

The deregulation trend of the past 20 years has gradually stripped away the power of regulators. Once again, a handful of companies are rapidly taking over energy, communications, and water. Size is becoming evermore critical to success, both for utilities and their customers, and the price of utility services is once again fluctuating with supply and demand.

The good news is that investment is once again starting to flow back into these industries, providing critical improvements needed for America's economy into the twenty-first century.

THE SHAPE OF CHANGE

The architects of the current brand of deregulation, of course, sold the public only on deregulation's good points while ignoring its bad ones. As they persistently lobbied state and federal politicians to get what they wanted, they fed the public platitudes about how deregulation was guaranteed to bring low rates, as it had for airlines and other industries. Hungry to bring down rates, consumer groups swallowed it hook, line, and sinker.

Ironically, the only real opponents of deregulation were the utilities themselves. As their objections were brushed aside as self-serving, though, they began to focus on getting the best possible deal on the transition to deregulation.

As the deregulation debate unfolded, there was no real discussion of the most important issue: what kind of system would evolve under deregulation. As they crafted the rules for the transition to competition, the negotiators ignored the lessons learned from utilities' preregulation era. Consequently, they were woefully unprepared when markets began to shape events.

In the natural gas and electric industries, the initial proponents of deregulation were principally large users of energy, who were anxious to bring down their utility bills to make themselves more competitive globally. Multinational corporations, especially heavy industry like automakers, had chafed for years under the monopoly system that subsidized small consumers at their expense. Deregulation was their chance to bring down their own rates, they thought, and whether the resulting burden fell on consumers or utilities did not matter.

During the 1980s, the big boys' mouthpieces were professional lobbying groups like the Electricity Consumers Resource Council (ELCON), who tirelessly argued their cause with anyone who would listen. Their breakthrough came in late 1993, when California regulators floated a plan to open the state's electricity market to all comers. The proponents intended for the burden of the transition to be borne by the utilities, supposedly as the price for decades of bad management.

After the California bombshell, dozens of states announced their intention to bust up their utility monopolies. Swiftly recognizing a threat to their very survival, utility companies leaped into action. Led by a chorus of lobbying groups, including the Edison Electric Institute, utilities mounted a swift counterattack, claiming radical deregulation would be an unlawful taking of private property, and threatened to tie up any change they didn't approve in the courts. Many used their substantial influence in state capitals to quash or at least delay legislation.

In California, the utilities' point man was John Bryson, CEO of SCE Corp., parent company of Southern California Edison. A former regulator, Bryson saw from the beginning that deregulation was inevitable and instead focused his firepower on ensuring utilities would recover their "stranded costs." These were investments made under the monopoly era, such as nuclear plants and renewable energy technology, which Wall Street predicted would be "uncompetitive" without regulatory protection.

Bryson quickly found an ally in California State Senator Steve Peace, who ultimately became the principal architect of the state's 1996 deregulation law. Peace was aware that utilities could still disrupt the state's plans for deregulation. By joining forces with Bryson, he dramatically increased the odds of competitive legislation passing and made less likely a challenge by the state's other major utilities—Pacific Gas and Electric and San Diego Gas and Electric.

Like most adversarial agreements, the compromise reached offered something for everyone involved. Consumers were required to shoulder the burden of stranded costs, which were reduced by a combination of sales of power plants and the issuing of bonds to refinance the supposed uneconomic assets on utilities' books. In return, utilities granted consumers an unprecedented up-front 10 percent rate cut and a rate freeze until their stranded costs were recovered. Competition was phased in quickly, beginning with the large users who had most pushed for change.

The California compromise shifted the tenor of the deregulation debate around the country. And, after the Republicans' 1994 electoral coup on the state and federal level, the deal was sealed. Negotiations primarily between utilities and their largest customers have produced deregulation plans, based on the Golden State blueprint, in more than two dozen states. The Federal Energy Regulatory Commission, the federal watchdog of the energy industry, has adopted a similar tack for cases under its jurisdiction. Proposed legislation on the federal level, though deadlocked by Washington's general gridlock, has basically followed the same lines.

Unfortunately, the California compromise, and many of the similar deals inked around the country, had a fatal flaw: The players all took for granted one of the central tenets of deregulation theory— that power rates would automatically fall following deregulation. Worse still, there was no fallback plan in case they were wrong. As a result, the compromise was extremely vulnerable to what was rapidly emerging as the country's biggest energy problem: the lack of new power plants, the natural gas to run them, and transmission lines to carry the electricity to market (see Figure I.3).

Tough environmental standards and uncertain deregulation plans gave American utilities a strong incentive not to build power plants in the 1980s and 1990s, particularly in the Northeast and California. Many companies that built nuclear plants in the 1980s, for example, saw a large percentage of their construction costs ruled unrecoverable by regulators, forcing them to write off billions in previously booked assets and ultimately to commit the most unforgivable sin in investors' eyes: cutting dividends.

By the early 1990s, credit-rating agencies like Standard & Poor's and Moody's were routinely downgrading utilities that were building power plants, in anticipation of regulator-ordered writeoffs. In fact, one of my criteria for picking utility stocks back then was finding companies that didn't need or didn't plan to build power plants.

In California, the disincentive to build reached a peak when the deregulation compromise forced the former monopolies to sell their existing generating capacity. Other states again parroted California's mandate, with the idea that selling plants would pre-

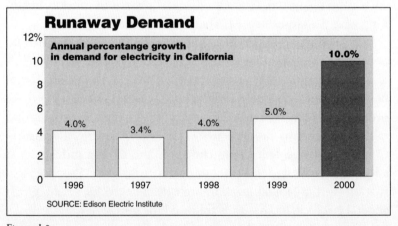

Figure I.3

vent utilities from unfairly favoring their own generation in a deregulated market. In theory, utilities would become pure distributors of power, treating all generators equally to provide only the lowest-cost electricity to consumers.

However, the reality was quite different. With perfectly good plants up for sale, power companies anxious to enter the Golden State, like Carolina-based Duke Energy, bought existing power plants instead of building new ones. Then, when population growth and the rise of e-commerce set off an explosion in demand for electricity, the state still lacked the new power plants to meet it.

Misunderstanding the fundamental nature of what deregulation really meant, therefore, had the worst possible result. The players were unable to meet their most important responsibility: ensuring there was enough power generated to keep the lights on. That's the essential problem that's buried California's utilities in a sea of red ink, triggered statewide blackouts, and created a huge financial liability that ultimately will be borne by consumers and taxpayers.

The good news is shortages are not so acute elsewhere, particularly with other states encouraging the development of new plants to avoid following the Golden State's example. The bad news is that the blame game has prevented California from solving its problems and, despite new plants coming online, severe weather could still set off a similar crisis in other states.

While energy deregulation has been a state-by-state story, the federal government carried out the overhaul of America's communications system. The Telecommunications Act of 1996 was one of the most intensely lobbied bills in history. The impetus was a desire by politicians and others to bring the benefits of lower rates, brought by competition in the long-distance telephone business since the breakup of AT&T, to the local phone industry.

Just as with energy, the players and policymakers fundamentally misunderstood what they were doing by replacing regulation with markets. The Act eventually boiled down to a compromise between the principal combatants, the two parties with the most to gain or lose: local phone monopolies led by the Baby Bells and the long-distance phone oligopoly led by AT&T. The result was identical to what happened under energy deregulation. Each party won enough concessions to keep it happy.

After the Republicans took control of Congress in 1994, the political capital of communications providers rose dramatically. The most significant change was probusiness Virginian Thomas Bliley Jr., replacing proconsumer Massachusetts' Edward Markey as the principal telecom mover and shaker in the U.S. House of Representatives.

Bliley's goal was to pass long-stalled legislation to bring the benefits of competition to communications before the 1996 election. With him in charge, the key question became who would get more from the act, the local service monopolies or the long-distance oligopoly. After the Clinton administration gave a final push, the 1996 Telecommunications Act literally had something for everyone, protecting the Baby Bells while opening their markets.

Since 1996, long-distance rates have continued to fall, and competition has made major inroads into the former local monopolies, as well. Much of the country, however, has been left out in the cold. In fact, while wealthy Americans are more connected than ever, a growing minority is finding itself doomed to higher rates for basic services while unable to afford the wonders of the Internet age. Most important, power in the industry has become increasingly concentrated in the hands of a few companies, those forecasted by deregulation proponents to suffer the most under competition: the Baby Bells themselves.

TAKING ROOT

Power outages, clean-water scares, downed phone lines, and soaring communications costs are stark reminders of just how essential energy, communications, and water services are to twenty-first-century American life. Unfortunately, these problems are likely to grow more prevalent over the next decade.

Not all the blame can be laid at the foot of deregulation. In fact *real* competition is likely to rectify many of the problems we're seeing now. Solving the problem of electricity shortages depends on attracting the capital to build more power plants. That's most likely to happen if energy utilities are allowed to grow large and powerful enough to deploy resources on a national, and even global, scale.

Technological advances that ensure better delivery of cheaper, more reliable, essential services are also far more likely to be made under competition than regulation. Fuel cells and other technologies to improve the reliability of power flows will be developed only if electricity is relatively scarce and prices are high. Ditto with alternative energies like solar, wind, and geothermal, which have been too expensive relative to natural gas and other fuels. Again, they're far more likely to be developed by giants with the cash to do the job than impoverished pygmies.

In telecommunications, the growing digital divide between those who can afford to spend $400-plus a month on communications and those barely able to afford local service will also narrow over time as new products proliferate and technology increases the number of ways to make a call. This, too, is far more likely to take place under market rate deregulation than reregulation as the industry attracts capital and as companies gain the heft to deploy assets effectively. Wireless service in many developing nations is expanding at a torrid clip as a far cheaper alternative to installing new landlines. Multinational wireless providers like Vodafone are using their superior access to capital and global economies of scale to expand usage and market share.

In water, deregulation of distribution is unlikely, given the physical constraints of transporting the liquid, but municipal monopolies that currently dominate the industry are finding it too difficult to raise and spend the billions needed to meet rising water quality standards, so they're turning to investor-owned utilities to do the job. Here, too, increased concentration of power is allowing industry to deploy capital where it's needed most to provide a better product at a more affordable price.

TURNING BACK THE CLOCK

The alternative to continuing on the path to deregulation is of course reregulation. California's power crisis has already induced the state and the federal government to take a greater role. Even John Bryson has questioned whether consumers are ready to embrace a fully deregulated market, as have other Golden State deregulation advocates. Many states have put their energy deregulation plans on hold, pending evaluation of California's woes.

Putting the genie back into the bottle will prove even more difficult than changing the system in the first place, for every action government takes to regulate power prices risks scaring away new power plant development. The more dramatic the action, the less investment there will be and the worse future shortages will become.

In telecommunications, discontent has focused on the wave of industry megamergers, climaxing in U.S. and European regulators blocking Worldcom's prospective merger with Sprint in 2000. Officials cited overconcentration of market share in the U.S. long-distance market as the basis of their rejection. In the aftermath, stocks of all long-distance providers crashed and burned.

In addition, the two biggest long-distance companies—AT&T and Worldcom—seem to be plotting a withdrawal from the business via spinoffs or an outright sale of their operations. Consequently, the end result of just one merger rejection is even greater concentration of long-distance market power, very likely in the hands of Baby Bells, as they win federal permission to enter the business, or foreign telecom giants.

Industrywide attempts to overturn deregulation on the state or federal level could trigger panic-selling of utility stocks, causing a massive capital outflow from the industry just when the money is needed most to finance infrastructure growth. In 1993 to 1994, energy utility stocks suffered their worst bear market since the early 1970s, as investors worried that deregulation would produce dividend cuts and outright bankruptcies. Only the California compromise triggered their recovery. Telecom stocks suffered a similar meltdown in 2000, as did energy utilities in early 2001, when California's crisis raised reregulation risk.

There's also the question of whether turning back the clock is possible. Higher rates have aroused the ire of the public, particularly in California, and spurred demands for price controls, but there's nothing even approaching a consensus for fixing the underlying problem. Even in California, for example, tempers cooled along with the temperature in the mild summer of 2001. Referenda to overturn energy deregulation in California and Massachusetts in recent years have garnered little support, and the proderegulation Bush administration is certain to block anything on the federal level for at least the next few years.

Other barriers to reversing change include the considerable vested interests in maintaining and expanding deregulation, such as major multinational consumers and the utilities themselves. Any attempt to turn back the clock would require years of closed-door negotiations, or else risk even more time-consuming court challenges. More likely, we'll see federal legislation, particularly in energy, to tackle the obvious problems of deregulation while leaving its essence intact.

BIGGER IS BETTER

The bottom line is that utility deregulation is here to stay, which means the utility industry will be governed by supply and demand. In the new order, size will spell success, and failure to grow will mean death.

Heavy users of energy and telecom services will enjoy the lion's share of lower rates and new services. Utilities will compete on a global basis for the business of large corporations, where a single new customer can bring billions of dollars in new revenue. Well-heeled consumers will reap the benefits of telecom technology. They'll also have access to distributed generation and more reliable energy technologies designed to keep the lights on at all times, including during power outages.

Contrary to the pronouncements of free-market ideologues, the average consumer will enjoy few of deregulation's benefits, at least at first. Those accustomed to paying less than $100 a month for energy and communications will keep paying higher rates as fewer providers compete for their business. Service quality will be similarly lopsided, with the most affluent enjoying the best and others competing for scraps. Those in the poorest areas could find themselves increasingly in the dark as power blackouts and brownouts become more frequent for less-preferred customers.

Competition in the utility business won't help the little guy either. Large companies able to control their supplies and costs will increasingly win out over small ones, who have little influence over either. Companies with the reach and resources to compete on a global playing field are increasingly dominating the fastest-growing, most competitive and potentially lucrative utility businesses, such as

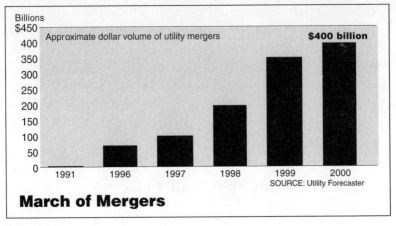

Figure I.4

cellular and electricity trading, as small players withdraw or are taken over. The need for size is what's behind the ongoing tidal wave of utility mergers. See Figure I.4 for dollar volume of utility mergers. Fry that don't find a partner soon are doomed.

This book will serve as a guide for navigating this new era. The first few chapters examine how the energy, communications, and water industries are shaping up for the future, including the challenges they face and the opportunities they present. I spotlight who's likely to win and lose, and where we're likely to go from here.

As consumers have found out all too painfully in the past few years, deregulating communications, energy, and water doesn't mean lower rates, at least not immediately. However, there are considerable opportunities to profit from the changes in essential services by investing in select companies.

The remaining chapters identify big and small companies offering long-term investors the prospect of massive returns in coming years, as they grab the lion's share of newly opened markets. I'll also show how to construct your own model portfolio of these stocks commission-free.

The need for companies to get bigger to survive and thrive in the new era means there will be many more utility mergers. I profile two great ways to take advantage of these mergers, as well as strategies that helped readers of my advisory *Utility Forecaster* profit enormously in the past few years.

CHAPTER 1

....

A Shock to the System

In the late 1970s, America was gripped by a paralyzing energy crisis. Gasoline was suddenly breaking the family budget. Gas lines and outright shortages were common. The public was nearing open revolt.

President Jimmy Carter declared the "moral equivalent of war" on the nation's growing dependence on imported oil, and the country turned down its thermostats in winter, up in summer, and bought smaller cars to meet the challenge.

A generation later, we're on the brink of an energy crisis even the Saudi Arabians are calling more serious. Oil prices have been on the move, breaking through 10-year highs. Even with the world's economies slumping in late 2001, humanity's appetite for black gold continues to increase, particularly in China. Despite oil-producing countries' willingness to pump to the last drop, and the slowdown in world growth in 2001, prices are more than twice those of the late 90s.

Oil supply isn't the only challenge, however. Today's looming energy crisis has another especially sharp edge: volatile electricity prices, punctuated by severe shortages of power in many regions of the country. For the first time since the Great Depression, the very ability of the nation's electric system to provide reliable power is at risk, even as it's needed more than ever to power the new economy.

In California, the summer of 2000 and the following winter brought the issue home to millions. Razor-thin reserve margins,

1

the cushion utilities have traditionally maintained in production capacity to meet emergencies, shrank to near zero. Rotating blackouts, transmission and distribution congestion, and price spikes as much as ten times normal levels were the result.

Only mild temperatures prevented similar breaches elsewhere in the country. Nonetheless, electricity prices spiked along the East Coast and throughout the Midwest as soaring demand overwhelmed supply. With demand rising at twice the rate of just a few years ago, these markets are also becoming extremely vulnerable to wild spikes, outages, and even full-scale shutdowns of overloaded systems.

A NEW PARADIGM

All this was part and parcel of the energy crisis of the 1970s. Just ask New Yorkers who survived the great blackout of 1974.

What's different this time around is deregulation and the effect it's having on power producers, investors, and especially consumers. With competition and market prices for power replacing regulated monopolies, consumers are no longer insulated from changes in electricity prices, and they're starting to feel the bite.

In San Diego, power prices tripled in summer 2000 from prior-year levels before the state imposed a freeze. Upstate, a shortage of power triggered rolling blackouts. Wholesale power prices have spiked to ten times the levels that prevailed in 1999. The Golden State's largest utility—PG&E—has filed Chapter 11 due to rolling up $9 billion in debt by purchasing power at sky-high prices and selling it at legally fixed rates to consumers.

With more power shortages looming in coming months, the crisis now threatens to literally black out the California economy, upsetting the nation's already weakened e-commerce industry and banking system. Politically pressured politicians and regulators have imposed price caps and mandatory rate cuts. Some are pushing for a complete overhaul of the state's deregulation plan. Whatever the government decides, chaos is sure to continue.

Farther up the coast, consumer discontent is raging in Washington and Oregon. Though neither state has yet opened its markets to competition, electric rates have soared over the past year.

The reason: Regional power producers have been exporting as much energy as they can to meet demand in California. Coupled with poor hydropower conditions, that's put a strain on local supplies and forced local utilities and their customers to pay up to three times the price for electricity of just a few years earlier.

As yet, the East has avoided energy shortages. Still, utilities from New York City to Maine have passed huge rate increases on to their customers due to the spiking price of purchased power. In summer 2000, for example, Consolidated Edison pushed through a 43 percent rate hike to cover its energy costs, provoking the ire of regulators and consumers and launching a government investigation of the company's rates and power suppliers. All this occurred in the context of a relatively mild summer. Things could get really ugly when the weather takes a more extreme turn in either winter or summer, as it surely will.

Runaway price increases and shortages have led to an epidemic of finger-pointing. The U.S. Department of Justice is investigating alleged energy price fixing in New York, New England, California, and the Midwest, where gasoline prices burst through $2 a gallon in early summer 2000. State regulators have joined in, particularly in California and New York, where some are calling for the government to limit utility profits.

Consumers and regulators alike are starting to eye the record earnings reaped by power generators across the country. States that have not yet broken up utility monopolies are asking Congress to exclude them from any future federal deregulation legislation. And even reregulation—derided as dinosaur socialism just a few years ago—has moved to the realm of respectability in industry debates.

The bad news is there's no end in sight for either volatile electricity prices or shortages. In fact, given the severity of the crisis and the deep-seated factors behind it, the situation will get worse before it gets better. The more dramatically regulators act to stanch rising rates, the greater the potential for disaster.

DEEP ROOTS

The roots of the current crisis run very deep in two directions. One is the ongoing explosion in demand for electricity, due mostly to the growth of the Internet, as well as population and economic growth. The other is the series of extremely disruptive changes that have turned the U.S. electric and gas utility systems on their ear over the past 20 years, dramatically shrinking power supplies.

Explosive demand for electricity in the latter 1990s came as a complete shock to most energy analysts. As recently as 1996, the Energy Information Administration projected power demand would grow just 2 percent a year in the world's developed countries through 2010. Their estimate was well below the 2.6 percent rate that prevailed between 1970 and 1993. Instead, power demand is increasing nearly 4 percent a year in many parts of the United States and shows every sign of accelerating even more. Despite sluggish economic growth in 2001, power demand still rose more than 3 percent (see Figure 1.1).

By some estimates, computers now consume 13 percent of power used in the United States, up from just 1 percent in 1993. If current trends hold, they'll suck down nearly half the nation's power by 2010.

A typical desktop computer consumes no more than a couple of lightbulbs of power. The key is volume. There are more than 100 million computers in the United States alone, with some 45.2 million sold in 1999. The more powerful these machines become, the more energy they use. The biggest energy users are web

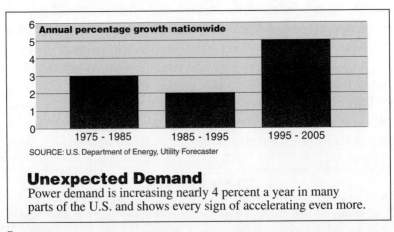

SOURCE: U.S. Department of Energy, Utility Forecaster

Unexpected Demand
Power demand is increasing nearly 4 percent a year in many parts of the U.S. and shows every sign of accelerating even more.

Figure 1.1

servers, the powerful computer banks that run the Internet, the average one using enough power to run 25,000 homes, or eight 40-story office buildings. (See Figure 1.2.)

Even with the rest of the economy just holding its own, growing computer industry use adds up to a quantum leap in power demand. Annual demand growth nationwide will likely peak close to 5 percent over the next few years, as long as the economy avoids a severe recession. Even then, demand growth will be merely delayed. Based on that, the U.S. Department of Energy projects some 1,200 new power plants will have to be built by 2020 just to meet that new demand. That estimate could be even greater if the 10 percent demand growth recorded in California in 2000 returns.

DOE projections also don't include plants scheduled to be shut down over the next few years due to old age. Over 35 percent of the power plant capacity currently online in the United States is 35 years or older. In New England, 75 percent of the plants came online before 1972. Some estimate as much as 90 percent of current capacity will have to be replaced by 2015, and evidence suggests 40 percent of the nation's nuclear plants will be shut down before their licenses expire.

Put into perspective, we need almost half as many new power plants to be built in the next few years as are currently operating, just to meet conservative estimates of what new demand will be.

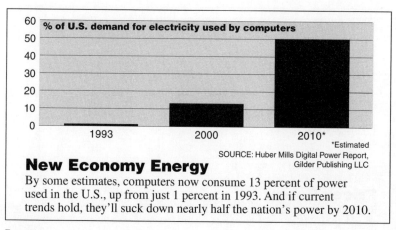

New Economy Energy

By some estimates, computers now consume 13 percent of power used in the U.S., up from just 1 percent in 1993. And if current trends hold, they'll suck down nearly half the nation's power by 2010.

Figure 1.2

The result has already been the biggest power plant building boom since the 1960s. Unfortunately, it won't come close to increasing supply enough to keep prices from rising.

During the last energy crisis, utilities were monopolies holding government-sanctioned franchises to provide electric and natural gas heating service to set territories. Coal was the fuel of choice for most power plants, but oil was used heavily. As oil prices soared, so did the desire of management, regulators, and consumers to shift to fuels with lower, more dependable costs. The result was an unprecedented building spree of nuclear power plants, with nearly 120 reactors licensed by the early 1990s.

Building these plants, however, proved costlier than in even the wildest imaginations of the industry's severest critics. Building cost overruns and expensive construction delays were common even before the 1979 near-catastrophe at the Three Mile Island nuclear plant near Harrisburg, Pennsylvania. After Three Mile Island, safety concerns triggered an explosion in costs upward from $1,135 per kilowatt of capacity for plants completed in 1980 to $4,590 by 1990, a more than fourfold increase (see Figure 1.3). Power that proponents had dubbed "too cheap to meter" in the 1950s had become too expensive for consumers and regulators to swallow.

At the same time nuclear power costs were skyrocketing, the prices of oil and other fossil fuels were cratering. A decade of

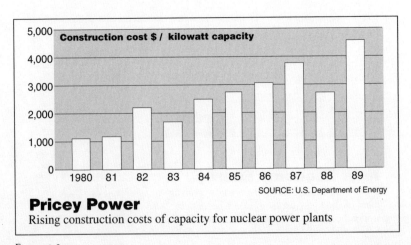

SOURCE: U.S. Department of Energy

Pricey Power
Rising construction costs of capacity for nuclear power plants

Figure 1.3

dramatically slower economic growth dampened oil demand worldwide, which combined with rising production levels in the North Sea to break the Organization of Petroleum Exporting Countries' (OPEC) stranglehold on oil prices. Oil took a final dive in 1986 from which it's only now recovering, as the Saudis abandoned their traditional role of propping up prices and triggered the collapse of OPEC.

Low fossil fuel prices and skyrocketing construction costs came to a head by the late 1980s and early 1990s. Under the monopoly franchise system, state and local regulators set electric rates. To recover their nuclear plant investments, utilities had to win regulators' approval for rate hikes.

Given that the public pays these officials' salaries—and elects them directly in many states—regulators' reaction was predictable: Nuke costs were met with skepticism that bordered on outright hostility. Starting with hefty writeoffs imposed on Union Electric for the cost of its Missouri-based Calloway plant, state regulators from New York to California and everywhere in between disallowed billions of dollars in utilities' construction expenses.

The result was nothing less than a financial catastrophe for dozens of utilities. Orders for new nuclear plants abruptly dried up in 1978, and some 60 plants on order were canceled. Companies were forced to cut and even eliminate dividends to reflect their reduced earnings power. Two companies—Public Service of New Hampshire and El Paso Electric—slid into bankruptcy. Utility stock prices plummeted and credit agencies like Moody's and Standard & Poor's slashed bond ratings across the board.

Worse still, the nuclear plant rate increases that regulators did grant provoked an outcry from consumers, particularly large industrial users. Even regulators in states like Oklahoma, where utilities had built no nuclear plants, began to launch so-called prudence reviews, questioning management decisions for even routine expenditures. Those found wanting by the often-shifting criteria were punished severely with rate cuts and customer refunds. Even companies that hadn't asked for rate hikes in years were forced to keep a constant vigil for fear of having their rates reviewed.

By the early 1990s, even the hint that a company would have to build power plants was enough to set off jitters on Wall Street. Most utility boards of directors avoided new building, preferring instead to buy the power they needed. What plants were built were smaller, peaking facilities designed to run only during periods of extremely high demand. New baseload capacity—huge plants meant to run all the time—was practically nonexistent.

ELECTRICS TAKE THE BAIT

It was in this environment that deregulation came to the utility industry. The urge to lift regulations on industry had been gaining steam since the late 1970s, when President Jimmy Carter, President Ronald Reagan, and British Prime Minister Margaret Thatcher first popularized it. In the United States, airlines, financial services, telecommunications, utilities, and others had operated under tight government scrutiny since the 1930s to guard against a repeat of that era's turmoil.

One by one, these industries were opened to competition as government controls lifted. The effect on consumers has been a mixed bag. Airline deregulation has brought the speed of air travel to the average citizen, while savings and loan deregulation triggered one of the greatest financial fiascoes of all time. Each opening emboldened the deregulators and encouraged industry players to seek change on their terms.

Electric utilities' turn came in the early 1990s. At the time, natural gas prices were scraping multidecade lows and new technology was emerging that allowed far faster construction of gas-fired plants than ever before. As a result, new power plants running on gas could be built and operated far more cheaply than the nuclear and coal plants that dominated electricity generation.

Deregulation proponents claimed that if the monopoly electric markets were opened to competition, a new breed of independent, savvy, and nimble nonutility producers would build a massive fleet of the state-of-the-art, natural gas–fired plants. The low-cost power generated would force utilities to cut the cost of power generated from their own plants, driving down rates and benefiting consumers and industry alike. All that was necessary, according to proponents, was to slash the regulations that had been in place since the Great Depression and allow the market to work its magic.

Estimates of the actual savings under full competition varied widely, but most projected a drop of at least 30 percent in consumers' rates, with the savings spread across the board to both large and small users. Some cited the experience in Argentina, one of the first electricity markets in the world opened to competition, where rates fell 40 percent as regulatory barriers came down.

Typical of the consensus of the times was Peter Navarro, author of the 1989 book *Creating and Destroying Comparative Advantage.* Navarro claimed in a winter 1996 *Harvard Business Review* article that rates would fall by 30 percent if the United States simply adopted less-onerous Japanese-style regulatory rules.

The D-men (deregulation-men or proponents) found a willing audience among major U.S. industrial concerns. Companies like General Motors and USX, for example, were facing ever-tightening global competition and were anxious to cut costs in all areas. Large users had long complained that they were subsidizing low residential rates by paying too much under the monopoly system, and since they used tremendous amounts of electric power, they were extremely interested in anything that would leverage their buying power. Under the umbrella of benign-sounding lobbying groups like the Electricity Consumers Resource Council, they used their political clout to bring about change in their favor.

Big users finally got their chance for change in April 1994, as California regulators announced a radical plan to transition the electric industry to competition. The state Public Service Commission proposed a system that would create a central spot market power pool into which all generators would sell their power. All customers were to have a choice of suppliers by 1997, and utilities were to sell their power plants and become pure transmission and distribution, or *wires-and-pipes,* companies.

In the weeks that followed, several states followed suit with their own plans to radically shake up the utility industry, and dozens more announced they were studying a potential shakeup of their local monopolies. Any expectation of rapid change, however, was soon dashed as problems emerged. The original

California proposal raised serious concerns about the state's interconnection with other states that were still operating under monopoly systems. That posed the danger of jurisdictional disputes with the Federal Energy Regulatory Commission (FERC), which directs federal energy policy.

The proposal had an even bigger problem: It completely undermined Wall Street's confidence in the utility industry nationwide. The key issue was stranded costs, capital expenses made by utilities under the monopoly era that, according to Wall Street, would not be economic under competition. Nuclear power plants were the most visible of these assets, but they also included contracts to purchase renewable energies that utilities had been forced by law to enter under the Public Utility Regulatory Power Act (PURPA), passed in 1978 as a way to get the country off imported oil.

By some estimates, stranded costs were equal to nearly half of utilities' total capital, and several times shareholder equity. Being forced to write off these costs outright would theoretically trigger dividend cuts, drastic restructuring, and even potential bankruptcies for the most heavily impacted, as formerly rock-solid companies suddenly would be in violation of financial covenants with lenders.

Stranded cost worries gave California utility stocks a quick 50 percent haircut in 1993 and 1994, but even companies in states not considering regulatory changes crashed and burned. The once safe and slow-moving Dow Utility Average fell from a high of 256 in autumn 1993 to a low of around 170 in late spring of 1994.

Bond ratings entered freefall as the credit agencies revised their rating systems to reflect what they thought was the emerging reality. Terrified, many of the safety-first investors who had traditionally purchased utility stocks and bonds panic-sold.

Even the utilities themselves had little confidence in their future under deregulation. In a 1995 survey of industry executives taken by the Washington International Energy Group, only 19 percent believed higher profits were likely in the changing environment, while 62 percent looked for falling earnings. Half of respondents forecasted an increase in utility bankruptcies and 73 percent predicted price wars, with companies forced to cut rates to the bone to keep customers (see Figure 1.4).

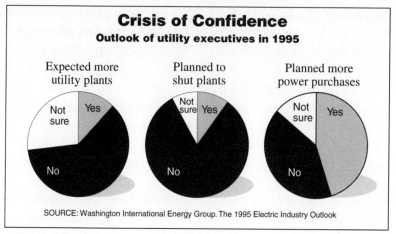

Figure 1.4

After the California proposal, utilities across the country found it more difficult to raise capital. Meanwhile, the growing uncertainty about what changes would occur made utility boards even more reluctant to approve large capital expenditures for new power plants.

Even the nonutility producers, whom deregulation proponents expected to flood the market, saw their capital sources wane. Most of these actually owed their livelihood to PURPA, which required utilities to buy independents' output at a premium in order to encourage new power sources. They were worried that deregulation would end PURPA and the profitable subsidies that kept them in business.

The level of panic peaked in 1997, when the U.S. Department of Energy released a study forecasting a wave of utility bankruptcy filings. Utilities, the study said, would be forced to "absorb revenue reductions exceeding 30 percent in some cases." And while the DOE stated its belief that the utility industry would remain solvent, it nonetheless reinforced the idea that these stocks were far too risky for the conservative investors who had traditionally owned them.

The crisis of confidence in the industry had a direct and chilling effect on the construction of new power plants. For example, a summer 2000 California Public Utility Commission report showed only 672 megawatts of new generation had been added to the state's system since 1996, compared with a 5,500-megawatt increase in demand. The situation was similar in other regions of the country.

The utility industry's crisis of confidence has persisted even under the new order for the utility industry. The result: Despite clear runaway demand for power, utilities and other power producers have been slow to commit the resources to meet it. While some companies like Calpine have been on building sprees in recent years, overall industry spending to build plants continues to lag behind projected demand growth, despite the overwhelming evidence that volatile power prices are here to stay.

The California compromise of 1996 basically set the rules for the new order nationwide. Led by Southern California Edison CEO John Bryson and the lobbying group, the Edison Electric Institute, the utilities fought and eventually won the only battle they really cared about: the issue of stranded cost recovery. Utilities were allowed to recover these by issuing stranded cost bonds in the amount of their estimated stranded assets. The bonds themselves were guaranteed by a surcharge imposed on all California residents, regardless of whether they chose a competitor for service.

Other states where utilities had large stranded costs—such as Illinois, Michigan, New Jersey, New York, Ohio, Pennsylvania, Texas, and most of New England—also allowed companies to issue stranded cost bonds financed by a rate surcharge. The result is that the financial risk to utilities of stranded costs has essentially been eliminated. In fact, for many companies recovery has amounted to a multibillion-dollar cash windfall that they've used to pay off debt as well as to make profitable new investments.

While they gave ground on the stranded cost issue, the most radical D-men ruled the day. In California, as elsewhere, consumers were granted an immediate 10 percent rate cut and five-year rate freeze. Competition was phased in immediately, with the objective of total deregulation in 2002. Utilities sold their power plants to third parties and turned their transmission systems over to an independent system operator, or ISO, and regulators' power to set rates was dramatically curtailed to emergencies.

Over the past six-plus years, some 25 states have enacted deregulation based on similar parameters. As a result, competition on the retail level is creeping in for two-thirds of the U.S. population, though two out of every three Americans were unaware of electric deregulation as recently as late 1997.

WHOLESALE CHANGES

Deregulation of America's wholesale market has happened even more quickly. Using powers gained from the Energy Act of 1992, the FERC has been pushing the envelope for change, shaking up transmission policy to make it easier to ship power around the nation. The lack of federal legislation for retail electric deregulation—due largely to a combination of ambivalence, general party politics, and gridlock—has limited the scope of what FERC can do. Nonetheless, the competition in the wholesale market continues to grow rapidly and shape the overall industry.

Under the monopoly system, wholesale power sales, which are mostly bulk power transactions to utilities, municipalities, and large industrial concerns, were largely conducted as a gentleman's agreement. Power-short utilities could count on power-rich neighbors to provide sufficient output in times of need, and at a rock-bottom price. Wholesale transactions were very low-margin deals, mostly transacted under long-term contracts between companies.

In contrast, wholesale markets today are one of the bloodiest shark pools in the world. Customers are fought over not just for their power sales, but for myriad other services as well. Profits depend on how well power marketers anticipate market changes and weather, control their costs, hedge their exposure to unforeseen conditions, maintain their financial strength, and above all build reservoirs of talented traders who understand the market.

On the retail level, things continue to move slowly, even in deregulated states. Most consumers have been reluctant to switch power suppliers even after being informed of their choices.

On the wholesale level, even a few minutes can be a lifetime for those buying and selling power. In fact, a rapidly growing percentage of this business is being transacted on the Internet through such companies as EnronOnline, now the largest e-commerce site in the world and arguably the most profitable as well.

Over the next five years, the fast-moving wholesale market will transform the larger retail market. Some companies will remain vertically integrated—both producing and distributing power—particularly in states where deregulation has been delayed, but most will decide to specialize in one area or another. Utility profits will be set by market forces, rather than established by regulators based on their costs.

In most of the 25 states opening to competition, the wires-and-pipes side of the business—managing the network that connects plants to customers—will remain regulated. The reason is no one wants multiple power lines running down their street. Operators of networks will receive a fee, set by regulators as a return on investment, from customers to access their networks. In contrast, the business of generating power will be fully competitive, with profits determined by a company's efficiency and the market price of power.

As is the case in the wholesale market, power marketing is the linchpin of the new retail system. Marketing companies line up the generators and the consumers of power, competing with each other to provide the most reliable and inexpensive service. Some own and operate their own power plants, while others simply buy what they need on the wholesale market. How much they'll earn depends on how well they manage their costs and risks, as well as on how many customers they attract (see Figure 1.5).

Pure wires-and-pipes companies are the lowest-risk segment of the new electricity industry, with extremely predictable revenue and profit streams. They're also the slowest-growing, since regulators still control their profitability. In fact, their only road to growth is signing on new customers.

Marketing and generation companies will reap huge rewards if they correctly perceive opportunities and capitalize on them. Companies like Duke Energy, Mirant, and UtiliCorp have already used their smarts to make a fortune in the wholesale market, particularly as electricity prices have gyrated wildly in recent years.

The downside of unregulated marketing is, of course, that returns are not set. Adverse market conditions, a poor decision, even a freak power plant outage can mortally wound a marketer if it's unprepared.

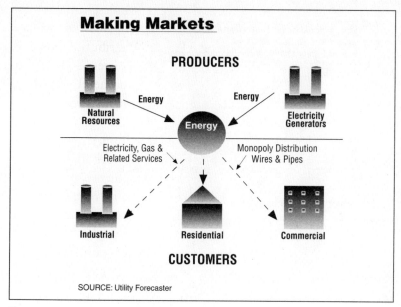

Making Markets

PRODUCERS

Natural Resources — Energy →

Energy ← Electricity Generators

Energy

Electricity, Gas & Related Services

Monopoly Distribution Wires & Pipes

Industrial   Residential   Commercial

CUSTOMERS

SOURCE: Utility Forecaster

Figure 1.5

Competing effectively also means marketers must continually add to their expertise to meet changing market conditions. For example, natural gas and electricity have become virtually interchangeable as energy sources. Gas's clean-burning capabilities have made it the fuel of choice to both generate electricity and heat homes. Scores of industrial companies are swapping gas for electricity and, though still a niche market, fuel cells using gas could become a substitute for grid-generated electricity. To compete effectively selling electricity, marketers must now be adept at selling natural gas, and vice versa.

Utility managements have coped with these changes in different ways. Some withdrew early on from the more competitive generation and marketing sectors of the business, selling their power plants. Others made that decision after learning some painful lessons in competitive markets. The remaining few continue to build national and even global operations to produce and sell energy in deregulated markets.

Regardless of the path they've chosen, however, utility managements have come to the same simple conclusion about their mode of travel: Size spells success (see Figure 1.6). Since 1986,

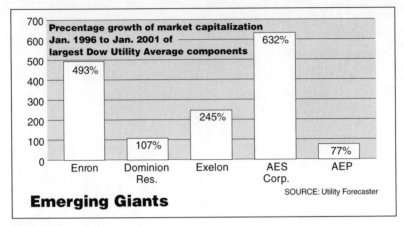

Figure 1.6

there have been more than 100 utility mergers, and some dozen more were pending in late 2001. Since 1998, the number of energy utilities has shrunk by nearly half.

Distribution companies have merged to pool capital and spread costs over a wider area to become more efficient. Gaining heft will also potentially allow them to offer a range of new products such as telecommunications service, boosting growth.

The rationale behind generation company and marketing company mergers is even more compelling. Only large companies have the size and strength to ride out the inevitable setbacks in the industry. These include events within a company's control, like ill-placed bets on the weather and inadequate hedging, but as the summer power crunches of 1998 through 2001 attest, events beyond a player's control can be just as catastrophic.

A TASTE OF ARMAGEDDON

Before the summer of 1998, there were a record 400-plus power marketing companies in business. The typical player's portfolio was a diverse mix of purchase and sale contracts, mostly with other industry players. Everyone assumed everyone else was following the rules and had the financial power to make good on any errors.

How wrong they were. On June 26, 1998, America's power marketing companies got their first taste of the danger of unbridled electricity competition. A series of major power plant outages, combined with record high temperatures in the Northeast and Midwest, launched power prices into orbit.

Caught betting the wrong way on prices, a number of overly aggressive, underfunded power marketers defaulted on their contracts to provide power. The traders and utilities doing business with them were forced to look for alternative supplies at any cost. As a result, electricity that had been selling for $30 per megawatt hour a few days before traded as high as $10,000 per megawatt hour.

Both the nation's 13th-largest marketer—a unit of investment bank Barr-Devlin—and the city of Springfield, Illinois, were in default for millions in broken contracts to marketers. Both had bet heavily on falling or at least steady power prices. The price spike forced them to make good on low-priced contracts by buying power at sky-high prices, and their money soon ran out.

The marketers hurt by the crisis included several of the biggest and savviest players, like Southern Company, who suffered sizable losses despite betting the right way on power prices. As temperatures cooled, these players began to freeze out the weaker marketers. The result has been a dramatic shrinkage in the number of significant energy marketers, with larger players increasingly dominating the market.

That concentration is likely to increase further in coming years as loss-plagued firms like Washington state–based Avista, Delaware's Conectiv, and Kentucky-based LG&E exit the business or at least scale back their efforts. And even healthy, small players like NiSource have sold out as well, to focus on areas in which they're large enough to compete long-term.

Huge capital needs and concerns about the future of electricity prices have made consolidation in the generation business even more striking. The same small group of buyers has dominated the dozens of utility power plant auctions around the country in recent years. And they've dominated permits for new construction as well.

According to a study by global law firm Baker & McKenzie, the 10 largest generators have increased their share of America's power plant capacity from 36 to 51 percent since 1992. The 20 largest firms—several of which are currently merging with each other—own 73 percent, up from 56 percent.

Like large marketers, larger generators are able to spread their risks more effectively than smaller firms. Owning a mix of plants burning different fuels limits the risk of cost increases in the price of a single fuel—natural gas for example. Owning several plants in a single territory increases a company's economies of scale, while owning plants spread geographically reduces exposure to weather swings or regional economic downturns.

In contrast, having only a few plants leaves a company vulnerable to unexpected outages, fuel cost swings, the collapse of a major power sale contract, weather, and unexpectedly tough regulation. That's why, of the hundreds of nonutility power producers that sprang up following PURPA, the only survivors are AES, Calpine, Dynegy, and Enron—all of which found a way to get much bigger, fast.

The jury is still out on how well today's merged utilities will perform, but thus far the record has been very positive. That makes it a certainty more deals lie ahead as the partners cope with changes gripping their industry.

Size will ensure the survival of the best companies, and it should lower the cost of running America's electricity and natural gas systems. Unfortunately, as you'll see in the next chapter, it won't stop electricity rates from rising.

....

INDUSTRY PROFILE: JONATHAN GOTTLIEB

*When Jonathan Gottlieb graduated from New York Law
School in 1985, he was one of a rare breed: attorneys with
energy experience. Today, he's at the top of a rapidly growing legal specialty that's become one of the major forces
reshaping the power industry.*

*Gottlieb's resume includes a stint advising the all-
powerful Federal Energy Regulatory Commission, a role in
developing the first natural gas futures contract, and his
current position as partner at Baker & McKenzie, the
world's largest law firm.*

*He has represented clients in the development of power
plants in 24 states and 17 foreign countries, totaling some
14,000 megawatts of capacity, enough energy to light 14
million homes. His clients are a virtual industry who's who,
including the world's largest power developer AES Corp.,
U.K. energy giant Scottish Power, French water conglomerate Suez Lyonnaise des Eaux, Calpine, Dominion-Virginia
Power, PPL Global, and PSEG Global.*

Q: WHAT'S THE BIGGEST CHANGE IN THE ENERGY
   UTILITY INDUSTRY IN THE PAST 20 YEARS?

A: Management. Before 1995, the typical utility manager was an engineer who had spent 20 to 30 years at
their company, often starting as a meter reader. The
company culture was extremely local- and regional-
focused, even parochial, with most employees, including
executives, growing up within 25 miles of headquarters.

Visionaries were scarce among chief executives. In
fact, there was an industry herd mentality. In the early
1990s, major business consulting firms like McKinnsey,
Arthur Andersen, and Price Waterhouse sold these execs
on a business model that said they had to diversify overseas. You had people who had never been more than 25
miles from home, let alone ever traveled abroad, trying
to make deals in countries they knew nothing about. The
results haven't always been good.

Beginning in the mid-1990s, we've seen a tremendous change. Traders and financial people have taken over the management of power plants and every other competitive aspect of the business. These people are focused on opportunity and growth and, as competitive wholesale markets grow, they're building and acquiring more generating capacity to back up their financial commitments.

By the way, this convergence of the paper deal and the physical deal parallels what happened with natural gas in the early 1990s. As the free market for the commodity grew, so did the need to lock up new supply. Competition-focused managers are now in complete control of that industry.

Q: WHERE DO YOU SEE THE BIGGEST OPPORTUNITIES
     IN ENERGY TODAY?

A: As a lawyer, generation is best because it's the most legal service–dependent area of the business. We're heavily involved in drafting and negotiating the various agreements needed to buy and build power plants. Every deal typically involves ownership structuring, obtaining necessary permits, contracts with construction firms— most of which are now global concerns like Bechtel and GE—lining up fuel supplies and above all financing. Greenfield projects, which site and build entirely new plants, are the most intensive of all.

From the client's point of view, however, I'm not sure which end of the business is best. Generation is basically a commodity business. Your profit is subject to so many variables that are beyond your control like the market price for your power or fuel. But the potential for huge unregulated profits is tremendous, so this end of the business attracts some of the best and the brightest. T&D [Transmission and Distribution] isn't nearly as sexy, but it's far steadier and very likely recession-proof. You're basically just standing there at the gate, collecting a toll and punching the ticket to let people through the door.

And you're spending more time talking with the customer and trying to find ways to increase your throughput.

By the way, I believe the best opportunities in both generation and T&D are right here in the U.S., rather than overseas. Our existing infrastructure is old and tired. The way we're running utility infrastructure in this country now is like taking a 1964 Chevy station wagon and loading up Mom, Dad, the kids, and the dog, tying all the luggage on the roof and going out on a two-week summer vacation and where you run that old Chevy 12 hours a day. Chances are it will break and you won't be able to find parts. And I'm not just talking about California. In New England, 75 percent of all the power plants operating were built before 1972.

I believe California puts the spotlight on all of this. Smart regulators are comparing California and Texas—where they did build enough capacity—and are making it much easier to build new generation and transmission. We're also looking at a tremendous opportunity in natural gas development. Just 4 percent growth in annual demand for electricity is expected to nearly double demand for gas by 2010. That's a lot of new gas we've got to find.

Then there's the merger angle. The competitive utility business is in a mature stage. Just as there were once 200 car companies, there were 200 independent power producers just a few years ago. Now we're down to two or three car companies and we're rapidly getting down to a dozen or so major power producers like Calpine, AES, and Duke Energy. Only companies with access to large pools of low-cost capital can compete long-term. Little guys can't handle it and that means more mergers, including more across international boundaries.

Q: WHAT DO YOU FOCUS ON WHEN YOU ANALYZE A
   POTENTIAL PROJECT FOR A CLIENT?

A: Often the single most important factor for both domestic and international deals is structure. Taxes are a big part of this, as are things like special accounting rules. Whether it is a domestic or foreign project impacts both the structure and the tax analysis. How much the host government takes of the proceeds will make or break any project. How tax questions are dealt with is vital for structuring any successful deal.

Due diligence is a very important part of what we do. In the case of acquisitions, we go through all the records of the business to make sure there are no major defaults or potential liabilities that could impact the client.

Regulatory issues are becoming an increasing concern again here in the U.S. FERC has taken on a more central role in the success of new generation projects and the states are increasingly active as well. With the current boom in new power plant construction, environmental activists are finding new ways to delay projects and we are spending increasing time managing these complex issues.

Transparency issues are less of a problem now overseas than they were a few years ago, particularly when it comes to the language barrier. But cultural barriers can be just as daunting. You've got to be extremely careful that what you mean to say doesn't imply something else to the person you're negotiating with. That was a major problem for companies investing in China in the early 1990s and it remains a huge problem in India, where the vast majority of companies investing have had a terrible time.

For international deals, much currency risk can be hedged with forward contracts or by being paid in dollar-denominated accounts. Government risk is more difficult. There are no free rides anywhere. Clients will often ask where they can invest without worrying whether the government will take their property away and I say yeah, like the U.S.? Several years ago, the Bonneville Power Administration canceled a contract with a power plant developer after construction had already started. Confiscation doesn't just happen in India, it can also happen here at home.

Q: WILL THE ENERGY INDUSTRY EVER REREGULATE?

A: One of the first guys I worked with in this business represented the old American & Foreign Power Company back when the wave of nationalizations was taking place in the late 1950s and early 60s. We ended up working on the privatization of some of those same companies in the 1990s, often by subsidiaries of the former owners. I'll never forget that guy telling me that he hoped to live long enough to be around for the next wave of nationalization. I don't think we'll see that any time soon, except perhaps in California.

These things always move in cycles. But there's no doubt free markets are still on the ascendancy. In fact, California's ongoing disaster is likely to actually speed up the deregulation of wholesale markets in this country. It's simply the best way to encourage investment in energy, and we need a lot of it right now.

CHAPTER 2

The High Price of Power

Deregulation will ultimately bring down electric rates and boost utilities' profits in the bargain. That's what happened in the 1920s in this country, as dominant utes increasingly gained economies of scale. In the 1990s, Argentina and Britain—the first two countries to open their monopolistic energy utility industries to competition—had a similar experience. The price of Argentine electricity dropped 40 percent from preregulation levels immediately after opening its market.

In addition, the larger and more powerful companies become, the easier and faster they'll be able to deploy assets in areas of greatest demand. That will help prevent future crises similar to what's happened in California in 2000 and 2001.

Change must be allowed to take root if we're going to get to the promised land of efficient, low-cost, and plentiful energy from the present of volatilely priced, scarce power. The transition isn't going to be easy. In fact, it may not happen at all.

First of all, runaway power demand growth is unlikely to halt any time soon, barring an economic meltdown. The Internet is becoming an increasingly large piece of the economy, reaching 100 million users in a matter of a few years.

By mid-decade the wireless Internet will increase usage even further, new e-businesses will start up, and new applications will proliferate. Evermore giant computer farms or web servers will come online to handle an ever-growing volume of data needs for corporations. That translates into more demand for power. All those rechargeable cellular phone batteries will need to be charged that much more frequently for wireless Web users.

A full-blown recession would certainly slow power demand growth, but the effect would only be temporary and, given the fact that people will keep their electricity flowing long after they've canceled a trip or cut back other expenses, demand is unlikely to slow much. Rather, demand growth is a glacier; only a paradigm shift will change its course. In addition, any drop in energy prices will only increase demand and induce consumers to become even more complacent during future price increases.

Second, dozens of utilities are still recovering billions in stranded costs through surcharges that have required them to freeze their rates, despite higher energy prices. In California, Southern California Edison and PG&E and later the state itself swallowed skyrocketing wholesale power costs due to rate freezes put in place as the price of stranded cost recovery.

As a result, even as wholesale prices were spiking and outages were becoming commonplace, retail prices held relatively steady. Utilities themselves rolled up billions of dollars in losses from buying power high and selling it low, and were ultimately driven into default. Effectively insulated from higher power costs, the average consumer had little incentive to significantly alter his or her habits. Despite the threat of brownouts, California's power demand rose to scary heights.

Nationwide, conservation incentives designed to encourage less use of electricity have lost the popularity they enjoyed in the late 1980s and early 1990s. They've been eliminated in deregulating states and appear to be on the way out elsewhere as well. In an age where the most popular mode of transportation is a gas-guzzling sport utility vehicle, there's little incentive to pinch pennies on power, at least where the price is still low.

Even in areas where power costs have risen, conservation has lagged. California's first response to spiking power costs was to impose caps on wholesale electricity prices. As the state's power system spun out of control, Governor Gray Davis and the legislature delayed rate hikes, even at the cost of completely overhauling the 1996 compromise and committing billions of dollars in state funds.

This subsidizing of lower rates is hardly a long-term prescription for slowing demand growth. Rather, it's seen by the less sophisticated consumer as a government guarantee of cheap power.

State and federal investigations of power price spikes elsewhere in the United States will have the same effect. While there is a good case some abuses of market power may have been committed, the wide publicity the inquiries are getting is adding to the public's misperception that there is no supply/demand crisis.

The prevailing consensus seems to be that if the bad people profiting from the current situation are stopped, all will return to normal. With the tenor of the investigation presuming someone is in the wrong, there's little to set the record straight.

HELP WANTED: POWER PLANT BUILDERS

Demand growth is not slowing. That leaves boosting supply as the only way to keep power prices under control, but here, too, the situation is far more complex than simply putting up a plant and hooking into the grid.

The first hurdle to building a power plant is finding a power generation company willing to do the job. This was difficult enough during the halcyon days of the monopoly era. Franchised utilities could forecast well in advance of demand, but their ability to recover their costs through rate hikes was iffy with regulators putting their operations under a microscope to check for flaws. That made utilities increasingly reluctant to build.

In the era of deregulation, the list of potential builders has shrunk even more. The handful of companies that increasingly dominate generation will build only if they are assured of generating a profit. Because they now face the threat of competition, most demand a hefty return on investment before they'll part with dollar one, up to twice the rate utilities typically earned during the monopoly era. Builders also demand a faster payoff to limit the long-term risks of participating in a particular market.

Any attempt to clamp down on generating profits is also a deterrent to building new capacity. California's threats to "disgorge" the profits of generating companies, for example, induced many of its largest investors to move aggressively into the Northeast and Midwest. Money that could have been invested to meet runaway demand in the Golden State was deployed elsewhere.

Power plants now comprise less than 40 percent of utility assets—down from 49 percent in 1994—a clear testament that generation is viewed as increasingly less important to companies' success. In fact, Enron, one of the industry's biggest and most profitable players, has staked its growth to getting rid of most of its power plants.

Operating under a concept making the rounds in business schools called *optionality,* Enron's success depends on knowing the value and function of utility assets better than their owners. That way, it can create a virtual-energy empire, cashing in on the most lucrative areas while eliminating the risk of actually owning or building anything. The company's legendary success in what amounts to a pure trading strategy has spurred others to adopt similar approaches, further shrinking the pool of potential builders.

Not everyone will stop building plants, but the implication is that electricity will have to be at least relatively scarce in a state for companies to even consider building a power plant there. Over time, that will limit the amount of capacity developed in any market and, barring a recession, will keep power prices high, especially given the runaway demand sweeping the nation.

The second hurdle is siting a plant. Except for a few states like Texas—which is having major problems with air pollution—most would-be builders face strict controls on where and how power plants and high-voltage transmission lines can be constructed. "Not in my backyard," or NIMBY, has been the battle cry of more than one community that used its political clout to block an unwanted plant.

Governor Davis has signed legislation in California designed to dramatically reduce the time needed for plant siting reviews in the state to just 100 days, but opposition to new power plants isn't likely to go away either in his state or anywhere else.

Even in the teeth of the state's 2000 power crisis, a citizens group succeeded in derailing a planned gas-fired power plant, due to concerns about how it would affect the nearby water supply. Concerns over global warming, the impact on traffic congestion, and community health where plants are built are further hurdles that will only become more severe in coming years.

If new plants do get built, there's the question of having adequate transmission capacity to carry the power to market. According to a recent study by the Electric Power Research Institute—a research group serving the industry—much of the nation's grid is over 50 years old and in need of dramatic new upgrades. Periodic voltage sags and surges already cost the U.S. economy more than $50 billion annually, and the level of damage is rising as electricity demand rises and places ever-greater demands on the system.

Problems siting new power lines are nearly insurmountable, even along existing utility right-of-ways. The controversy in the early 1990s over the purported health risks of electromagnetic fields, or EMFs—allegedly generated from high-voltage power lines—has died down for the moment, but it was a major threat to utilities' financial health for several years. The key event was the highly publicized and emotional Zuidema case, in which the plaintiffs alleged their daughter's kidney cancer was the result of negligence by utility San Diego G&E regarding EMFs from its power lines.

The case was ultimately thrown out after a long legal battle. But the court's decision was based more on the impossibility of proving utility negligence than on whether or not EMFs are indeed carcinogenic agents. In addition, the case dramatically increased public awareness of EMFs and made utilities highly unwilling to build new power lines.

If scientists find conclusive proof that EMFs cause cancer, any new building could be taken as proof of willing disregard for the public health, opening them to potential lawsuits that would make today's tobacco lawsuits look like chump change.

Most utility managements would rather do anything than take on the task of building new transmission lines. In fact, many have taken advantage of deregulation to exit the business altogether, shifting the management (and therefore potentially the legal liability) of operating the lines to quasi-government entities (as done in California) and/or large regional transmission organizations (RTOs) pooling the lines of several neighboring companies.

This opening of lines is sanctioned by FERC as a way to promote competition. An effort was launched in mid-2001 to force consolidation of transmission line management into four superregional organizations. Yet the major beneficiaries thus far have been transmission-owning companies, who have been able to exit a very low-margin and high-risk business almost painlessly. This raises serious questions about who will finance needed, new transmission capacity. As long as there aren't any clear answers, power will have a hard time getting to market efficiently in times of crisis.

IT'S GAS, GAS, GAS

Any power plants that make it past these hurdles are almost certain to be natural gas–fired. Some 95 percent of the new power plants in development are slated to burn gas for one main reason: Gas plants can be built far more quickly than plants using other fuels, typically now in one year or less depending on the development of the site, so construction costs can be better controlled. Projections call for 50 percent of America's power grid to be run on gas by 2010.

Gas plants also emit very few pollutants, making them far easier to site as well. And large electric/gas companies like Duke Energy can easily supply them (see Figure 2.1).

Gas's growing dominance in generating power means changes in its price will increasingly trigger corresponding changes in the price of electricity. When gas supplies are tight and demand is great, power prices will rise. Conversely, when electric demand is high, gas supplies will tighten, which will drive up gas prices and, in turn, electricity prices.

Another major reason for gas's growing dominance as America's generating fuel of choice is the decline of alternative fuels. Nuclear power currently provides around 20 percent of the country's electricity needs, but no new nuclear plants have been ordered since the Three Mile Island near-meltdown in 1978, due to safety concerns and costs.

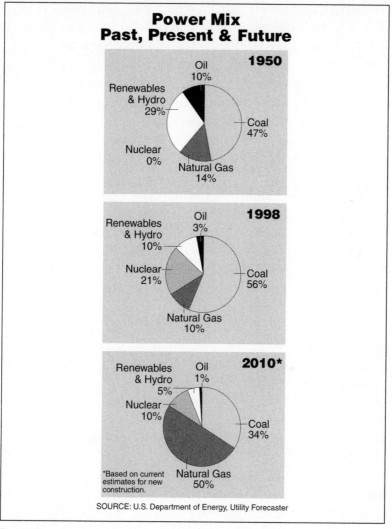

**Power Mix
Past, Present & Future**

1950
Oil 10%
Renewables & Hydro 29%
Coal 47%
Nuclear 0%
Natural Gas 14%

1998
Oil 3%
Renewables & Hydro 10%
Nuclear 21%
Coal 56%
Natural Gas 10%

2010*
Renewables & Hydro 5%
Oil 1%
Nuclear 10%
Coal 34%
*Based on current estimates for new construction.
Natural Gas 50%

SOURCE: U.S. Department of Energy, Utility Forecaster

Figure 2.1

In addition, there's now the growing problem of where to store the growing stockpile of nuclear waste building up at the nation's 100 or so operating reactors, now that the federal government's Yucca Mountain facility has been mothballed. And the cost of decommissioning nukes remains a potentially extremely expensive wild card.

Last but not least, nuclear power has a disastrous financial legacy. Once declared too cheap to meter, nuke construction costs rose fivefold in the late 1980s. Nearly every company completing a nuke in the past 20 years was forced to write off billions in unrecoverable costs. Dozens cut their dividends and two went bankrupt.

More than a dozen utilities have taken advantage of stranded cost recovery under deregulation to sell their nuclear plants, and a half dozen others are in the process of selling theirs. The handful of companies doing the buying, including Exelon and Dominion Resources, have realized big profits as power prices have risen, but they'd need considerably more incentive to authorize building a new one.

Coal is still the nation's dominant fuel for generating electricity, with a 50 percent share. Under current policy direction, however, the fuel's share is projected to decline to just 10 percent by 2020, according to EPRI. For one thing, the vast majority of coal-fired power plants were built in the 1950s and 60s and are in need of substantial upgrades or else should be shuttered.

Most also face increasing scrutiny from the public and federal regulators, particularly the Environmental Protection Agency, which has sued seven big coal utilities for skirting the rules requiring them to install pollution equipment on 17 plants to prevent acid rain. Three of the companies have already settled their disputes. If the EPA's claims are upheld without settlements, the remaining offending companies—particularly American Electric Power—will dish out several billion dollars in damages.

Some companies, like FirstEnergy, have made great strides in developing new, clean, coal technology. Yet only a handful of plants now use it, and the costs remain prohibitive for many smaller coal plants. Mercury emissions are another potential death knell for coal, as are mining safety concerns. Ditto global-warming concerns, due to coal plants' heavy emissions of greenhouse gases like carbon dioxide.

Renewable energies such as hydroelectric, solar, geothermal, and wind power have been touted since the 1970s as ultraclean alternatives to natural gas, and without the exposure to volatile prices. Unfortunately, despite their appeal, their development has been ignored and even opposed by many in industry and government (see Figure 2.2).

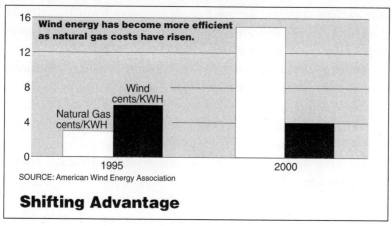

Figure 2.2

As a result, the money has not been spent on research to make them economically viable, except as niche providers of energy. Despite skyrocketing fossil fuel prices, the entire federal budget for renewable energy research for fiscal year 2000 was just $362 million. That was less than two-tenths of a percent of the market value of high-tech favorite Oracle that same year.

Hydropower is actually on the decline around the country, as environmental concerns have prevented the relicensing of scores of dams. Consequently, despite the promise of such new technologies as solar panels and new, more efficient wind turbines, even Clinton administration energy secretary Bill Richardson—a fan of renewables—projected only 5 percent of energy will come from such sources by 2020. That's despite the fact that several states, Maine for one, have mandated that a certain percentage of generators use renewable fuels. Bush administration renewable projections are even lower.

Many technology fans have touted fuel cells and other forms of distributed generation as the answer to the country's energy needs. In early 2000, word that Microsoft chairman Bill Gates had bought 5 percent of Avista Energy—a utility with a subsidiary that makes fuel cells—set off a buying spree in fuel cell developers. At the peak, investors drove up the shares of several fuel cell companies as much as 20-fold, despite the fact that they were still years away from profitability.

Fuel cells theoretically take business away from the electric grid, but their systems are supported by many utilities as a way to take advantage of e-commerce's need for more reliable power.

In contrast to an ordinary industrial company, an e-commerce company absolutely can't do without electricity for any length of time. For some, a prolonged outage could literally mean extinction. Fuel cells provide that extra degree of reliability, keeping the lights on regardless of the grid's woes (see Figure 2.3).

Fuel cells and microturbines—which are individual, small-scale generation units—will undoubtedly enjoy robust demand in coming years, and they'll be a profit center for the utilities and other companies that develop them. Some are even being developed for use in transportation. Two factors, however, will keep them from displacing enough power demand on the grid to make a significant dent in power prices.

The first is cost. Even the least expensive systems still require an initial investment that the average homeowner would probably never recoup. In addition, since most fuel cells and microturbines run on gas or some derivative thereof, their operating costs will be affected by energy prices, just like ordinary grid power.

Most fuel cells also use increasingly pricey platinum-group metals to operate. Extreme pricing volatility for this resource is

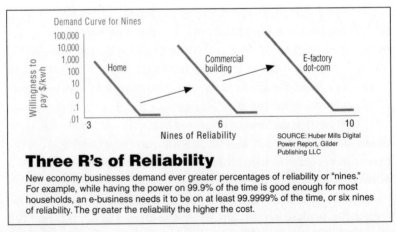

Three R's of Reliability

New economy businesses demand ever greater percentages of reliability or "nines." For example, while having the power on 99.9% of the time is good enough for most households, an e-business needs it to be on at least 99.9999% of the time, or six nines of reliability. The greater the reliability the higher the cost.

Figure 2.3

yet another key reason fuel cells will remain only a niche market for the few who can afford them and whose livelihood makes them worth the expense.

The second concern is reliability. There are literally dozens of fuel cell designs. Until one emerges as dominant, it will be hard to win market acceptance. Plug Power, for example, has been forced to redesign its fuel cell product due to problems meeting the criteria of its major backer, General Electric. The delays and general disenchantment with the company from the investment public could make it difficult for Plug and other fuel cell companies to gain the necessary funding to make their plans a reality. Despite their state's problems, few Californians have switched off the grid to date.

In sum, environmental advantages, speed of construction, and the lack of alternatives add up to long-term dominance for natural gas in generating electricity. The problem is the fuel is in increasingly short supply just as demand is taking off.

Total U.S. gas demand is expected to rise by 50 percent over the next decade, largely driven by power generation. There's now a serious question if new sources projected to come online in coming years will keep up with projected demand for both electricity generation and home heating. That adds up to rising natural gas prices, which will flow directly into higher electricity prices.

The tipoff that natural gas has entered a new pricing paradigm is its behavior over the past couple of summers. Traditionally, gas prices have peaked in the winter months as supplies tighten due to rising demand for home heating. Summer prices sagged as supplies expanded and demand fell. In the past two years, however, prices exploded in the summer months as demand for generating electricity stretched supplies thin. Now there are both winter and summer periods of peak demand for the fuel, keeping upward pressure on prices year-round and creating the real possibility of a shortage in coming years.

Alarmingly, however, there's little recognition of this fact in the marketplace. Gas-producing companies are rewarded on Wall Street for maximizing quarterly earnings, rather than boosting

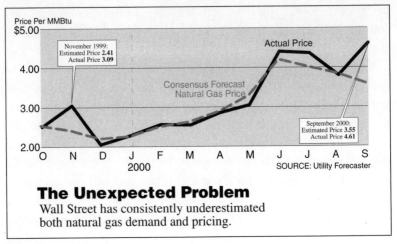

Price Per MMBtu

November 1999:
Estimated Price **2.41**
Actual Price **3.09**

Actual Price

Consensus Forecast
Natural Gas Price

September 2000:
Estimated Price **3.55**
Actual Price **4.61**

O   N   D   J   F   M   A   M   J   J   A   S
              2000   SOURCE: Utility Forecaster

The Unexpected Problem

Wall Street has consistently underestimated
both natural gas demand and pricing.

Figure 2.4

reserves for future production. Major producers like Burlington Resources are actually producing less gas than they have in recent years.

Worse, according to the Energy Information Agency, natural gas reserve replacement in the U.S. was just 83 percent in 1998, 89 percent in 1999, and fell below 100 percent again in 2000. Despite a dramatic increase in new gas-drilling rigs, new exploration isn't even keeping up with reduced levels of output. One reason is the increasing difficulty in locating cheap, new reserves. The companies themselves doubt prices can stay high and are reluctant to invest in new production that would not be profitable at much lower prices. Their very lack of action ensures tight supplies and higher prices (see Figure 2.4).

Finally, gas prices will continue to find support in the rising price of oil, increasingly its main fuel rival. From 1998 to 2001, oil prices nearly tripled as demand in the world's developed and developing economies mushroomed. The fact that China—a net producer of oil as recently as 1993—is now importing a growing percentage of its oil from the Middle East, indicates the trend of rising demand has only just begun. Remarkably, this price action has occurred in an era of relative peace in the Middle East. Things will really get ugly if politics turn nasty (see Figure 2.5).

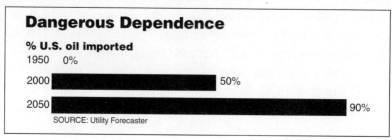

Dangerous Dependence

% U.S. oil imported

1950   0%

2000   50%

2050   90%

SOURCE: Utility Forecaster

Figure 2.5

CRISIS OF CONFIDENCE

Today's volatile electricity prices will ultimately be brought under control—despite runaway demand and rising natural gas prices—provided market forces are allowed to take effect on the electricity industry. Higher natural gas prices are the best way to encourage development of renewable energy and conservation efforts. High electricity prices are the only way to promote the building of new power plants and transmission lines to alleviate the nation's budding supply crisis.

Unfortunately, there's a growing possibility that electricity deregulation could be derailed, not just in states where it hasn't yet occurred but in states now open to competition. In the former group, a Georgia Public Service Commission member in early 2001 stated unequivocally that "if deregulation comes here it comes out of Washington," despite the fact that the Peach State has already successfully opened its natural gas market to full competition.

Those sentiments have been echoed in Minnesota, Nevada, Wisconsin, and other states. Regulators have put aside deregulation to focus on improving the reliability of the current monopoly system. Troubles in California have induced legislators in North Carolina and Louisiana to put deregulation studies on hold, and Arkansas and Oklahoma have delayed their plans as well. In deregulation's favor, both Texas and Ohio have pushed ahead with plans in recent months. Regulators in most states seem to be waiting to see if California can pull itself out of its supply crisis without reversing its restructuring.

The first two states to deregulate were California and Massachusetts. Voters there overwhelmingly rejected proposals in the November 1998 election to overturn deregulation. Reregulation proponents, however, were vastly outspent by utilities that feared the loss of their hard-won stranded cost recovery. A period of higher prices could make it very hard to defeat future initiatives, particularly in the Golden State, where a radical proposal for a complete industry overhaul will be on the ballot for the 2002 elections.

Companies, consumers, and regulators alike have looked to the federal government to end the deregulation uncertainty by passing comprehensive energy legislation to establish the same set of market rules nationwide. One of deregulation's greatest proponents, Enron CEO Ken Lay, is a personal friend of President Bush and has already exerted considerable influence on federal policymaking, including the administration's current energy plan.

Since the mid-1990s, however, Washington has been paralyzed by gridlock, leaving few in Congress willing to take on such a potentially sensitive issue. As the 2002 election approaches, the likelihood of action will diminish, as the parties jockey for partisan advantage. As a result, the window of opportunity is probably too small for comprehensive national deregulation. Instead, whatever happens will be designed to fix specific problems, such as the dearth of power plants. The risk remains high that the crisis of confidence in the energy utility industry that's prevailed since the 1970s will continue.

The longer the country goes without settling the issue, the greater the potential for the greatest threat of all to the system: Reregulation. Britain's double cross of U.S. utilities in the past few years is a stark example of what can happen when the regulatory environment abruptly changes. There, the Labour government hit the U.S. companies that had bought the country's utilities with an unexpected "windfall profits tax," followed by stiff rate cuts. The same thing happened in Australia, as regulators suddenly cut allowed returns in half.

Were reregulation to prevail in the United States, consumers would doubtless enjoy an upfront rate cut that would prove immensely popular. The impact on the supply/demand crisis, however, would be catastrophic. Australia, for example, is now mired in a supply shortage, and wholesale prices are on the move in Britain as well. But companies are reluctant to invest heavily to solve it. Real or inflation-adjusted required returns for new power plant projects could soar at least into the low-20 percent range to compensate for greater political risks and uncertainty. That would make it very difficult to bring in new power plant investment, worsening the crisis, and dramatically increasing the threat of systemwide shutdowns in periods of peak demand.

Some states, like California, could take the draconian step of taking over their utility systems, but here taxpayers would be saddled with the burden of building supply to match runaway demand, even as consumers continued to pay more. The ultimate casualties would likely be the politicians foolish enough to propose such action.

Whether deregulation continues to progress, consumers face at least several years of volatile electricity prices. The only question is whether the transition will be relatively smooth—if the industry changes now under way are allowed to run their course or (better) are eased along by federal legislation—or rocky, if politicians decide to throw the whole system into chaos by reregulating.

Regardless of which way things go, there will be a huge number of winning investments in the emerging energy utility industry. The shrinking circle of electricity generators, for example, have an opportunity to sell as much power as they can produce for the next few years. The correspondingly tiny group of major marketers will enjoy a once-in-a-lifetime chance to crack open retail markets. Producers of fossil fuels, particularly natural gas, are almost guaranteed a high price for their output. And several makers of fuel cells and microturbines are likely to be big gainers as technologies that improve the reliability of power supplies become increasingly popular.

The gains consumers will earn as investors will more than offset the higher prices paid for the essential service of energy. Highlighting the best bets is the focus of the latter chapters of this book. In the next chapter, we'll turn our attention to a far different industry, communications, which faces a very similar challenge.

. . . .

INDUSTRY PROFILE: RICHARD OSBORNE

*Richard Osborne joined Duke Energy's predecessor, Duke
Power, in the mid-1970s, fresh from earning his MBA at the
nearby University of North Carolina. His 26-year tenure
with the company has included a variety of finance positions, including Treasurer for eight years beginning in 1981
and Chief Financial Officer starting in 1989.*

*In recognition of his value to Duke, as well as the massive
changes in the energy utility industry, Osborne was named
the company's Chief Risk Officer in 2000. It's a position he
himself says wouldn't have existed a decade ago at an
energy utility, but which he relishes.*

Q: WHAT'S THE BIGGEST CHANGE IN THE ENERGY
UTILITY INDUSTRY SINCE YOU STARTED WITH DUKE?

A: The industry is no longer homogeneous. We've evolved
from vertically integrated regional companies to a largely
segmented industry where the key challenges vary widely.

Ten years ago, I think 95 percent of utility executives
would have told you managing regulatory risk was their
most important objective. Today, there are a number of
companies trying to aggregate distribution and, to a
lesser extent, transmission wires to put together large
systems of retail customers. For these companies, regulatory risk is still paramount. By the way, they include our
Duke Power unit, which serves 2.2 million electric customers in the Carolinas, as well our transmission group.

In contrast, other segments have developed that have
far different concerns. Our merchant generation business, for example, is chiefly focused on commodity
prices, the state of the economy, and the credit risk of
those we do business with.

Q: HOW DOES DUKE ENERGY MANAGE RISK ON A
COMPANYWIDE LEVEL?

A: Our operations and assets cover almost the entire
energy value chain. Consequently, one of our greatest

challenges is to compile the information needed to aggregate risk in an intelligent and meaningful way.

Our exposure to natural gas prices is a good example. We're exposed to changes in gas prices through our merchant energy group which buys and sells gas, our gas-fired merchant power plants, our regulated gas-fired power plants, and our field services unit, which essentially has to buy gas for its customers.

Our pipeline systems themselves are very much tied to the value of natural gas in final user markets. How much someone is willing to pay our Texas Eastern unit to move gas from the Gulf to New York, for example, depends on the difference in price between those locations. And we're exposed to gas prices as to how they impact fertilizer, which is essentially made from gas.

Our first step is to assess the gas price exposure of each of these operations. Then we can aggregate, assess, and consolidate information about the risk of price fluctuations to Duke as a whole, rather than try to hedge the exposure of each unit by itself.

Since some of our operations benefit from higher gas prices, they offset those that are hurt by them. We factor out these cancel-outs to determine whether the remaining exposure is acceptable for Duke. If it is, we'll continue to monitor it, but we won't take any action. If it's not, the most efficient way to deal with it is to ramp up new business origination.

If we find Duke has bought too much gas, we'll find a way to either sell some or use more. That could mean building a new generating plant. If we're short gas, there are also several options. For example, we could go out and buy a long-term purchase contract, or we could use the derivatives market. The NYMEX Henry Hub index is the most commonly traded. We've used all of these techniques in combination.

Q: WHAT IS DUKE'S CORE BUSINESS STRATEGY?

A: Our basic thrust is to be the provider of choice for energy solutions, especially in natural gas and power, for large wholesale customers in particular. We've shown we can do that in regulated utility operations over the years, as well as unregulated merchant energy, gas processing, and global development of power projects in Australia, Latin America, and now Europe.

Outside of our core businesses, we have a number of support business investments. Our Duke Fluor Daniel venture is the largest EPC contractor—engineering, procurement, and construction—for generating plants in the U.S., with by far the largest market share.

We also try to take advantage of what we feel are market distortions. For example, we've bought equity participation in gas-producing properties in the Gulf of Mexico. And we'll do it again from time to time when we feel market conditions are compelling, though exploration and production are not part of our core business expertise.

Generally speaking, however, we're very focused on all parts of the energy value chain. Investments outside it, such as in telecom, are not a significant part of our business strategy.

Q: WHAT ARE THE BIGGEST CHALLENGE AND THE
   GREATEST OPPORTUNITY YOUR INDUSTRY WILL FACE
   IN THE NEXT FIVE YEARS?

A: They're really one and the same: how to deal with an industry that's transitioning from homogeneity and tight regulation to broad segmentation between highly regulated and very competitive operations. There are a number of ways to profit in both the competitive merchant and regulated retail sides. Duke intends to take advantage of opportunities in both.

Deregulation has had varied success thus far across the country, with the California debacle being the worst example of failure. But the state is an unusual case and its problems won't change the general course or direction for the industry. Instead, I suspect we'll all learn from it to improve the model and go forward.

This is a very exciting time for the energy industry in this country, and particularly for those of us involved in it. In fact, the whole world is evolving on a similar model. State-owned or highly regulated monopolies are becoming companies that are tightly controlled in some areas but really much more market-oriented in others. I think it's a healthy trend that will create a more economic and efficient energy business.

. . . .

....
Toward the Next Ma Bell

A generation ago, a single company—AT&T—dominated telecommunications. Easily the world's most dependable network, Ma Bell's wires connected virtually every home and business coast-to-coast, but its reach was global. With a brand name that was a revered symbol of America's emergence as the leading power of the latter twentieth century, its Bell Labs unit pioneered nearly every major breakthrough on which today's new economy is based, from cellular phones to the microchip.

As late as the 1970s, AT&T seemed invincible, able to hurdle any challenge at home or abroad. On Wall Street, it was considered the ultimate, one-decision stock, with a century-old track record for strong growth and destined for at least another hundred years of success.

Today, Ma Bell is a shell of her former self. Regulators and feisty competitors have stripped its dominance of local and long-distance telephone service. Mismanagement has eroded its once vaunted edge in technology and customer service. The AAA credit rating, which had stood for decades, is rapidly sinking toward junk status. For the first time in over 100 years, the company has slashed its dividend. Under an ongoing plan to divide into four parts, what's left of the old tree may not last out the decade.

The destruction of AT&T is a direct result of the deregulation of the communications industry. The process began slowly in the mid-1970s, picked up steam in the 80s, and reached its conclusion in the latter 90s.

The deregulators achieved their goals: the end of AT&T's reign as the world's preeminent telephone company, and the unleashing of market forces to spur industry competition, investment, and innovation. In some ways, breaking up Ma Bell has delivered the goods of better, cheaper, telecom services.

In the past 20 years, dozens of competitors have sprung up to vie for the country's communications dollars, driving down the price of services like long distance to a few cents a minute. E-mail and cellular phones have become ubiquitous, and a new generation of wireless communications is on the way, promising everything from the wireless Internet to smart wireless appliances.

There have also been consequences not dreamed of by the deregulators. Far from saving money, America is spending more on communications services than ever before. While heavy users of services have seen their rates drop, the price of basic local and long-distance service to the poorest citizens has actually risen, as the profit motive has replaced the pledge of inexpensive universal service. A rising number of Americans are being caught on the wrong side of a growing digital divide, threatening to cut them off from the benefits of the new economy.

The greatest surprise has been deregulation's winners. All but a handful of the upstarts that sprang up to challenge the old AT&T have disappeared, either to mergers or obscurity. Instead of creating a world ruled by myriad small companies locked in tight competition, deregulation has cleared the path for the rise of Ma Bell's eventual successor.

The second Ma Bell will be among the most powerful enterprises the world has ever seen. Over the past eight years, U.S. telecom revenues have tripled, with sales surging in every segment (see Figure 3.1). That growth continues to flow to a handful of companies that are growing steadily bigger and richer while smaller rivals flounder.

As the new empire's power grows, some governments will act to stanch its rise. By the time they do, though, their actions may in fact speed along its development by thinning the field.

The identity of the second Ma Bell is as yet unknown. In fact, it could well be several large companies acting as a global oligopoly. The best candidates for the role have already emerged: the very

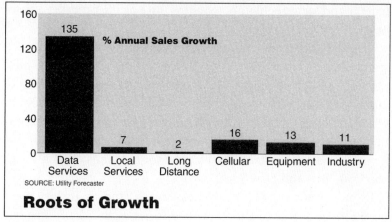

SOURCE: Utility Forecaster

Roots of Growth

Figure 3.1

same local phone units the first Ma Bell was forced to divest in 1984, the so-called Baby Bells.

THE RISE AND FALL OF AT&T

Founded in the late nineteenth century by the telephone's inventor, Alexander Graham Bell, AT&T's unquestioned rule over American communications began in 1907. Its president at the time, Theodore Vail, convinced trust-busting U.S. President Theodore Roosevelt that telephone service's best chance to develop universally would be if his company were granted a nationwide monopoly.

According to Vail, one company acting as a monopoly would enjoy the security of return needed for attracting investment to build and maintain needed infrastructure. Parallel networks would be a costly waste of resources and a financial failure over the long haul. Only a monopoly would have the economies of scale to keep costs down and rapidly develop new products. And only a monopoly could offer truly universal service, subsidizing quality in poor urban and rural areas that were more costly to serve.

In short, Vail held that only a nationwide monopoly could ensure all Americans first-rate communications service, essential if the country was to develop into a profitable economic whole. To compensate for the lack of competitive checks and balances, federal and state regulators would ensure against market abuses by overseeing service and rates.

With T.R.'s blessing, Vail's concept was enshrined into law, and spurred one of the greatest capital spending booms in history. Over the next half century, AT&T connected millions of homes and businesses coast-to-coast with a seamless network of copper wires. In doing so it transformed America. No longer would commerce rely on the telegraph or, worse, the mails. Instead, communications became instantaneous, even for locations as far away as San Francisco and New York.

By mid-century, AT&T's success, reach, and financial power were indispensable to the nation's well-being, but Vail's historic compact was already unraveling. Americans came to take for granted the speed and convenience of being able to phone anyone, anywhere. Instead, the focus became the company's power over the economy, alleged abuses of the public trust, and gaps in service. The shift in perception was captured in the 1967 satiric film, *The President's Analyst,* in which the archvillains are megalomaniacal telecom executives.

Bashing the monopolistic phone company gained new strength with the rise of deregulation ideology in the 1970s. Deregulation proponents acknowledged the incredible achievements of the Bell system—namely universal, affordable, telephone service for all Americans—but they argued competition would open up a new world of lower rates, better service, and technological advances for all, just as it had done for previously regulated airlines and trucking.

Critics cited AT&T's sheer size as evidence the monopoly had outlived its usefulness. Its layers of bureaucracy were painted as insensitive to customers' needs and, in fact, downright wasteful. A host of smaller, more nimble competitors, deregulation proponents said, would be able to do what Ma Bell did far more cheaply if given the chance. That would in turn force AT&T to become more efficient and cut its rates.

The movement to break up AT&T crested when Ronald Reagan, one of deregulation's greatest champions, won the U.S. presidency. The new administration gave a final push to an antitrust lawsuit filed in 1974 by the U.S. Justice Department, resulting in the landmark January 1982 consent decree from the U.S. Supreme Court. The decree ordered AT&T to divest its seven local phone units, thereafter dubbed the Baby Bells, which remained monopolies. AT&T's long-distance market was thrown open to full-blown competition.

The next stage of deregulation came with the passage of the Telecommunications Act in 1996. Just as the consent decree was intended to smash AT&T's unquestioned industry power, so the 1996 Act was aimed at breaking the local phone monopoly grip of its offspring, the Baby Bells. Deregulation proponents held up the so-called last mile of communications as a bottleneck to progress. They argued that forcing open local networks would at last force down local phone rates. Eliminating the access fees the Bells charged long-distance companies to complete long-distance calls, they maintained, would cut long-distance rates even more.

The deregulation debate began in the Democratic-led Congresses of the late 1980s and early 90s. By the time Republicans took over in 1995, the debate had reached critical mass. By 1996, smarting from a series of devastating political defeats at the hands of President Clinton, the new Republican leadership was anxious for a legislative victory. They found an eager ally in Clinton, who was also up for reelection. Together, they pushed for landmark communications reform, and with Representative Thomas Bliley (R-VA) as the point man in Congress, industry was able to write the rules.

As expected, the key provision of the Act was the opening of Bell local phone monopolies to competitors. In return, the Bells were allowed to enter the long-distance business, once state and federal regulators certified they had met a checklist of requirements.

In Wall Street's eyes, the Act was the death knell for the Bells. Few gave the local giants much chance of holding their own markets against the muscle of the long-distance Big Three: AT&T, MCI, and Sprint.

A survey of local service rates released by The Chicago Corporation in October 1996, for example, boldly predicted long-distance carriers would "be able to profitably enter the $100 billion local exchange service market" regardless of what pricing rules were set down by the Federal Communications Commission or the courts. The consensus was that the Bells would lose up to 30 percent of their customers in the first few years of deregulation, with more to follow as more nimble new entrants picked off business.

The Bells' chances of making up for the loss with long-distance revenue were similarly discounted. One influential analyst asserted the Bells would have to gain four times as much market share in long distance as they lost in their core local franchises just to break even. This, he believed, would be virtually impossible, given the likely delays in meeting the FCC's checklist. Reflecting the Street's consensus at the time, he also doubted the Bells could hope to compete against the marketing machines of the long-distance giants.

Adding to the Bells' woes was the makeup of the Federal Communications Commission itself. Chairman Reed Hundt was an avid proponent of breaking up the Bell monopolies. He and his colleagues were prepared to aggressively tilt the competitive playing field toward new entrants and against the incumbent Bells whenever they could.

VAIL'S REVENGE

Only Theodore Vail could have predicted what really happened since. The Act proved the final deathblow to the old AT&T. Its core long-distance telephone business has continued to crumble while its new businesses have failed to pick up the slack. Its Big Three peers have fared little better and, despite the best efforts of the FCC and billions in Wall Street money, hundreds of industry upstarts are biting the dust.

The only real winners have been the companies expected to lose the most: the Baby Bells. Of the original seven, four Bells now remain (see Figure 3.2). The largest, Verizon Communications, is the product of mergers between two Bells—Bell Atlantic and NYNEX—and GTE, a company with very similar characteristics to the Bells. SBC Communications is comprised of three Bells—Southwestern Bell, Pacific Telesis, and Ameritech—as well as Bell look-alike Southern New England Telecom. U.S. West is now a wholly owned subsidiary of long-distance giant Qwest

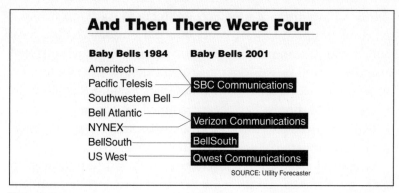

And Then There Were Four

Baby Bells 1984	Baby Bells 2001
Ameritech	
Pacific Telesis	SBC Communications
Southwestern Bell	
Bell Atlantic	Verizon Communications
NYNEX	
BellSouth	BellSouth
US West	Qwest Communications

SOURCE: Utility Forecaster

Figure 3.2

Communications. Only BellSouth remains in its original form, though it's considered a very eligible takeover target.

Regulators allowed the wave of Bell mergers in the late 1990s mainly to speed local phone competition. Approvals were conditioned on Bells' promises to boost service and improve network access to rivals. SBC's merger with Ameritech even carried the obligation for the new company to launch a competitive effort in the territory of other Bells.

As it turned out, these measures have had almost no impact on Bell dominance of their local phone markets, which remains at 90 to 95 percent nationwide. Additional efforts to open their networks have forced the Bells to make upgrades that are rapidly reducing the incentive for building competing networks.

Once-rampant service quality problems, especially in the Northeast, have been largely corrected. In fact, it's Bell rivals who now draw most of the complaints. In addition, increased economies of scale have sharply driven down costs. And Bells have actually found a way to make money from rivals as well, fashioning immensely profitable wholesale businesses that sell capacity and network services to upstarts.

The result: Would-be rivals are fast disappearing as a major threat to Bells' health, growth, and dominance. Following the 1996 Telecom Act, numerous cable television, long-distance telephone, and competitive local exchange carriers (CLECs) attempted to launch local phone services. Wall Street poured out its coffers to finance them.

Today, long-distance providers are focused solely on winning the local phone business of commercial customers. Few have launched any meaningful effort to snare lower-margin residential customers, even in wealthier areas, and despite pledges to offer universal service by many companies, critics charge that less well-to-do neighborhoods have been redlined by the new entrants. None has managed to turn the local business into a profit center from which to launch future growth.

As for the cable television systems, they've been engaged in their own death battle with satellite-based entertainment providers. Some have continued to spend billions to upgrade their infrastructure to carry telephone and Internet service. But here, too, winning enough market share to generate significant profits has proven elusive.

Even AT&T, now the biggest U.S. cable player with some 40 percent of connections, seems to have failed in its efforts to provide full telephone service over its cable lines. Consequently, most cable television companies are now focusing on more profitable endeavors like digital cable, relegating telephone service to an afterthought.

The CLECs have proven to be the most tenacious of the would-be Bell rivals. From their origins in the early 1990s, the groups' primary focus has been building communications networks of high-capacity fiber-optic cable, connecting primarily office buildings. Fiber is capable of carrying far more information far more quickly than the Bells' conventional copper networks. Consequently, the group has enjoyed no small measure of success snaring commercial customers who are ever more dependent on timely, efficient flows of information.

CLECs, however, have an Achilles heel: their insatiable need for new capital to expand. Until 2000, Wall Street was all too happy to buy the stock and bond offerings of any would-be network builder on the premise that exploding demand for broadband capacity would ultimately ensure immense profits. With some $20 billion in stock and bond offerings flowing, dozens of start-ups hit the scene, promising unique strategies to beat the big local and long-distance phone companies. Initial public offerings soared to stratospheric heights, though profitability was years away even in a best-case scenario.

As it turned out, reality proved far from a best case. By mid-2000, Wall Street was anxious to see some results for its investment. But the upstart CLECs' revenue targets proved tougher than expected to reach as the Bells fought back by building their own high-speed networks. The proliferation of other CLECs began to threaten their ability to raise equity capital. Profitability projections were pushed ever further out in the future, and the mountain of debt CLECs had accumulated suddenly started to cave in.

When the end came, the fallout was worse than anyone could have imagined. Once red-hot names like Covad, GST, ICG Communications, Intermedia, Level 3, PSI, RCN, Teligent, Viatel, and Winstar have fallen 90 to 99 percent from their highs. A growing number of CLECs are headed for bankruptcy. The rest have abandoned their growth plans in order to preserve capital and prevent bankruptcy. Only those CLECs lucky enough to be taken over are assured of survival.

The result: Six years after industry deregulation, new entrants have yet to grab more than a sliver of market share from the local phone companies. Even that share is endangered, as the Bells continue to build out their networks, and any new rivals are virtually certain to depend on Bell networks to survive.

Bells' local phone revenues have also gotten a big boost from offering additional services. Features like caller ID and call waiting have gained huge penetration rates around the country. Demand for second phone lines has also mushroomed. In addition, network access fees, which are billed to long-distance companies as a cost of using Bell networks, have declined to a fraction of pre-deregulation levels. As a result, this once powerful incentive to build alternative networks to bypass the Bells is rapidly evaporating.

Even more impressive has been the postderegulation Bells' ability to attack new markets. Supposedly dull, visionless management has made one right move after another while rivals have floundered; the pull of Bell names in unregulated markets has blown the doors off even the most optimistic projections.

Under the Telecom Act, the Bells can offer long-distance service only after they prove to federal regulators that their local markets are open. Delays in meeting the required checklist have been extensive as critics expected. In fact, from 1986 to late 2001, only two Bells had won the right to offer long-distance service, Verizon in Connecticut, Massachusetts, New York, and Pennsylvania, and SBC in Texas, Kansas, and Oklahoma.

Based on the record in those states, however, the Bells should have no problem grabbing market share from both long-distance giants and other new entrants alike, once more markets are opened—and they may not have long to wait. With Republicans in charge at the Federal Communications Commission for the first time in eight years, the agency is listening to Congress, where leaders in both parties have called for speedier approvals of Bell long-distance applications. And the U.S. Department of Justice's intensive reviews are loosening up as well.

The result: Over the next couple of years, the Bells will pour into long distance, as well as the high-speed data market from which they're also barred at present. The 30 percent or so market share they'll achieve will instantly place them among the dominant players. Ultimately, they're likely to buy the consumer long-distance franchises of AT&T and MCI WorldCom, both of which are planned as spinoffs due to their flagging performance. That will shift long-distance industry power, which is still 86 percent controlled by the four largest players, into the hands of the Bells.

In the realm of new industry products, the growth of Bell dominance is even more impressive. Cellular telephones are without doubt the industry's most successful new product in the last half century. Since 1989, the number of cellular phone users in the United States has risen from about 3.5 million to over 100 million (see Figure 3.3).

Penetration rates are rising even faster in developing nations, such as China, and in Latin America, where the fixed-line network is spotty at best. With new innovations such as the wireless Web coming onstream in the next few years, the market is set for another major sales explosion. In fact, wireless phones are already replacing fixed lines in much of the world, as well as for most mobile Americans.

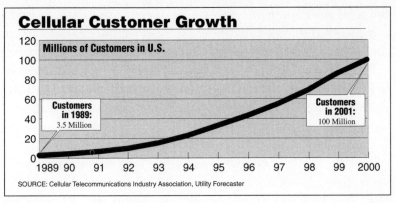

Cellular Customer Growth

Millions of Customers in U.S.

Customers in 1989: 3.5 Million

Customers in 2001: 100 Million

SOURCE: Cellular Telecommunications Industry Association, Utility Forecaster

Figure 3.3

Five years ago, the decaying AT&T empire boasted the largest cellular company in the United States, AT&T Wireless. Sprint PCS and Craig McCaw's Nextel were considered its most formidable rivals. In contrast, Bell company wireless efforts were discounted as Johnny-come-latelies with little chance of being anything more than regional operators.

Since deregulation, however, the Bells have grabbed the upper hand. From the thousands of individuals and companies who won spectrum licenses in the government auctions of the 1980s, the country's two largest cellular providers now are both Baby Bell efforts.

Verizon Wireless, which is 45 percent owned by British cellular giant Vodafone, reaches nearly 30 million customers nationwide. The company is a combination of the cellular systems of the former Bell Atlantic, GTE, NYNEX, Pacific Telesis—spun off as Airtouch in the mid-1990s—and U.S. West, which sold its systems to Airtouch a few years later. SBC Communications has fused its wireless systems—which include those of Southwestern Bell, Ameritech, Southern New England Telecom, and the digital cellular operations of Pacific Telesis—with BellSouth's to form Cingular Wireless.

In 1995, the top five wireless companies in the United States controlled less than 50 percent of the market. By 2000, that share had risen to 80 percent and it's still rising. Together, Verizon and Cingular control some 50 percent of the entire U.S. cellular base, and, given their unmatched reaches, economies of scale, and the financial power of their parents, that share is rising daily. The two companies dominated auctions of cellular territory in late 2000 as they continued to fill in their networks (see Figure 3.4).

Data communications is the industry's other major innovation of the late twentieth and early twenty-first century. Here, too, the Bells were late out of the gate in the new market competing with cable television companies, but again, they've more than made up for it, quickly consolidating market power in their hands.

To date, Bells have been shut out of the long-distance data market. Verizon, for example, was forced to divest the Internet backbone of high-capacity fiber-optic cables and switches of GTE when it merged with that company in early 2000. It will be able to buy back the unit, known as Genuity, only if it's allowed into the long distance business throughout its 14-state local phone territory by 2005. Instead, a handful of major companies, including WorldCom, own the majority of the world's Internet backbone. The business of Internet service providers (ISPs) is similarly concentrated in a few big names.

The Bells, however, are coming to both markets in a hurry. Though Congressional efforts are stalled, they're gathering strength in other areas of the exploding data markets. Verizon, for example, is rapidly building a massive fiber-based network in the Northeast, while SBC has inked a major alliance with Williams Communications' nationwide network.

Once derided as inferior to cable television modems and the like, Bells' offerings of DSL, or direct subscriber line—high-speed

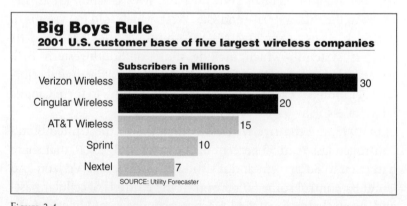

Big Boys Rule
2001 U.S. customer base of five largest wireless companies

Subscribers in Millions

Verizon Wireless	30
Cingular Wireless	20
AT&T Wireless	15
Sprint	10
Nextel	7

SOURCE: Utility Forecaster

Figure 3.4

Internet access that's always on—are also growing, thanks to a superior combination of low prices and aggressive marketing.

That's putting the squeeze on all of their competitors in the business from cable providers to ISPs. Verizon's recent abandonment of its proposed merger with DSL upstart Northpoint Communications testifies as much to its own success at signing on new customers as to Northpoint's failure to profitably grow its own operations, which ultimately condemned the company to bankruptcy.

The Bells' data dominance will only increase in coming years as the wireless Internet—which they already dominate—takes hold. According to research from The Strategis Group, the number of respondents saying they would use their local phone company for Internet service has increased from 19.9 percent to 30.6 percent over the past year, a greater share than that of the pure-play ISPs. Moreover, remaining competitors will have to rely on the Bells' emerging network of high-speed connections, earning them additional wholesale revenues.

SECRETS OF SUCCESS

Why have the Bells succeeded where their critics predicted only abysmal failure? Because they shared the primary strength of the old AT&T monopoly: money. The local phone offspring of the late, great AT&T empire are still the best-capitalized communications companies in the world, and they're set to be well into the new century.

Running a network has always been expensive. The cost of installing and servicing thousands of miles of copper wire was a major reason Theodore Vail was able to convince Theodore Roosevelt, a trustbuster at heart, to allow his company to build a monopoly.

Since the mid-1990s, the quantum leap forward in communications technology, as well as demand for new services, has dramatically upped the ante for network operators. The cost of building and running competitive networks has soared to levels that would have made Vail blush. Meeting future demand for speed and capacity—particularly in the transmission of reams of data—requires previously unheard-of levels of bandwidth or raw network capacity. Laying thousands of miles of fiber-optic cable, installing state-of-the-art digital network switches, and building web servers that computer farms needed to process and store huge volumes of data, has already cost billions and will cost billions more.

As Bell bashers pointed out, the Bells' copper wire networks are vastly inferior to the new technology in terms of both capacity and speed. They overlooked one simple fact, however: The copper network was already in place and paid for. The new technology would be able to compete only after billions were spent to build new networks.

The key question was not who had the best technology when the postderegulation race began, but rather who had the money to put the technology to use once the standards were in place and demand for the cutting-edge products—like high-speed data—was reaching critical mass. The answer was clearly the cash-rich Bells.

With little or no sales, Bell competitors borrowed heavily to construct new networks to generate revenue for the future. In contrast, the Bells financed network upgrades using safe revenue streams from their copper networks. Bells were able to simultaneously bring their networks up to speed, keep their debt down, and cut costs. Consequently, they're now far more competitive than their smaller, heavily indebted rivals, enabling them to cut rates to regain market share and keep profit margins high at the same time.

Superior economies of scale is the second factor behind the Bells' success. As Theodore Vail understood, a company's network becomes cheaper to operate the bigger it grows. Bigger discounts are possible for the procurement of new technology and equipment. Labor and regulatory agreements can be negotiated with fewer complications. Lobbying and political clout is greater. The ability to market more products to a broader reach of customers grows exponentially, and the most lucrative customers can be pursued more aggressively.

The effectiveness of the old AT&T empire makes this point quite well in telecommunications. The bigger the company grew, the easier it was for it to finance more growth. Major capital expenditures were spread out among more people, limiting their impact on rates. Ditto subsidies of less profitable customers. More recently, the Bell mergers make the same point. Starting with the Bell Atlantic/NYNEX union and continuing through the SBC/Ameritech deal, every combination has produced billions in cost savings, synergies, and accelerated profit growth.

Economies of scale will only become more important in coming years as the industry's technology threshold continues to rise. Marketing spending will be increasingly critical in an age where technology permits several providers to coexist, but only the best-known names grab the spoils. No one is better positioned than the Bells, particularly as they use their superior financial position to make more acquisitions and expand.

The third reason Bell critics missed the boat was overestimating the role of technology on the evolution of postderegulation communications industry power, and underestimating the Bells' ability to absorb and profit from new technology.

At the time the Telecom Act of 1996 was passed, for example, a debate was raging over the fundamental nature of future communications. At issue was the role of *Internet protocol*, or IP, a system of communications in which information travels in *packets* over the Internet.

Since the founding of AT&T, communications has been designed around circuit switches. These go back to the old days when switchboard operators would connect two phone lines with patch cords to create an electric circuit. Today, the circuits aren't actual physical wires, but are still based on the fundamental principle of setting up a connection.

IP is an entirely different concept. The best way to think of it is as electronic mail or e-mail. With e-mail, no connections need be set up ahead of time. Instead, the caller's message is sent as a packet of information that wends its way through the network to its ultimate destination. With IP, the call's route to the receiver follows the path of least resistance to arrive at its destination.

IP represents a vast advance over circuit-based communications in several respects. First, it allows more information to flow faster. Second, it can be done with far less bandwidth or communications capacity, since the packets don't have to follow any specific routes. Third, while a circuit communication can be broken if there's a problem anywhere in its designated route, IP communications will continue to flow as long as any route is available.

IP's key drawback is in voice communications. For starters, both conversers must be online. The real problem, though, boils down to network capacity. Packet flow works fine as long as there's sufficient bandwidth. The problems start when bandwidth is in short supply, resulting in the quality concerns that plague Internet phone calls today, like e-mail backing up or slowing down on Christmas or Mother's Day.

The 1996 consensus was the Bells were wedded to circuit-switched communications and would be unable to adapt when IP took over. In reality, their initially visionless approach has served them well. As dozens of startup, IP-based, service providers have struggled by trying to compete immediately against the Bell circuit-based networks, the Bells have learned from their mistakes and are beginning to employ the technology in their own way. Thanks in large part to their superior financial firepower, they're moving quickly and effectively.

Management was considered the Bells' greatest weakness when deregulation opened their monopolies in 1996. Decades of protection from competition had left most very top-heavy. Big bureaucracies and multilevel management stifled creativity and made executive promotion mostly a function of pleasing the higher-ups. Innovations were few and far between, and top executives were mostly discounted as apparatchiks and hacks.

In contrast, several Bell competitors had top executives who were considered visionaries on Wall Street. Bernard Ebbers, for example, built WorldCom into one of the world's most powerful communications providers through more than 100 mergers and acquisitions over five years. William Esrey brought Sprint from obscurity into the limelight in similar fashion.

The brain gap between the Bells and their competitors was alleged to go all the way to the bottom. While Bell companies offered relative job security, their rivals offered the bright and ambitious the promise of busting into new markets and incentivized them with soaring stock prices. The result was a flow of many of the Bells' most capable employees to their upstart rivals, which turned into a flood when the Bells began laying off employees to cut costs.

Ironically, it's been the so-called visionaries who have stumbled in the postderegulation communications world. After failing to acquire Sprint in 2000, Ebbers has seen WorldCom fall short of its revenue and profit targets, forcing him to dramatically scale back his former expansion plans. By early 2001, the company's share price was more than 70 percent off its highs. Esrey has endured a similar fate at Sprint.

Worst of all has been the performance of C. Michael Armstrong at AT&T, who was viewed as a virtual celebrity on his arrival. After putting together an empire including 40 percent of America's cable television connections, a 50 percent share of the long-distance market, and the nation's leading cellular phone provider, he's now done a 180-degree turn to divide the company. In contrast, the hacks and apparatchiks at the Bells have slowly and surely moved their companies into a dominant position, with the best yet to come.

Ivan Seidenberg of Verizon Communications and Edward Whitacre of SBC Communications recognized something their more flamboyant rivals did not: the importance of the last mile of communications.

While others positioned for the more exciting growth areas of their industry, like cellular and data, hinging their future on the latest technologies, these men stuck to basics: building unassailable economies of scale through acquisitions and technological upgrades. As a result, they now have the foundation to dominate all communications markets, including those on the cutting edge of technology. In the end, it was their chess game skill that's beaten the entrepreneurial approach of their rivals.

All of these strengths were critical to the Bells' rise to industry prominence, but it's the marketing power of their brand names that has come as the biggest surprise to many.

Before the 1996 Telecom Act, it was assumed that AT&T, WorldCom, and Sprint were the most recognized telecom brands, and that, if given the choice, consumers would opt for their service rather than the Bells'. In practice, just the opposite has occurred. Both Verizon and SBC have been enormously successful marketing their wireless services nationwide against the long-distance Big Three, and they've greatly exceeded expectations in grabbing new customers where they've been allowed to enter the long-distance market.

Most impressive, however, has been the way they've held service in their core local phone markets. Even in the first rush of deregulation, competitors made little headway. Now, in a direct contrast to the early 1990s, surveys show the public has far more confidence in local phone companies than in any of their rivals, including the marketing powerhouses AT&T and WorldCom.

Part of that is due to the fact that, in an era of so many choices, many consumers find it comforting to stick with a familiar name. While AT&T's brand name is still rated as more powerful, the Bells apparently have done a good job distinguishing themselves in the years since the 1984 divestiture.

Bells have also substantially bolstered their reputations for quality of service. As recently as the mid-1990s, for example, NYNEX was considered one of the worst companies in the country for service quality and was roundly despised by its customers in New York and New England. As a result, it was widely considered an easy target for would-be rivals in the local phone business, including AT&T and Time Warner's cable television system. Since its takeover by Bell Atlantic in the mid-1990s, however, quality has improved to the point where a growing number are now using its long-distance service rather than AT&T's. There's been little erosion of local phone revenues either.

THE NEXT MA BELL

Is communications truly a natural monopoly as Theodore Vail postulated nearly a century ago? The ascendancy of the Baby Bells to the top of the industry—and the retreat of even their largest competitors—seems to say yes.

It's far from certain whether a Baby Bell will actually emerge as a new Ma Bell, though. The Bells' unexpected strengths have pushed them into the lead, but there are a host of other companies, both within and outside the United States, that have benefited from the same trend toward the powerful.

In this country, Alltel Communications and Century Communications, for example, have built Bell-like franchises in less densely populated areas of the country. Operating in rural areas, they have the additional advantage of facing relatively little competition. WorldCom has built a considerable lead in business-focused, high-speed data markets worldwide. Broadwing has built one of the nation's most advanced Internet backbone networks with very little debt, thanks to a Bell-like hold on the Cincinnati communications market.

The framers of the 1996 Telecom Act envisioned cable television companies as key competitors of the Baby Bells in local phone markets. The chief component of their infrastructure, coaxial cable, is vastly superior in bandwidth potential to the existing copper networks, and the technology to complete phone calls over cable lines was ready in the form of set-top boxes. The advantage was especially acute with Internet connections, where cable modems were considered vastly superior to the high-speed offerings of the Bells.

Proponents underestimated the cost of upgrading cable networks to handle phone calls and overestimated the ability of cable companies to pull away Bell phone customers. Today, however, cable providers like Cox Communications and Comcast still own valuable infrastructure and enjoy cash-rich franchise positions that make them potential Bell rivals.

Overseas, most of the government-owned monopolies have been privatized and now face competition. Several, including Telefonica, which dominates the Spanish and Portuguese speaking world, have financial power and economies of scale rivaling any of the U.S. Bells today. Some upstarts, like Vodafone, have transformed into giants.

Unlike during the twentieth century, these companies are increasingly able to compete with each other across national boundaries. The result is communications companies are truly becoming multinational, just as their counterparts in other industries have been for decades.

As big companies have repeatedly prevailed, merger mania has accelerated throughout the communications industry (see Figure 3.5). Governments have become more skeptical of new deals; that's one reason the pace slowed in 2001, but more are coming.

Industry globalization is a key reason the next Ma Bell will be far more powerful than its predecessor, with a network spanning the globe forged by acquisitions and growth. Any of today's leaders striving to be the next Ma Bell could easily wind up as just a part of another company.

Although its importance has been overestimated, communications technology is another wild card that could still shift the power structure. Wireless, for example, has the potential to supplant wireline communications for many uses. It's possible we'll see industry entrants from other industries as well take a prominent place in the communications picture. The development of alternative networks by electric utilities and others could still enable upstarts to take on the Bells with a high-tech advantage, though that window is rapidly closing. WorldCom's data-intensive network remains one of the world's most powerful.

Ultimately, the creation of a new Ma Bell depends on whether the world's governments will allow it. During 2000 and 2001, European and U.S. governments became more skeptical of communications mergers, nixing the planned marriage between WorldCom and Sprint. The ultimate arbiters of how much more consolidation happens—and how strongly governments will move to fight the inevitable—will be consumers.

Thus far, deregulation has been a mixed bag for consumers.

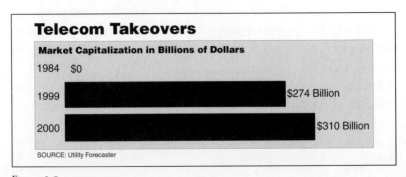

Figure 3.5

Complaints about poor service and misleading telemarketing by service providers are rising. Rates for lower-dollar users have actually risen, as companies focus on serving the most lucrative clients. Despite pledges to maintain universal service, evidence is mounting that a growing part of America is being left on the wrong side of a digital divide. If uncorrected, they'll be left out of the new economy.

On the other hand, deregulation has noticeably benefited the world's well-heeled consumers. As long as this process translates into lower rates, better services, and more products, they'll continue to embrace it eagerly, regardless of whether it leads to further concentration of power in the hands of future Ma Bell candidates. That's why few have mourned the death of upstart CLECs and DSL companies.

The growing satisfaction of the wealthy has produced a consensus between the Bush administration's Federal Communications Commission and Congress to intervene far less than the Clinton FCC did in the first years of deregulation. With Michael Powell as FCC chairman, prior attempts to tilt the playing field away from the Baby Bells—at least partly for less wealthy consumers' protection—have been abandoned in favor of letting the fittest survive. Without an effective regulatory check on their growing financial power and economies of scale, the rise of the Bells and their brethren around the world will be hard to resist.

Once the march toward a few or even one powerful provider starts to impact service, consumers—and very likely lobbyists for affected industries—will demand some sort of government action. That, however, could just as easily be the recreation of a regulated monopoly system as it could a full-scale breakup. Future politics will set the tone, but for the better part of this decade at least, the march to a second Ma Bell will remain inexorable.

. . . .

INDUSTRY PROFILE: JIM LINNEHAN

Jim Linnehan has played a variety of roles during his career in the communications industry. Perhaps the most formative was his 11-year tenure at AT&T's Bell Labs, during which he worked on market trials for Ma Bell's consumer division. Participating in the development of direct subscriber line (DSL) high-speed Internet access, interactive television, telephony, and video-on-demand, Jim learned firsthand about the industry's most promising technologies, as well as how they should and should not be marketed.

These trials followed a pattern Linnehan now describes jokingly as "the tail wagging the dog," spawned from the inventions of Bell Labs itself rather than market research. They basically involved taking a new technology developed by Bell Labs and inventing a potential use for it. Linnehan and his team would attempt to build enough support among executives for the solution within the company to drum up the cash for an actual market test. This approach earned the company the moniker of one of the world's worst technology companies, despite producing most of communications' major innovations over the past half century.

Now an industry analyst at Thomas Weisel Partners, Jim's focus for the past two years has been covering telecom services, mostly large-capitalization, long-haul players. Coupled with a stint at Montgomery Securities analyzing satellite company services, he's now one of the most knowledgeable sources on the rapid evolution of the communications industry in America.

Q: WHAT'S THE BIGGEST CHANGE IN THE
   COMMUNICATIONS INDUSTRY IN THE PAST 20
   YEARS?

A: Without doubt the development of the Internet as a global platform for communications, especially for business. The Net has frankly changed every way we communicate by eliminating the distance between people. We're now able to purchase and sell goods and services from anywhere to anywhere, which just was not possible before. The magnitude of that dwarfs everything else that's happened, including the Telecom Act of 1996, which only changed things in the U.S.

Incidentally, I look for a complete rewrite of the Telecom Act of 1996 in the next few years. Federal Communications Commission Chairman Michael Powell is in danger of building a legacy of being only big business–friendly. I expect he'll try to change that by promoting competition with some very Internet-friendly changes to the Act.

Q: WHAT IS THE ROLE OF CAPITAL IN TODAY'S INDUSTRY?

A: Over the past five or six years, companies have spent billions to deploy a new telecom fabric, basically optical technology. Over the next five years or so, there will be new generations of technology, but for the most part the fabric has been built. Instead, new spending will go toward making things run better. That means increasing customer satisfaction—especially from experiences on the Web—by making things stronger, faster, and cheaper.

The biggest beneficiaries in my view will be the global companies, particularly those heavily involved in cross-border traffic with a lot of cost-effective bandwidth. The greatest area of inefficiency in telecom is the disparity in pricing between countries, particularly among the single-nation telecoms. The globals who are most effective in breaking down those barriers by being able to complete calls all on their own networks are going to reap a windfall as these barriers come down and pricing outside the U.S. begins to standardize. I also look for a huge upswing in the flow of international voice and data traffic.

Q: HOW CRITICAL IS SIZE TO SUCCESS IN COMMUNICATIONS?

A: Very. It's simply going to be very tough for small players to compete going forward. But the key is brand-name recognition, rather than some financial measurement.

There are basically three types of communications customers in the U.S.: consumers, small business, and large business. Most consumers don't even realize there are alternative providers of phone services, so that market is extremely difficult to crack. Large businesses are completely brand- and quality-sensitive. It's extremely important for them to be able to trust that their provider will be around a year from now. In addition, they tend to command a lot of buying power, so they get the best deals and have little financial incentive to switch providers. That basically leaves small business as the only market for small tels to compete for. Small businesses are far more price-sensitive, so they're more likely to switch to a smaller provider in hopes of getting a better rate.

Financial strength is important. But despite the well-publicized failures, there are a number of competitive local exchange carriers that are well-funded. The problem for them is simply market share. They're limited in who they can sell to. It really boils down to this: If you can walk into a customer's office and they've heard good things about you, you're in. If they haven't, you can forget about getting their business. Some CLECs have market share in the teens in their home markets. But if you take them where no one has yet heard of them, where they have zero brand recognition, it's going to be very tough.

Q: WILL INDUSTRY CONSOLIDATION CONTINUE?

A: Yes, but in a different way. Despite the change at the White House, I don't think we'll see many mergers between big U.S. companies to produce more scale at this point. Instead, the action will be among distressed companies, which will be absorbed by stronger ones looking to add a new product or technological expertise to their arsenal. One good example is WorldCom's recent takeover of little CLEC Intermedia in order to take control of web server farm company Digex. Basically, the acquirers will be big companies that recognize they're missing a club from their bag and can get it cheaper by buying rather than building. In other words, we'll see a good many more $1 billion transactions than $50 billion ones.

As for cross-border transactions, I don't think there will be more of the joint ventures that have failed so spectacularly in the past few years, such as Global One and the AT&T/BT Concert deal. I do think, however, that we'll see more non-U.S. companies making investments in this country. Vodafone's wireless venture with Verizon is a good example. And we're also likely to see mergers between major phone companies outside the U.S.

Q: WHAT'S THE FUTURE OF WIRELESS
   COMMUNICATIONS?

A: Four years ago it looked like everything in the world was going wireless. We may still get there, but it's become clear that there are a lot of hurdles. Basically, the wireless spectrum doesn't exist to provide the level of quality and service we've become accustomed to on our desktop. We can't even successfully complete a wireless phone call with the same quality as a landline phone!

There are a couple of interesting dynamics happening in the wireless industry though. First, wireless voice pricing seems to be following a similar path as consumer long-distance pricing, which is sharply down. Second, the business market for wireless services continues to grow very strongly, with a number of employers starting to pick up the tab.

Interestingly, I don't see, outside of a couple of companies, anyone who has really cracked the business market yet. And that market is really poised to grow much faster, particularly once 3G (third-generation) wireless technology hits the scene. U.S. companies, however, still have a problem their European rivals don't. People perceive the service as inferior to landline service and that will inhibit their growth until it's resolved. U.S. wireless companies must deliver on the promise of wireless.

CHAPTER 4

....

The New Politics of Water

Pure and plentiful water—lakes, streams, and wells—was once the birthright of every American. Unfortunately, in barely two generations, abundant clean water has largely become a myth.

Unbridled development, the relentless spread of suburbs, the destruction of wetlands and forests, industrial discharge, agricultural runoff, acid rain, and a hundred other forms of pollution have degraded the nation's water supplies to dangerous levels. Hazardous elements have turned up in dozens of cities' and towns' watersheds across the country, and, despite the best efforts of government and industry in many areas, the danger of new toxins seeping in is ever present.

In 1999, 25 percent of New England's water systems and 39 percent of New York City area systems were cited for health violations. The Environmental Protection Agency's 1998 National Water Quality Inventory Report to Congress reported 35 percent of assessed rivers and streams did not meet basic water quality standards. Moreover, 45 percent of lakes and 44 percent of estuaries were found impaired, including 4,700 miles of Great Lakes shoreline.

The health costs of unsafe water are staggering. Water-borne diseases—such as the 1993 outbreak of cryptosporidiosis in Milwaukee that killed 50 and hospitalized 4,000—are thankfully still rare. Scores of other elements found in ordinary drinking water supplies, however, have been linked to everything from cancer to birth defects. Arsenic levels found in some areas, for example, were cited in a 2000 U.S. Environmental Protection Agency report as the cause of a wide range of respiratory failures, as well as liver cirrhosis, rectal cancer, and cerebrovascular disease.

As the horror stories pile up, the American public has increasingly demanded cleaner, safer water. In response, the federal government and a host of individual states have dramatically tightened standards in recent years. One of the last acts of the Clinton administration, for example, was to implement the toughest standards yet for arsenic. Though the Bush administration has scaled back the standards, the level of pollutants is still rising, and so will the number of rules governing drinking water supplies.

The financial cost of pollution is equally steep. Industry, utilities, and government are now dishing out some $64 billion a year to ensure clean water supplies (see Figure 4.1). With EPA continuing to discover more dangerous pollutants, the costs are rising. In fact, EPA estimates an additional $260 billion will be spent over the next 20 years on improvements to U.S. water and wastewater infrastructures.

The rising cost of operating systems is turning the politics of who controls water on its ear. Under the old system, massive government-owned monopolies ran most of the nation's urban systems, while a diffuse group of more than 60,000 systems served the smaller towns, more distant suburbs, and developments.

Under the emerging order, the rulers will still be monopolies, but rather than governments, their owners will be a small but rapidly growing band of investor-owned utilities with the finan-

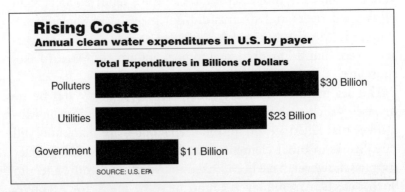

Figure 4.1

cial power, economies of scale, and management expertise to build national water empires.

The change is still in its early stages. With both state and federal regulators backing their rise to power, water utilities will wind up wielding as much industry power as their energy and communications counterparts did in their halcyon years. The opportunities for investors will be enormous. Consumers will also benefit, though, as these growing empires ensure safer water supplies and simultaneously keep costs low.

THE MUNI MONOPOLY

From its beginnings more than a century ago, America's water industry has been built on the premise that the liquid would always be clean, cheap, and plentiful. With potable water readily available throughout most of the country—except in the West— the cost of building and running water systems has been relatively low. The business, consequently, has been a cash cow.

In rural and small-town areas, there are still some 60,000 individual systems, 90 percent of which serve fewer than 3,000 people. In addition, much of the rural United States continues to be served by backyard wells that cost nothing more than the time and effort to dig them.

In the large cities, there was a heavy initial cost to build systems capable of bringing enough water to market to meet the needs of large populations. Once the needed economies of scale were gained, the massive financial power and reach of the urban systems made them even cheaper to operate, and every successive expansion brought costs down further.

The development of America's urban water systems basically parallels that of big city electric, natural gas, and communications utilities. Early on, communities decided that water service was a natural monopoly, in large part because of the sheer difficulty in moving it around. Building multiple competing systems was quickly discovered to be ludicrous. Instead, communities built single systems of pipes, mains, and treatment plants serving all of a town's inhabitants. That remains the case today and won't change anytime soon.

In water, however, it was municipalities, not utilities, that quickly became the dominant players. One reason muni water monopolies—which today control 85 percent of U.S. water supplies—won out was rooted in ideology. Even as laissez-faire capitalism reigned supreme in the early twentieth century, water was viewed in a different light, even from phone or power service. In fact, to many, water was a gift from God, essential to life itself. Allowing companies to profit from its sale was considered immoral.

Trust was another reason munis won the day. As cities grew, potential interruptions in water service became all the more intolerable. After the Great Depression bankrupted several power utilities, it seemed only governments backed by a community's tax dollars could be relied on to provide clean, plentiful water in even the worst crisis. Municipal governments' ability to issue low-cost, tax-free bonds to finance infrastructure growth was also cited as further security that investor-owned companies could not match.

As the muni monopolies grew, they developed a third great advantage over their investor-owned rivals: an extremely powerful constituency in the halls of political power. By mid-century, the biggest water systems had become very cheap to run (see Figure 4.2). Consequently, they were cash cows for their owning governments. They also provided a prime outlet for patronage in construction and contracting jobs, giving city gov-

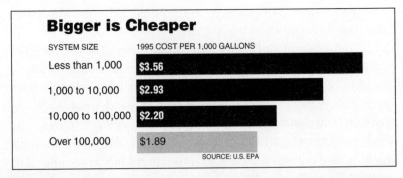

Figure 4.2

ernment administrations a powerful weapon for maintaining
political power.

While small towns and farms relied on a single well or wells,
municipalities tapped into rivers and later constructed large reservoirs from which water was piped to residences and businesses.
Treatment of sewage and wastewater soon developed alongside, as
did fire-prevention systems, and the technology of water pressure—practiced in some form since the days of ancient Rome—
was established to keep water flowing throughout systems.

In the early days of running water systems, municipalities were
basically concerned with extending their reach and expanding
available sources from groundwater supplies, reservoirs, lakes, and
rivers. The challenge increased with the country's rapid urbanization following World War II and the subsequent move to the suburbs, prompting the U.S. Army Corps of Engineers to take a major
role in development.

Throughout, the munis proved up to the task. As their size and
reach grew, their operating costs fell, and their ability to grow
increased. Tax-free bonds provided an almost painless way to
finance new infrastructure when needed. By granting their own
franchises, governments ensured against any competition as well.

In contrast, utilities were effectively barred from the most lucrative water markets, big cities. Instead, they made their living serving the small towns and suburbs outside the purview of the large,
city-owned systems. One of the oldest water utilities in America,
for example, was little Elizabethtown Water, which maintained its
independence on the outskirts of one of the world's largest systems serving the New York City area. As a result, utes were mostly
very small enterprises up until the 1990s, even as their counterparts in the power and phone businesses blossomed into multinational corporations.

The graph (Figure 4.3) breaking down the water industry's
early 1990s ownership structure tells the story. Municipal systems served nearly 85 percent of Americans nationwide. The
rest was divided among a handful of utilities and some 60,000—
mostly small—systems, 90 percent of which serve less than
3,000 people.

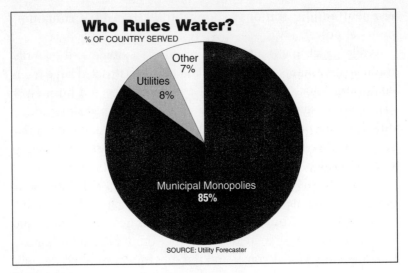

Figure 4.3

THE WORM TURNS

By the 1960s, the triumph of the munis was complete. Not only did they serve all the major population centers, but the ethos that public systems were the lowest-cost and most efficient way to provide water service was almost universally accepted. In contrast, utilities were often viewed with suspicion as profiteers, and state regulators closely monitored their safety and quality.

While utilities' lack of economies of scale kept their rates relatively high, muni water rates were so low that few consumers or businesses cared how much they used or who provided it. When a major project or expansion was needed, it was the munis who had the access to capital via tax-free bond issues. Investor-owned companies were considered insignificant also-rans and accessed capital markets only rarely.

Ironically, the muni monopolies were already starting to lose their grip, the reason being a quantum leap in operating and capital improvement costs for which they proved shockingly unprepared, despite their formidable economies of scale.

Decaying infrastructure in the inner cities—the first areas to build systems—was the first danger sign. Water mains began to break and piping started to erode; while the problems were first confined to more impoverished areas, they soon spread.

Worse, the side effects of nearly a century of Industrial Revolution began to show up in water supplies in the form of dangerous chemicals. Hazardous pesticides such as DDT began to appear as well from agricultural runoff. Acid rain changed the chemical balance of rivers and streams. Most alarming, deadly bacteria began to turn up as 100 years of environmental degradation finally began to take its toll on America.

Pressure began to mount on cities to dramatically upgrade their water treatment facilities to meet these new challenges. Unfortunately, they couldn't have been more unprepared. Beyond adding new customers, cheap water supplies and low operating costs had long discouraged meaningful new investment in systems.

In many cases, money had been siphoned off to other projects and uses. Now that it was needed, it was nowhere to be found. As for raising new capital, the massive population growth of the past two decades had already placed a great strain on many municipalities' borrowing ability. At the same time, the massive migration of more affluent citizens to the suburbs eroded their ability to tax, further undermining their financial positions.

By the early 1970s, clean water had become a hot-button issue. Confronted with evidence of deteriorating waterways and weakened by the Watergate scandal, the Republican White House at last bowed to the demands of Congress for tough action. The result was the 1974 passage of the landmark Safe Drinking Water Act (SDWA).

The SDWA was a response to uneven water quality, as supplies in many areas became more contaminated. For the first time, the federal government—operating through the nascent Environmental Protection Agency—had the power to force state and local water systems to eliminate or at least severely limit the occurrence of dozens of substances in drinking supplies.

Systematic testing of wells, reservoirs, lakes, rivers, and other bodies of water was put into place, and the EPA was charged with collecting reams of data on every aspect of the nation's water supply. Consistent national standards were established, with maximum allowable levels set for a wide array of substances enforced by the EPA.

The SDWA's tough new rules didn't halt what amounted to a century-long deterioration in America's water quality. They did, however, have one indelible legacy: establishing procedures for detecting and monitoring the dangerous pollutants creeping their way into the nation's drinking water supplies, setting the stage for more dramatic action later on.

That came in 1986 when Congress amended SDWA to require the EPA to publish standards for 83 specific contaminants. In addition, it authorized the agency to regulate 25 new contaminants every three years and come up with standards as needed. Under the Act, the EPA first reviews data concerning health effects of substances found in water supplies. It then sets Maximum Contaminant Level Goals (MCLGs), depending on whether the elements are known or probable carcinogens.

Generally, MCLGs for carcinogens are set at zero. Everything else is set at a level where no adverse health effects would occur, with a margin of safety. The EPA also sets a Maximum Contaminant Level (MCL) as close to the MCLG as possible, creating the standard that's enforceable by law.

After 1986, the EPA had the power for the first time to be proactive in ensuring clean water standards by seeking out and regulating scores of new substances, even before they actually caused damage. The result was unprecedented progress improving water quality. The price was a dramatic rise in the cost of water treatment, as providers were forced to consider and test for scores of new substances in the water they sold.

The third great revision to the nation's clean water laws came in 1996 with the Safe Drinking Water Act Reauthorization Amendments, signed into law by President Clinton on August 6. The amendments were intended to simplify standards for clean water, provide flexibility to systems in how to meet the requirements, and boost enforcement of penalties for noncompliance.

The amendments removed the requirement for the EPA to identify and regulate 25 new substances every three years, but they also created more vigorous enforcement of standards for substances already deemed harmful. Over the past five years, the

EPA has waged war on polluters and substandard water systems alike, imposing sharp penalties and going to court to defend its prerogatives when necessary.

The amendments also gave the EPA a mandate to research three particularly troublesome substances increasingly found in water supplies—arsenic, radon, and cryptosporidium; identify the health risks they posed; and prescribe new limits on their occurrence in the water. The result will continue to be the enactment of tough limits on all three substances in the future.

THE NEW ORDER

As the cost of clean water continues to rise, the old politics of water is changing rapidly. As under the old order, size is king and access to capital is queen, but under the new order it's the long-ignored investor-owned utilities that are the best positioned for dominance.

Toughening clean water standards have slowed the deterioration in America's water quality over the years. As Figure 4.4 shows, the percentage of U.S. water systems in compliance with EPA standards steadily rose over the decade of the 1990s.

Though more dangerous contaminants have been discovered, the framework is in place for their discovery and treatment. Water scares such as what hit Washington, D.C. in the mid-1990s—

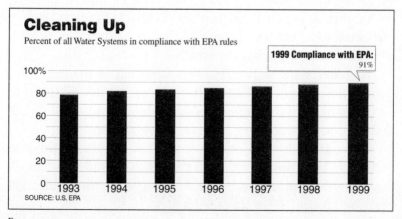

Figure 4.4

when supplies run by the U.S. Army Corps of Engineers were declared unsafe for bathing, let alone drinking—are rare, and there's every reason to hope they'll remain that way.

In addition, greater appreciation for the value of wetlands and watersheds, fewer overt leakages of toxins into rivers and streams, more strict air pollution standards, and ongoing cleanup programs are gradually improving water quality around the country. While our waterways won't be safe to drink from directly for years to come, if ever again, there are some remarkable emerging success stories, such as the cleanup of the Potomac River that runs through our nation's capital. These efforts will continue as awareness grows of the toll of dirty water on industries such as fishing and logging, as well as recreation.

The cost of cleaning up water, however, has been considerable. As more hazardous substances become a threat to supplies, it's likely to head a lot higher before it again comes under control. Barring a miracle, the days of cheap, plentiful water are over, at least for our lifetime. Even the Bush administration, which has worked to loosen environmental standards in power generation and energy production, has continued to enforce tough clean water standards. And we're just one water scare away from far tighter rules.

At the same time clean water standards have toughened up, the infrastructure of water systems has steadily decayed. Today, thousands of miles of piping, particularly in the inner cities, need replacing. Older water treatment plants have become increasingly outmoded, as higher standards have demanded greater levels of performance. Even the breaking of water mains has become alarmingly common in many areas.

For water systems, the keys to succeeding in the ever more costly environment of the twenty-first century are still the same as they were in the high-growth twentieth: size and access to capital. With standards rising and ever more pollutants threatening to contaminate supplies, greater economies of scale and financial power are increasingly critical to the health of water systems. By necessity, those able to meet the challenge will grow rapidly. The weak will flounder in a sea of red ink.

The financial challenges of the emerging era are sounding the death knell for the 50,000-plus U.S. systems serving less than 3,000 people. Like the cities, water supplies of rural and small-town systems have been massively degraded in recent years by everything from agricultural runoff to acid rain. Worse, many are still using water treatment technology that was likely outdated during the Eisenhower administration, and they simply don't serve enough people to spread around the costs of upgrades without driving their communities into depression.

With their power to tax and issue tax-free bonds, the municipal monopolies still have formidable weapons at their disposal for dealing with the rising costs. However, there's also little support for the kind of tax increases required to finance these actions. In fact, there's a growing consensus that—as in other industries—the private sector can do the job better.

A study by the Reason Foundation in the mid-1990s concluded that California consumers using muni monopoly water service pay an average of 28 percent more than they would from a utility. That rationale has found a friendly ear in the Bush administration, as well as with state regulators across the country who are at this point forbidden from overseeing muni-run water systems. In fact, the muni monopolies themselves have largely abandoned expansion.

Like other water systems, utilities have faced rising costs. Smaller utes in particular have been forced in recent years to ask the state regulators who oversee their operations for particularly large rate increases to cover the costs of water treatment and infrastructure improvements. In many cases, at least some of the requests have been disallowed, leaving the companies weakened with high levels of debt.

The difference is, unlike the munis, utilities' regulator-sanctioned capital improvements are immediately added to their asset bases, which in turn are used to calculate their rates. As a result, the more building they do, the more money they make. Rather than weaken them, new building increases their economies of scale and financial power to grow even more (see Figure 4.5).

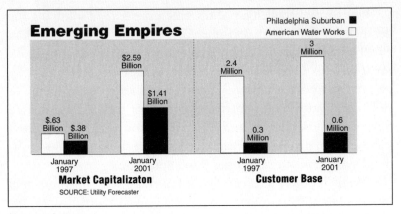

Figure 4.5

As a result, utilities are the heirs to the riches of water's new era, and they're taking full advantage of their rivals' weaknesses to grow as never before. As this industry shakeout runs its course over the next five to ten years, they'll come to dominate the water industry more thoroughly than even the muni monopolies of the old order.

WATER'S WINNERS

Water utilities are gaining control of their industry in two ways. The first is by absorbing numbers of small, cash-strapped systems. The second is by taking over management of municipal systems for a fee under contract. Both avenues to growth will remain wide open and mostly problem-free for years to come.

Acquisitions are the most straightforward way for utilities to grow. Systems serving less than 3,000 people simply don't have the resources to upgrade their infrastructure let alone ensure against a growing array of contaminants. Most have become increasingly cash-strapped in recent years, trying to keep up with or hide from EPA regulations; many now are simply tapped out.

The easiest way for these systems to ensure clean water supplies to their customers is to combine with a larger system having economies of scale to easily absorb them. Consequently, they've been willing targets of acquisition-hungry utilities, often approaching would-be acquirers with offers.

From the utility's point of view, these deals are attractive from both a short- and long-term perspective. In the short run, they usually add to earnings immediately. Willing, cash-strapped, small systems rarely sell for much more than their book value, the value of their assets less their debt. Since utilities sell well above their book values, adding these new assets is immediately accretive to profits.

In addition, costs of absorbing such small systems are generally very low. Constructing and upgrading treatment plants is the biggest capital cost that water systems face today, but big utilities construct water treatment plant capacity to serve huge numbers of potential customers. All that's generally required to absorb a new system is to hook the existing pipes into the treatment system.

Even the costs that are incurred in making acquisitions are generally recoverable, thanks to cooperative state regulators. Unlike the energy and communications industries, officials have never wielded much power over water, even to ensure clean water standards. The reason is most systems have either been too small to oversee or else municipal monopolies were out of their purview.

In contrast, regulators directly oversee operations of utilities. So expanding the utes' reach directly increases their own power, considered critical in an age of increasing clean water standards.

Takeover requests for the smallest systems are routinely approved, usually in a matter of a few weeks, and most states also allow for the recovery of merger premiums in rates as well. To further incentivize takeovers, Pennsylvania has granted acquiring utes automatic rate hikes to cover the cost of absorbing new buys. Other states have ordered small systems to justify why they should remain independent.

The long-term benefit of buying small systems is even more important. Due to conservation incentives, the average American's water use has remained roughly constant to falling in recent years, leaving acquisitions as the primary road to growth.

The more utes grow, the greater their heft and financial power to grow even larger. Just as the muni monopolies became unassailable by growing larger, so are investor-owned utilities. Getting bigger helps to cut system operating costs and rates by allowing a ute to spread out its expenses over a wider population, particularly when it comes to constructing water treatment plants.

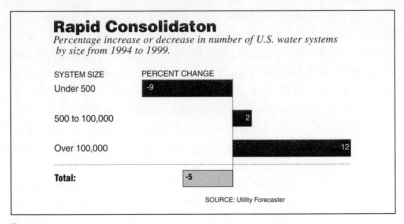

Rapid Consolidaton
Percentage increase or decrease in number of U.S. water systems by size from 1994 to 1999.

SYSTEM SIZE	PERCENT CHANGE
Under 500	-9
500 to 100,000	2
Over 100,000	12
Total:	**-5**

SOURCE: Utility Forecaster

Figure 4.6

In addition, growth improves access to capital by bringing a company to Wall Street's attention. It allows a ute to attract a higher caliber of management; it increases diversification as a bulwark against a sudden deterioration in regulatory relations in a state, as well as unfavorable shifts in the weather; and it makes the company more attractive as a potential merger partner for small systems.

The ongoing consolidation of the water industry is only in its beginning stages, and the potential for further growth is staggering. As of early 2001, water utilities served only around 8 percent of the U.S. population. With nearly 60,000 systems for sale, that share is growing rapidly (see Figure 4.6).

The more water utilities expand, the faster their rate of absorption. For example, the two biggest water utes, American Water Works and Philadelphia Suburban, have already boosted their growth rates toward double digits, almost purely from acquisitions.

DILUTING THE COMPETITION

The second way water utilities are gaining industry dominance is through management of the municipal systems that still serve some 85 percent of the U.S. population. Despite the obvious inability of the muni monopolies to keep up with twenty-first-century standards, the old quasi-religion that public water is best still has many followers.

The level of opposition to utility takeovers of muni systems was showcased most recently in 1995. Bowing to intense public pressure, the Santa Margarita Water District in Orange County, California, turned back a plan by American Water Works to buy it. In recent years, towns in New Hampshire and New Mexico have taken over their water systems on the pretext they could do the job better than the utilities. American Water is faced with a similar threat in Chattanooga, Tennessee, where its long-standing franchise has been challenged.

Nonetheless, the superiority of utilities to muni monopolies is gradually winning acceptance for cost savings as well as safety. During the U.S. Army Corps of Engineers' Washington, D.C., water scare, for example, the only system in the capital area that continued to provide clean water was in Alexandria, Virginia. That was the only system in the area run by a utility, American Water Works.

Boxed in by critics of takeovers and rising system costs, city governments are increasingly taking a third route: turning their systems over to the utilities under long-term management contracts, even while keeping legal control. Utes are charged with bringing and keeping systems up to EPA standards, as well as supervising all needed improvements in piping, mains, and water treatment plants. For this, they collect a fee that typically includes incentives for increasing efficiency and keeping rates as low as possible.

Under this arrangement, the cities carry the financial risk of running their systems, and they're responsible for funding all the needed capital improvements. The contracted utility is responsible only for competently running the system. Its capital costs are very low, especially compared to the expense of buying a system outright, and it can walk away once its contract expires.

Since the mid-1990s, system management contracts have become wildly popular across the country. Atlanta and Milwaukee are now both managed by utilities, as are scores of smaller cities and towns. Hundreds more are set to follow, enabling contract management to emerge as a major growth engine for water utes. The best is yet to come.

Ultimately, many of these system management arrangements will likely become outright acquisitions for the utilities. As their funding needs for other purposes grow, many municipalities will undoubtedly attempt to escape the still-formidable financial risk of owning their systems.

Others will find tempting the prospect of reaping a windfall gain from a system sale. They'll likely get their chance as the fervor for public water fades in many parts of the country in favor of demand for anything that will make drinking water supplies safer and more reliable.

Either way, investor-owned water systems—some of which are now foreign-owned (see the next chapter)—will continue to increase their reach in coming years by acquisitions and management contracts. That will establish them as the kingpins of an industry destined to remain a monopoly for years to come.

....

INDUSTRY PROFILE: ANTON GARNIER

At the ripe old age of 28, Anton C. Garnier followed his father and grandfather as president of California-based Southwest Water Company (Nasdaq: SWWC). Since then, he's made this business—which started as a sheep ranch in the early 1870s— a model of innovation in an historically sleepy industry.

Since the mid-1980s, Garnier has been a pioneer in the business of managing municipally owned water systems under contract. Southwest's specialty is systems of 5,000 to 50,000 people, which are generally too small for larger industry players to pursue. He's also leveraged the expertise of his employees in little-known but lucrative businesses such as automated meter reading and manhole repair, making Southwest one of the fastest-growing water companies in the country. Earnings growth has exceeded 20 percent for the past five years.

Q: AFTER 33 YEARS OF RUNNING SOUTHWEST, WHAT INTERESTS YOU MOST ABOUT THE WATER BUSINESS?

A: Relationships. We're in the business of doing things in water that give us ongoing revenues. In the utility business, when a customer moves into your geographic area, they stay your customer until they move out. The field operations in our unregulated businesses are similar. We won't get into anything where we can't sign someone on for a long period of time. Our goal is not to have to go out and sell all the time, but to build a relationship with each customer.

The key to our success in the contract management business is developing relationships with the right people. Once we win a contract, odds are great we'll keep it because we do provide great service. But to get the contract, those making the decision must trust us that we're going to do the right thing for them. We're very sensitive to the needs of city council members and their need to get reelected. Our goal is to convince them we can be a help by running a utility system they can be proud of.

The need to build relationships is a big reason why our sales cycle is 6 to 36 months. We're constantly in the process of developing the right contacts. In fact, some of the projects we're working on now may take up to six years to come to fruition. When you're dealing with a public agency, it's very difficult to predict when it's going to happen and a lot of things can go wrong, like the departure of the city manager or a city council election.

Q: HOW IMPORTANT IS THE CONTRACT MANAGEMENT
   BUSINESS TO SOUTHWEST?

A: More than half our revenue now comes from contract management services, and that number is likely to grow. Eighty-five percent of the U.S. water and wastewater industry is still controlled by government agencies and municipalities. In fact, their share has probably grown over the past few years despite the consolidation of investor-owned utilities, simply from population growth.

Most governments don't want to sell their systems. We tell them go ahead and own it, set the rates and make the needed investments and we'll manage the system for them.

The private sector has always been able to operate these systems more efficiently than have government agencies. Many municipalities still operate their systems the same low-tech way they did in the 1970s. We bring new management techniques, communications methods, and financing options they either can't afford, or lack the personnel and expertise to implement on their own.

Our focus on the small systems has several advantages. First, we've built up an expertise in building the needed kinds of relationships in this market that no one else can match, and every year we get better at it. Second, the market is below the radar of the big guys, so our competitors tend to be our size. Third, it allows us to be exceptionally diversified. Our average contract is less than $1.5 million and we have 200 of them, along with a backlog of $100 million. Even if we were to lose our biggest contract, it would have a negligible impact on profits. None of this would be true if we pursued only bigger contracts.

Keep in mind that we still get about 42 percent of our revenues from water utilities we own in California, New Mexico, and Texas. We've added a number of connections in this business and are still looking to make acquisitions, but only if they're accretive to earnings in the first year. And unfortunately the price you have to pay now makes that all but impossible, especially in California. For example, in early 2001 Sierra Pacific's water system sold to a government agency for more than 20 percent above its book value. In addition, systems that are for sale tend to be complex deals with serious problems.

Q: IS SOUTHWEST PURSUING OTHER GROWTH OPPORTUNITIES?

A: Submetering is a good example of a business that allows us to use our expertise in water and utility billing and lock in revenue from a customer for the long term. Basically, we contract with apartment owners to meter water use in individual residential units.

The resident gains control over the utility bill in a way that was never possible before, with potential savings of up to 25 to 30 percent. And the beauty is it's all done electronically, which holds down costs. Instead of a meter reader, a radio transmitter downloads information from the meter every day to a central computer. We send the bill, collect the money, and take out our fee. And we have no responsibility to collect from delinquent payers either. That's the landlord's job.

We expect eight percent of our 2001 revenue to come from submetering, with the share rising thereafter due to this sector's 30 percent annual growth. It also takes us up another step in technology. It's a bit of a learning curve, but eventually we'll be able to apply what we've absorbed to the rest of the organization.

Submetering has also helped us learn a lot of things about apartments. We can also allocate and bill for other services, such as heating and cooling, electric usage, and trash removal. For anything we do, however, we'll be looking to get long-term contracts so we can lock in our customers.

Another opportunity exists in sewer manhole repair. Millions of manholes natiowide were built using bricks and mortar and now, years later, require rehabilitation or repair. This creates a potential opportunity for us, especially as the regulatory environment grows increasingly strict.

Q: WHAT'S THE BIGGEST CHALLENGE FACED BY THE
   WATER INDUSTRY TODAY?

A: The misperception that tapwater is unsafe to drink. People now think twice about taking a drink from their faucets. But they think nothing of going down the street and paying 100 times that for bottled water. We're having to step up our public relations efforts in light of growing public awareness surrounding water quality.

The good news is that the technology exists so that we need never run out of water. The big question is cost. In rough numbers, groundwater costs $200 per acre-foot to produce and deliver. Surface water costs $500 per acre-foot, treated sewer effluent $900, and desalinized seawater $1200 to $1400. Currently, most customers receive groundwater, so it appears that use of the other sources and treatment options will add substantially to the cost of water. Americans will have to decide how much they're willing to pay to remove what level of contaminants from drinking water.

We believe Southwest can benefit from more regulations on water. In our regulated utilities, the additional regulatory costs tend to increase customer rates. Our contract operations business can benefit because more requirements make it difficult for others, particularly municipalities, to operate their own systems and meet all the required criteria. The fact is we're good at what we're doing and we can help.

CHAPTER 5

The Foreign Invasion

When power prices are spiking, there's nothing worse than an unexpected shutdown at a key power plant. That's what Utah's largest electric utility, PacifiCorp, faced in late 2000. Its executives scrambled to come up with new power supplies and devise a strategy to deal with regulatory scrutiny.

The final word, however, wasn't handed down from Salt Lake City, Provo, or anywhere PacifiCorp operated. Instead, it came from Glasgow, Scotland, the corporate headquarters of PacifiCorp's 100 percent owner Scottish Power.

Since the mid-1990s, giant, foreign-based utilities have poured into the U.S. market, plunking down billions of dollars in targeted projects, joint ventures, and outright takeovers of American utilities. As a result, they now own energy, communications, and water companies coast to coast, with more deals on the way.

In addition to Utah, Scottish Power controls the largest utilities in Oregon and Wyoming, and one of the biggest in Idaho. British electric company National Grid operates the largest power utilities in Massachusetts and Rhode Island, as well as a major New York electric. British utility Powergen services virtually the entire state of Kentucky.

French utility conglomerate Suez Lyonnaise runs America's third-largest water utility, United Water Resources, and is the country's largest manager of municipal water systems, including Atlanta, Georgia's. France's Vivendi Environment owns 20 percent of the second-largest water ute in the United States, Philadelphia Suburban, and is the country's dominant water purification company as well. British water utility Kelda runs the largest water utility in Connecticut, and German industrial conglomerate RWE owns the biggest public water utility in New Jersey. It's also buying American Water Works, the largest U.S. water utility.

Under a law left over from the Cold War, companies controlled by foreign governments are not allowed to own U.S. communications utilities, but former government-owned monopolies France Telecom and Deutsche Telekom stretched the legal limit in the mid-1990s, buying 20 percent of long-distance and local phone company Sprint. Canada's BCE and Britain's Cable & Wireless have also made large investments.

Despite some opposition in Congress, notably from Senator Fritz Hollings (D-SC), we're starting to see full-scale takeovers as well. Deutsche Telekom, for example, has purchased all of upstart wireless carrier VoiceStream. Japanese government–controlled NT&T DoCoMo bought 20 percent of AT&T Wireless, and may take complete control now that Ma Bell has spun off its once-prized asset. DoCoMo's parent NT&T is the owner of Verio, one of the largest U.S. web server farms that run the Internet.

Given the massive investment needed in energy, water, and telecommunications, foreign companies will continue to buy U.S. utilities, but the globalization of the utility business is far from one-sided. America's dominant utilities have also inked billions worth in deals abroad in the past decade, ranging from power plants and other infrastructure projects to buyouts of former national monopolies.

U.S. giants like Edison International's Mission Energy are key players throughout Latin America and Asia, and have established a strong presence in Europe as well. Most prolific is Virginia-based AES Corp., which garners two-thirds of its nearly $4 billion in annual revenue from overseas; the company will expand its empire of power generation and distribution assets from 32 countries to 46 by late 2002.

U.S. companies control most of Britain's power and natural gas grid in addition to much of Australia's. Duke Energy and AES have emerged as two of the biggest players in South America, owning utilities, pipelines, and power plants continentwide. American companies are providing a good chunk of the power plant investment in Asia, as well.

U.S. communications giants have put down stakes all over the world. WorldCom's high-speed business network is the envy of Europe, just as it is in the United States, and it's rapidly becoming the dominant Internet company in Latin America, thanks to its ownership of Brazil's former long-distance telephone monopoly Embratel.

Based offshore, Global Crossing operates the world's preeminent global fiber-optic network, with some 100,000-plus miles running; Baby Bell Verizon owns a quarter of Telecom New Zealand, as well as a third of Venezuela's former monopoly phone company CANTV; and SBC Communications rules a Europewide empire of telephone properties through its controlling interest in TeleDanmark.

Foreign-based companies have also moved in force to establish global empires outside the United States. Spain's Telefonica was first, buying newly privatized monopolies in Argentina, Brazil, Chile, Peru, and elsewhere more than a decade ago. The company now runs a network that dominates the Spanish-speaking world in everything from wireless telephones to the Internet. In the late 1990s, Iberia's leading energy utility Endesa followed in Telefonica's footsteps, buying Chile-based energy company Enersis, which in turn has assets continentwide.

In late 1999, British wireless magnate Vodafone staged the first hostile takeover ever of a European communications company, Germany's Mannesmann. Shocking their target's stodgy management, Vodafone relentlessly pursued its quarry until it won a settlement largely on its own terms.

In 2000, China's Li family, a major winner from the deal thanks to a big stake in Mannesmann, won a bidding war to buy former monopoly Hong Kong Telecom. And in 2001, Singapore Telecom entered the fray, outbidding a host of rivals for control of Cable & Wireless' Optus unit in Australia.

GOING GLOBAL

Welcome to the age of the utility multinationals. Like the United States, dozens of countries are finding themselves in ever more desperate straits to upgrade their energy, communications, and water infrastructure, or risk stifling economic growth. To encourage investment, national leaders are privatizing the former government-owned monopolies and opening their markets to competition for the first time.

For decades, countries kept foreigners out of their utility industries as a matter of national security. Now policymakers care less what language utility executives speak. Instead, they're focused on the color of the money they'll invest, and the more the better. As a result, longstanding barriers to foreign ownership of utilities are coming down, from Southeast Asia to Latin America and the United States.

Spain's fascist past is no hindrance to its biggest communications and energy companies carving out empires in its former colonies. America's history of dominating Mexico hasn't stopped U.S. telecoms from entering the country to compete with national champion Telmex.

The biggest turnaround has come in formerly communist countries, particularly in Eastern Europe. Long starved for investment, they've thrown open their borders; global utility giants have responded, investing billions in new power lines and plants, wireless and wireline communications networks, and clean, safe, water supplies.

When the global utility investment wave began in the early 1990s, the bulk of it was isolated investments from developed world utilities in the developing world. Today, overseas operations are fully integrated into several utilities' core businesses. Enron, Mirant, and Reliant, for example, are making a major push to market energy in Europe.

As confidence and expertise have grown, successful companies have made larger and larger investments. Energy utility Utili-Corp, for instance, has grown a relatively small investment in New Zealand into one of that country's largest utilities in less than a decade. The company has similarly built a major presence in Canada. Telefonica and Endesa both derive the lion's share of their growth from Latin America, and half the revenues of Powergen come from the United States.

Major cross-border mergers are still relatively rare, but their numbers are increasing, any company becoming a potential merger partner as the industry bulks up to compete on an ever-widening playing field. European firms are as likely to bid for U.S. utilities as American firms are for them. In fact, partnering with companies on a global basis through mergers will come to be seen as the only way to thrive in an increasingly global and competitive marketplace.

The stakes are enormous. The larger and more powerful companies become, the more easily and faster they're able to deploy assets to the places where demand is greatest. Size is already enabling utilities to better access low-cost pools of capital to pursue new growth opportunities. Diversification across national borders will limit regulatory and economic risk. In contrast, any major company that stays within its own borders risks being eaten alive by ever-growing global competitors.

If history is any guide, nationalist currents will ultimately resurface. Tough global economic times are fertile fields for antiforeigner rhetoric. There are no better targets than utilities, which have an extremely high profile as essential service industries.

California's threats to nationalize its utility industry are a sad reminder that rational discourse always breaks down when there's a convenient scapegoat at hand. India's treatment of foreign power producers is another case in point. Despite a desperate need for electricity, the country continues to squabble over price with those who might build plants. The result is more blackouts and less vital investment from overseas.

In addition, while the Bush administration is likely to approve most merger applications, the European Union may not, given its reaction to the failed WorldCom/Sprint deal in 2000. At least for the next few years, however, the laws of economics will hold sway, and globalization will accelerate (see Figure 5.1).

10 Major Cross-Border Utility Mergers

Acquirer	Country	Target	Country	Annual Sales Combined Company (bil$)
Vodafone	(UK)	Mannesmann	(Germany)	16.8
Endesa	(Spain)	Enersis	(Chile)	14.1
National Grid	(UK)	New England Elec	(US)	8.3
Powergen	(UK)	LG&E Energy	(US)	6.0
WorldCom	(US)	Embratel	(Brazil)	22.8
Deutsche Telekom	(Germany)	VoiceStream	(US)	39.5
Scottish Power	(UK)	PacifiCorp	(US)	8.7
National Grid	(UK)	Niagara Mohawk	(US)	8.3
Suez Lyonnaise	(France)	United Water Res	(US)	34.6
Mirant Corp	(US)	Bewag	(Germany)	13.3

SOURCE: Utility Forecaster

Figure 5.1

BACK TO THE FUTURE

This isn't the first time the utility industry has globalized. In the latter 1920s, investment by U.S. utilities in foreign-based electric utilities was the largest single component of U.S. direct investment abroad, dwarfing everything from banking to railroads.

The most prolific investor abroad was the old American & Foreign Power Company (AFP). AFP was a subsidiary of the high-flying Electric Bond & Share Company, one of the five giant utility holding companies that came to control virtually the entire U.S. electricity and gas industry during the 20s. Through AFP, Electric Bond & Share (EBS) acquired national utilities throughout Latin America and Asia.

EBS's move abroad began during World War I, when the U.S. government approached it to buy and operate electric systems in Panama to support the canal system. The purchase was completed in 1917, and was followed by the 1920 buyout of Guatemala's national utility. That same year, the company entered a series of investments in Brazil, and in 1922 it put up its first power lines in Cuba.

In response to its early success, EBS created AFP as its engine for global expansion in 1924. Following the principle laid down by Lloyds of London for over 200 years, management reasoned that it could both reduce its operating risks and boost its growth

opportunities by investing abroad. The new subsidiary set about
its task in earnest.

Over the next six years, AFP's assets expanded to over $1 bil-
lion, or more than $8 billion in today's dollars. It acquired prop-
erties from both governments and investors in Argentina, Chile,
Costa Rica, Ecuador, India, and Mexico, while expanding its holdings in Brazil. By 1929, it was staking a claim to China's electric
system with the purchase of Shanghai Power Co., that nation's
oldest and largest electric company, from the city government. A
related unit at EBS pursued similar investments in Canada and
Japan.

The first shock to the EBS/AFP empire came following Wall
Street's collapse in 1929. The company's expansion continued for
several years, but it became far more difficult to raise capital. As
the Great Depression swept Latin America, the growth of AFP's
subsidiaries slowed drastically. Forced rate cuts by regulators and
the sharp decline in host-country currencies against the dollar
squeezed earnings. By 1932, AFP had suspended common and
preferred stock payouts.

The company, however, weathered the storm and its subsidiaries continued to grow, with management actually restoring
dividends in 1939. Despite the loss of its China property in 1941,
AFP exited World War II more prosperous than ever. The 1950s
were glory years for the company. Though management sold the
India properties, the company continued to add customers and
participate in the explosive growth of Latin America. In 1953,
AFP President W. S. Robertson painted a picture to shareholders
of a company poised to take advantage of an industry where
growth potential was "virtually limitless."

Robertson proved right for several years. After learning from its
own mistakes in the early years, the company had seemingly hit
on a formula for explosive growth. Then came the second shock
to the company, one that ultimately proved fatal: the 1960 nationalization of its Cuban assets—the largest single component of the
company—by the newly ascendant Fidel Castro.

The nationalization took the wind out of the sails of American
& Foreign Power Company's expansion and, coupled with turmoil elsewhere in the world, management gradually became

convinced that Latin America and other developing countries were simply too unstable economically and politically to earn a reasonable return on utility investment over time. Over the next decade, the remaining assets were sold or liquidated and AFP was formally merged into EBS in 1967. The last investment in Ecuador was unloaded in 1976.

For most of the industry, the utility globalization movement ended decades earlier. The deathblow was the 1935 Public Utility Holding Company Act (PUHCA), which forbade foreign-based companies from owning U.S. energy utilities and ended nearly 50 years of investment from overseas that had helped build this nation's electric and gas infrastructure. Other major U.S. utilities had also given up investing abroad, concluding that the risks of pursuing the obviously stunning growth opportunities were simply too great despite the profitable example of AFP's 50-year history.

WHY GO ABROAD?

If the 1935 PUHCA stymied utility globalization, the deregulation of the 1990s has revived it. As utilities return to their state of nature—where the large and strong survive and the small and weak perish—the current move to go global is being driven by the same major forces that drove the first: growth and diversification. Given the possibilities, this globalization wave is a long way from cresting.

The primary motivation of any company to go abroad is explosive growth it can't get at home. The biggest opportunities are in the developing world, where needs for better and cheaper communications, energy, and water are immense (see Figure 5.2). Also, companies want to diversify their operations beyond their national borders to limit the regulatory, market, and economic risks of operating in a single country.

As I pointed out in the first two chapters of this book, rising demand and shrinking supply have added up to a chronic supply crunch for electricity, natural gas, and oil in the United States. A similar problem exists with our country's supplies of clean water, where rising pollution costs are rapidly outstripping

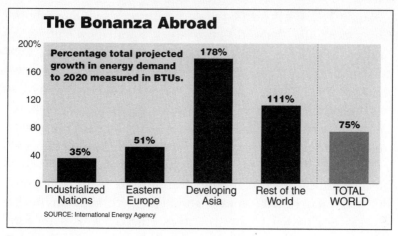

Figure 5.2

smaller players' ability to provide clean supplies for drinking. Communications infrastructure will also require a quantum upgrade in coming years as e-business becomes the norm and our nation becomes increasingly interconnected.

These trends are even more pronounced around the world. In the developing world, the opportunity and challenge is in bringing the wonders of modern essential services to economies burdened by antiquated infrastructure. Figure 5.3 displays the wide degree of difference in energy consumption between nations.

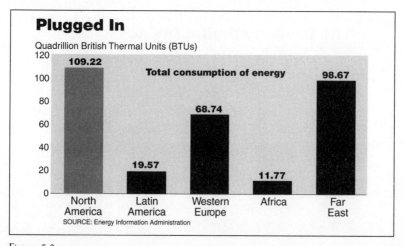

Figure 5.3

Barely half the world's people have ever used a telephone. China and India, the world's two largest countries, are projected to need 10 gigawatts capacity every year just to keep pace with current demand trends. That demand will accelerate as those nations add their own web servers, the giant computer farms that run the Internet. Clean water is scarcely a dream in many nations, including parts of the United States. With the ranks of the world's impoverished still growing, so are the ranks of the underserved.

Nowhere is the gap between rich and poor nations more yawning and critical than in communications. Access to computers, the Web, modern data storage, and high-speed/high-bandwidth systems is essential to any country's emergence as a modern nation in an increasingly integrated global economy. While access doesn't guarantee prosperity, lack of it ensures perpetual poverty.

France has nearly 30 times the number of basic wireline telephones and 99 times more cellular phones per capita than India, which houses nearly a fifth of the world's population. Singapore has nearly 10 times as many computers per capita as neighboring Malaysia. Israel has 26 times as many computers as nearby Egypt and six times as many as Lebanon. There's even some disparity in the developed world: The United States has almost twice as many computers per 1,000 people as Britain (see Figure 5.4).

Only a tidal wave of investment in coming years will meet these growing needs; large players with global reach are best positioned

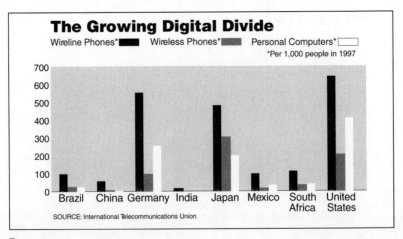

Figure 5.4

to meet them. In fact, given the depleted fiscal health of many of the world's governments, they're the only real alternative.

In the 1920s and 30s, AFP made a fortune buying, building, and operating the major utilities of Latin America. Armed with deep pools of low-cost capital and expertise delivering essential services, today's empire builders are following in its footsteps. Provided they learn from AFP's mistakes and successes, they'll capture a king's ransom from these explosive growth opportunities.

MANAGING RISKS

Rising political risks ended the first wave of utility globalization. Power plants, gas pipelines, phone lines, and water treatment facilities are all extremely high-profile assets that require a long-term commitment by their builders and operators. As a result, energy, communications, and water utilities are particularly at risk to regulatory politics, wherever they operate. As the history of AFP has shown, utilities have all too often fallen prey to politics.

With its long history of stable government, steady economic growth, and tradition of free enterprise, the U.S. market has long been considered among the most attractive places for utilities to operate. That reputation is stronger than ever today, particularly with our need for investment infrastructure.

Even here, though, there have been problems. PUHCA threw a huge bucket of cold water on utility globalization. More recently, during the 1980s and 90s the high cost of building nuclear power plants, and pressure from heavy industry to cut rates, induced regulators to disallow billions of dollars in power plant costs in dozens of states. The result was an unprecedented wave of write-offs and dividend cuts. Two companies, El Paso Electric and Public Service of New Hampshire, were forced into bankruptcy, and a half dozen others—including Long Island Lighting—were pushed to the brink.

In the era of deregulation and soaring demand for services, nuclear plant cost risk has diminished, but new dangers have taken its place. California's power crisis, for example, continues to fester, with one possible outcome being a 2002 referendum to nationalize the state's electricity system.

Other states could take similar action to keep down rates if the crisis spills over. In addition, while the Bush administration has taken a noticeably proderegulation approach, there's always the possibility that a future president could look at things far differently.

Horror stories abound of hapless U.S. utilities that lost their shirts investing abroad when the host countries' political winds changed. AFP's loss of its Chinese, Cuban, and Mexican assets illustrates in graphic relief what can happen when proforeign-investment regimes are overthrown by nationalistic ones.

With Communism discredited, companies that operate in the developing world today don't yet face serious nationalization risks. There's plenty of room for quarreling over rates, however, especially when foreigners can be blamed for raising them, and there's always the risk a host government will tap an overseas utility's investment for taxes or politically popular rate cuts.

These risks are faced even in developed nations with long pro-capitalist histories. In the late 1990s, for example, U.S. companies that had invested in Australia and Britain were bashed by unexpected rate cuts that turned profitable operations into barely breakeven ventures. Less than two years after allowing Americans to buy into its electric system, Britain imposed a one-time windfall profits tax, an act utilities charged was a double cross but which they were powerless to stop.

The upshot: When it comes to regulation in any country, the only constant is change. Utilities' visibility makes them uniquely vulnerable to a shift in government policy, public pressure to bring down rates, and in extreme cases even nationalization. The only way companies can truly protect themselves from potential regulatory problems in a single country—including their own homelands—is by becoming multinational. That's the major reason British water and power utilities, which have suffered several rounds of rate cuts from the country's Labour government, have invested heavily in U.S. utilities.

Diversifying globally also reduces economic and market risk. For example, several countries—including much of Europe—currently have large surpluses of electricity production capacity. As a result, generating companies there face falling profit margins and returns on investment, but companies who also diversified into markets with tight generating capacity—such as Brazil and the United States—have been able to shore up their results. The profits they earn in those high-growth markets will help them grow rapidly in their home markets as they recover in coming years. Diversifying also helps companies keep profits on steady ground during economic cycles, when some countries are growing while others stagnate.

The proof of diversification's value is in the performance of U.S. power-generating companies during California's power crisis. The global companies like AES, Enron, Mirant, NRG, and Reliant were hurt by the state's refusal to pay them for the electricity they generated and the threat of having to refund the state billions of alleged overcharges. However, since the Golden State accounted for only a tiny portion of their overall businesses, the impact on profits was minor.

In essence, the generators are more important to California than the state is to them. That adds up to bargaining power. In contrast, California's major utilities, Edison International and PG&E, are almost wholly reliant on the state. As a result, the crisis has stripped away their investment-grade ratings in a perilous slide towards bankruptcy.

WINNERS AND LOSERS

Ultimately, this round of utility globalization could end up the way the last one did, but it's unlikely to happen for some years to come. Over the past 20 years, the philosophy of laissez-faire capitalism and free markets has become increasingly accepted, even in formerly communist nations.

Nationalism itself has been channeled into helping national champions, major companies that have the best chance of becoming global competitors. Governments grant their champions favorable regulatory treatment to smooth their road toward expansion, and occasionally protect them from foreign competition. NTT in Japan, Telmex in Mexico, and Vivendi in France are good examples; all three have used the support of their home governments to grow beyond their borders.

Today, in most countries, gaining investment to fuel economic growth is viewed as a far more important social goal than maintaining control over basic industries. That view has been reinforced by the growing prosperity of nations embracing free enterprise. As a result, foreign control over utilities and energy, communications, and water services has come to be accepted in most countries. That's made utilities the world over increasingly confident about investing beyond their borders in search of growth.

Only a depression or world cataclysm is likely to change this positive environment. In very hard times, people look for scapegoats and money trees to shake. Given their high profiles and the secure cash flows from their control over essential services, utilities are obvious targets. The case of AFP shows that even the most powerful global empire can be rocked to its foundations by adverse conditions.

But, as the case of AFP also proves, those who can convert the developing world growth into utility profits will only grow in market and financial power. Global telecommunications, energy, and water are returning to their state of nature, where market prices set profits, and the largest win the lion's share of the spoils. Their size, as well as the profits the winners earn abroad, will go a long way to ensuring their strength at home.

Any company investing abroad faces several challenges. How they measure up will determine success or failure. The first is the language/culture barrier. Utilities investing abroad can get around the language part by hiring skilled personnel, going local to find employees, or sticking with countries that speak their same language.

Telefonica, for example, first launched its global empire by purchasing the monopoly phone systems of Spanish-speaking countries like Argentina, Chile, and Peru. The first major foray abroad by U.S. energy utilities was to purchase the electric and natural gas systems of the United Kingdom. This was followed by the buyout of several major Australian systems.

Unfortunately, a strategy of single-language investment may rule out some of the most explosive growth opportunities. Moreover, there's no guarantee that speaking the same language will limit the far more deadly sin of cultural miscommunication.

When the recent wave of U.S. investment abroad began in the mid-1990s, for example, some two-dozen-plus utilities jumped in feet first. Most did so on the advice of major consulting companies who counseled that with U.S. deregulation coming for energy and communications, companies needed to diversify abroad.

Unlike the disastrous utility diversification of earlier decades— in which companies lost billions in everything from real estate and savings and loans to thrift stores—this wave was viewed as different for one reason: The investing utilities would be expanding in a business they knew everything about. The problem was they were committing the far worse sin of buying into countries they knew nothing about. The results for many were calamitous.

One almost comical example of the cultural miscommunication of the era occurred in China, one of the world's most promising markets for electricity. In the latter 1990s, a herd of companies stampeded to Beijing, with the goal of securing "letters of intent" from the government to approve power plant projects. Not wanting to offend its would-be investors, the Chinese government gave the utilities' representatives exactly what they wanted. So when the negotiators returned, they found that the agreements they thought were exclusive were face-saving documents that meant little in reality.

To avoid these pitfalls, companies must be culturally savvy in scale and scope. AES has built the largest nongovernment-owned fleet of power plants worldwide by doing what other successful multinationals do, hiring local talent and delegating much of the day-to-day decision-making process to those on the ground overseas. The company's decentralized style has frightened some for its lack of control over its far-flung operations, but the company's record of consistently robust profit growth over the past decade is hard to argue with.

In contrast, the majority of other utilities that moved abroad were anything but multinational in scope or talent. Most of the herd in the mid-1990s was still ruled by the prederegulation mindset. The majority of managers were engineers who had made their way to the top by making sure their utility power plants and distribution systems ran well. The most significant negotiations were those conducted with regulators whom, as local businesses, managers already knew intimately.

Few of the top executives had ever traveled abroad. In fact, the typical utility employee had never lived more than 25 miles from headquarters. These managements were not up to the task of investing in overseas ventures in cultures and countries they knew nothing about. Five years after their big push abroad, more than half had shed their foreign operations, including several who were the most ambitious. More will likely follow them home in coming years (see Figure 5.5).

Those that remain must also have a wholly unsentimental approach about where they are invested, and be ready to cut losses quickly. The longevity of AFP is a testament both to the

Companies with a Major Commitment to Global Growth

Power Utilities Abroad in 1995	Power Utilities Abroad in 2001
AES Corp	AES Corp
American Electric Power	
CMS Energy	
Consolidated Edison	
Constellation Energy	
Dominion Resources	
Duke Energy	Duke Energy
Edison International	Edison International
El Paso Energy	
Enron	Enron
Entergy	
GPU Inc	
Hawaiian Electric	
PPL Resources	
Pub Serv Enterprise Group	Pub Serv Enterprise Group
Reliant Energy	
Southern Company	Mirant Corp
TXU Corp	TXU Corp
UtiliCorp United	UtiliCorp United
Xcel Energy	

SOURCE: Utility Forecaster

Figure 5.5

need to be willing to cast off unproductive or highly risky operations before disaster strikes, and to the dangers of waiting around too long. Companies must also be willing to shift assets around to maximize their global power.

Telefonica, for example, has been able to pool the wireless telephone and Internet subsidiaries of its Latin American possessions into a global unit, allowing it infinitely more financing for growth, as well as the ability to snare a larger share of the profits. Southern Company avoided the worst impact of Britain's windfall profits tax on utilities with some innovative financial engineering involving a bond issue and the sale of half its interest in its holdings to another utility, PP&L.

One country viewed as a troublespot today is India. Enron was one of the first companies to invest in the subcontinent, originally proposing to plunk down $10 billion for new power plants and fuel-related projects. After fighting for nine years about a single power plant, the company's future in the country is in doubt and it may have reached an impasse about even being paid for power from this plant it's already built.

That has serious implications for the other players in India, including AES, CMS, and Mirant. It also shows how companies must be quick to realize problems and prudent not to overcommit to development in a single country, regardless of how promising it seems.

For foreign companies buying U.S. electric utilities, the possible nationwide impact of California's energy crisis and potential shortages of natural gas loom as major potential risks. The large concentration of Britain's National Grid in the Northeast United States, for example, could come back to haunt it if a potential power shortage in the region becomes reality.

That's because its subsidiaries are primarily distributors of energy, with no power plants under management. These companies must buy energy on the open market at increasingly volatile prices. And regulators may not be as forthcoming in the future about passing those costs along to consumers as they've been in the past, particularly if the utility owner is based overseas.

With the utility globalization boom still in its early stages, there will probably be more expansion by the major players in coming years. The best of the biggest now have experience with the pit-falls of global investing. Most have developed formidable levels of expertise in host countries, as well as with obtaining financing needed to support growth.

The success of Southern Company's now spun-off Mirant sub-sidiary was in no small part due to the expertise its parent gained raising capital on Wall Street when it was building power plants in the 1980s and early 90s. In addition, the company's first major purchase overseas was to buy the power plant development arm of Hong Kong–based conglomerate Hopewell Holdings, which conferred instant expertise in Asia as well as new plant technolo-gies for use in the United States.

The ranks of European firms lining up to invest in this country are also dominated by a handful of names with global expertise. One of the most prolific is France's Vivendi Environment, which has water and waste treatment operations throughout Europe, Africa, and the Americas. As for communications, foreign com-panies are only beginning to buy and build the immense, high-speed data networks that will be needed to run the world economy of the future. The cross-border flows of capital are now almost as multidimensional as the Web itself.

In the years ahead, utility globalization will add a new urgency to the industry's ongoing changes. The former monopolistic util-ity fiefdoms will be increasingly invaded and ultimately absorbed by the ever-growing global dynamos. Even national regulatory power will melt before market forces, and free-flowing invest-ment capital will finance the greatest spending boom seen in energy, communications, and water since the early twentieth cen-tury. One of the driving forces—technological advance—is the subject of the next chapter.

....

INDUSTRY PROFILE: DENNIS BAKKE

When Roger Sant and Dennis Bakke launched cogeneration company Applied Energy Services in October 1981, it took them a year to raise their first $1 million. Most dismissed the pair as ivory tower academics from their work on energy conservation with the U.S. government, a Carnegie Mellon–connected think tank, and the book Creating Abundance: America's Least-Cost Energy Strategy.

Twenty years later, their brainchild—renamed AES Corp—is the world's largest investor-owned power producer with 64,000 megawatts of global generating capacity. Its energy distribution networks serve 18 million people. The Bakke/Sant premise that power generation is not a natural monopoly is now accepted industrywide, and their unique management style is a model for successful businesses operating internationally.

Q: WHAT IS THE AES STRATEGY FOR GROWTH?

A: When we started Applied Energy Services, our goal was to raise $3 million. Instead, we had to put up $60,000 of our own credit to get started, and finally raised $1 million to survive until our first project in 1983, a petroleum coke plant in Texas which cost more to clean up emissions from than to build. Up until 1989, we remained privately held and built about one new plant a year, all in the U.S. By then, we had changed the name to AES and had taken on our first foreign project in the U.K., where we learned about deregulation and privatization firsthand and really started moving internationally.

Basically, we believe the fundamental purpose of our business is to use the gifts and skills of our people and the other resources we have been given to serve the world. Our goal is to find places where we can make a difference providing electricity in a clean, safe, economically sound, and sustainable way. We're not giving electricity away. But it can literally take us anywhere in the world.

Q: WHAT ARE THE BIGGEST RISKS OF INVESTING
   ABROAD AS OPPOSED TO IN THE UNITED STATES?

A: In my view, the degree of risk is not significantly different from one country to the next. They're all difficult. In the past 20 years, for example, AES has suffered three political expropriations: in Florida, Nevada, and Britain. And right now our greatest credit risk is in California. That doesn't mean the U.S. and U.K. are riskier places to invest than Pakistan, which has not expropriated our property. It just means they're not necessarily less risky.

The point is you can't pigeonhole a country and say this is a bad place to operate. We don't say, for example, that Pakistan is worse than China, or that China is a riskier place than New York City. Our objective is to serve the world and if we're going to do that, we're going to take risks. So rather than start from the assumption that a place is too bad to invest in, we look for a way to mitigate the risks there.

Brazil, for example, is a good place for AES. The country has tremendous energy needs that we can fill. So while there are problems and difficulties from time to time, we have a huge investment there and are bullish on the country's future.

Q: WHAT MAKES AES' MANAGEMENT MODEL UNIQUE IN
   THE ENERGY INDUSTRY?

A: We have four values or principles, which govern everything we try to do: integrity, fairness, social responsibility, and fun. Fun tends to get the most attention.

Our outrageous goal is to create the most fun place to work in the history of the world. A key element of that is to maximize the number of individuals who get to make important decisions that make a difference. That boils down to having as many decisions made on the front lines of the business as possible, rather than back at headquarters. Everyone is required to solicit advice. But the final decision never leaves the person on the front lines.

This approach means bosses like me have to get out of the way and not make decisions. I try to limit myself to one a year—which is basically dividing up the world among the various operating groups. And I've tried to model that for all of our leaders around the world. Even our Board of Directors, which is very active in advising on numerous AES businesses, refrains from active voting in most business decisions.

We also don't have many of the organizational structures other companies do. For example, we don't have a Human Resources department or a Planning department or a Public Relations department or an Internal Communications department. In fact, only 40 of our 60,000 or so people work in our central office here in Arlington, Virginia. And most of them are in accounting and tax functions.

Incidentally, running a fun workplace has some very real economic benefits. In the 20 years since we started the company, we've only lost two senior people. The last senior person we went outside the company to recruit was in 1986. Coupled with the people we've gained through acquisitions, that means we seldom have to go through the time and expense of recruiting.

Q: HOW DOES AES MAKE A DECISION TO EXPAND?

A: Back in the early 1990s, all the various business groups at AES reported to me. Since then, we've expanded to some 130 separate businesses around the world, including power plants and energy distribution companies. My one decision a year involves deciding how these businesses and future projects will be divided among business groups, each of which is responsible for a particular area of the world. We've added two business groups a year since 1992 and now have 18 worldwide.

New projects or acquisitions are entirely the responsibility of those working in a particular territory. AES people are constantly out wandering around their regions looking for new opportunities to serve. Sometimes, a particular relationship will lead them to projects outside their own territories. The bottom line is you look for an opportunity, find a business, and try to develop it. Once it works, you can stay and help operate the business or move on to find another.

Q: HOW DOES AES USE ITS ECONOMIES OF SCALE TO ITS ADVANTAGE?

A: Our knowledge base of 60,000 employees is our most important asset. Thanks to the Internet, AES people have an unmatched network to tap into anytime they have an issue or problem anywhere in the world.

Because so many of our people make important decisions, they have a wealth of experience and knowledge to share. Whenever anyone has a major decision to make, they're required to solicit advice from the knowledge base. Everyone gets involved and the person will get a flood of e-mails. The key to fun, however, is the final decision never leaves the person on the front line who started the chain.

We have realized some benefits from scale in financing. Typically, however, the individual businesses or projects raise about 80 percent of their own capital. That has the additional benefit of keeping project control in the hands of those on the front line, who usually are very good at financing as well.

Q: WHAT'S THE BIGGEST RISK TO AES GOING FORWARD?

A: The biggest change in this industry over the past 20 years is the shift from government delivery of essential services to private delivery. Margaret Thatcher, the former British Prime Minister, gets the credit for starting that trend. And we've been able to take advantage from the whole privatization trend that has swept the world, albeit slowly.

There is some worry that California will slow this trend and maybe result in a few reversions to government control. But given the fall of the Soviet Union and

hundreds of other horrendous experiences of governments managing/controlling business activities, this
seems unlikely. People have realized that government
can't do as good a job as private, competitive industry in
providing essential services. In the long run, even with
hiccups like the California situation, society is much better off and essential services are still a whole lot better,
cheaper, and more secure when done in a private way.

. . . .

CHAPTER 6

....

Technology's Revolutionary Evolution

Faith in technology's ability to cure our ills is as American as apple pie. Throughout our nation's history, new inventions have solved almost every riddle and hurdled every obstacle to progress and prosperity. In the process, innovation has created and destroyed whole industries, and occasionally transformed the very nature of our society.

Take the automobile, arguably the single most transforming invention of the twentieth century. Before the internal combustion engine, personal transportation was a lengthy and often messy ordeal. Disposing of horse manure had become a major problem in many cities, and most movement was on foot. Barge travel was critical for transporting goods from country to city; entire regions of the country, especially western states like Utah, were barely connected to the population centers of the East.

All that changed as Henry Ford's dream of mass-producing cars became reality. Americans were suddenly able to carry themselves and their wares anywhere, anytime. As roads were built, the country was commercially and culturally linked as never before. Dozens of new industries sprang up, from steel to oil and gas. Mass transport of goods launched a new economic era where economies of scale replaced individual craftsmanship as the standard of progress.

The flip side was that scores of once-thriving industries shrank into obscurity, from the Chesapeake & Ohio canal system and the horse and buggy to the corner store. Eventually, fast, personal transport encouraged the development of vast suburbs, as city-dwelling Americans attempted to recreate the lost innocence of country living. And downtowns were transformed from the heart of community life into virtual ghost towns.

Thomas Edison's patenting and popularizing of electricity has similarly transformed America since the early twentieth century, as has Alexander Graham Bell's telephone. In barely a century, both inventions have become absolutely essential to modern life. Without them, hundreds of other industries we now take for granted—television, air travel, supermarkets—would not exist.

Our complex system for distributing goods and services would be impossible. We'd be almost completely dependent on food grown within a hundred miles of where we live. And our financial system would still be right out of Scrooge & Marley. Forget about day trading. In some places, even buying shares of a New York–listed company could take weeks.

Energy and communications are far from static industries themselves. In fact, the more important they've become for a functioning society, the more they're being transformed by technology. The proliferation of wireless phones and the Internet, for example, have turned the telephone industry upside down in the past two decades. Ultra-efficient combined-cycle gas/steam turbines, fuel cells, solar power devices or "photovoltaics," Internet-based communications technology, superconductors, and power semiconductors are shaking up the energy industry.

As they grow and evolve, these technologies will reshape the energy and communications industries into more responsive, efficient, clean, and cost-effective providers of essential services. Some will prove more useful than others and new ones will spring up to take the place of those that falter. Over the next 20 years, they're certain to have a transforming impact on how and where we get these services.

From an industry standpoint, the key question is whether these new technologies will be revolutionary or evolutionary. Will fuel cells transform America as automobiles did in the last century or simply enrich the energy industry's dominant players? Will cellular phones ultimately trigger the overthrow of the emerging, second Ma Bell, or simply smooth its rise to the top?

REVOLUTION'S EVOLUTION

In the 1990s, the U.S. government issued over a million patents for new inventions, 38 percent more than in the prior decade (see Figure 6.1). Only time can tell if any will have the impact of Henry Ford's dream. Chances are most will not. In fact, since the early Industrial Revolution, almost all new developments have been evolutionary, not revolutionary.

When a technology is revolutionary, it shakes the existing order to its roots. Fortunes are made and lost. Old companies disappear forever and new powerhouses are born. When a technology is evolutionary, the leaders of the affected industry evolve to absorb the advance, actually increasing their dominance. Throughout economic history, small companies have had most of the great ideas to drive change, but at the end of the day, they've lacked the marketing and financial power to lead revolutions, that is, to take over the industries they've reshaped.

If the innovators' shareholders were lucky, the leaders purchased their stock for a massive payoff. The less fortunate have failed as the technologies they pioneered invariably either lost their appeal or were replaced by better mousetraps. Either way,

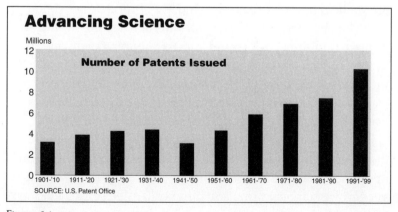

Figure 6.1

the would-be revolutionaries lost their way as those they wished to overthrow evolved and grew.

Not every big company, of course, has been able to evolve. For example, Western Union's franchise position in telegram communications was squandered because it didn't adapt changing technology. Xerox's failure to follow up on its Internet innovations has doomed it to extinction, and IBM's refusal to recognize the personal computer's potential was nearly fatal.

Most of the time, however, industry leaders have found a way to use their marketing and financial might to make change their friend. As a result, they've stayed on top of their industries.

In the pharmaceutical industry, several small developers have made it big by creating blockbuster drugs in recent years, but none has challenged the might of established players like Pfizer or Bristol Myers Squibb. The big boys are often late to the game but can quickly catch up and pass the creator of a successful product due to their superior economies of scale, distribution, and financial power. When all else fails, they buy out their smaller rivals and add the new product to their existing line.

In this generation, computer technology is the only industry where startups have broken into the ranks of the majors in large numbers. The launch of personal computers and the Internet has fueled the rise of major companies like Cisco, Intel, Microsoft, and Sun Microsystems, which before were largely unknown. Even here, the industry's oldest leaders—IBM and Hewlett Packard— have managed to remain dominant. Despite its new-economy image, Intel has been the microchip leader for decades.

In the late 1990s, the buzz was Internet startups would soon displace traditional bricks-and-mortar shopping malls and stores as the retailers of the future. Stocks like Amazon.com and eBay were bid to the sky on expectations of exponential growth. Stocks of non-Internet retailers—as well as the real estate investment trusts that leased them property—were knocked for a loop.

Just a couple of years later, many of those are broke who bet on the Internet to trigger a revolution in the retail industry where upstarts would unseat incumbents. Failure to meet ambitious sales growth targets, rising costs, and collapsing stock values have turned the dot-coms into dot-bombs. Internet retailing is alive and well, but it's in the hands of the retail sector's traditional powerhouses; it's an evolutionary technology for the industry.

The same will hold true for the new technologies now taking root in the energy and communications industries. Rather than shaking up the existing social order, these innovations are far more likely to make the leaders more lean, efficient, and profitable, even as they enjoy a wave of new investment interest.

THE WIRELESS EVOLUTION

Over the past 20 years, wireless phones have transformed the world's economy and culture. Visit even the globe's most seemingly impoverished places and you'll find millions of people in constant communication with business associates, stockbrokers, spouses, golfing partners, and anyone else who'll listen. In many countries, cellular has actually overtaken landline phones in terms of call volume.

For all their impact, however, wireless phones have emerged as an evolutionary, not revolutionary, technology for the communications industry. In fact, rarely has an innovation so increased the old leaders' dominance.

It wasn't supposed to be this way. When the U.S. government held a lottery for the wireless phone spectrum in the mid-1980s, its intentions were straightforward: Bring new investors and competition into the communications industry oligopoly.

The newly spun-off Baby Bells were also granted cellular licenses for their home territories, but safeguards were put in place to ensure competition would develop which the local monopolies wouldn't be able to squelch. The goal was for multiple competitors to force down prices and spur innovation.

Also, it was widely believed that advances would enable wireless phones to ultimately replace the old wireline system entirely, creating a whole new dynamic of industry power. Cellular technology, it was thought, would be so superior to the Baby Bells' networks of copper wire that it would make them obsolete. The new wireless providers, not the monopoly incumbents, would surge to the top of the industry.

As it turned out, wireless technology has moved ahead faster than most thought. The large, clunky, early phone designs have given way to sleek, credit card–sized units. Speed and spectrum have dramatically increased signal clarity as well as capacity, making it possible to access the Internet via wireless, something unimaginable just a few years ago. And the proliferation of cellular towers and satellites—as well as switching capability—has made it possible to call virtually anyone from almost anywhere.

Advancing technology has been matched by torrid global growth in subscribers. Over the past decade, the number of U.S. wireless phones in use has jumped 19-fold to nearly 100 million (see Figure 6.2). Growth has been even faster in Europe and eastern Asia, where 50 million–plus Japanese subscribers have made NT&T DoCoMo a bigger fish than its parent NTT. In countries like Mexico—where new landline phones can take months to connect—wireless phones are now the primary mode of communication.

And the best is yet to come. Over the next few years, the next generation of wireless technology, dubbed 3G, will hit the market. The result will be a dramatic increase in cell phones' data-delivery capability, with Internet access and financial information as targeted applications. Ultimately, 4G phones will enable users to electronically interact instantly with their homes, track down restaurant reservations while en route, order airline tickets online, and conduct a thousand other time-saving tasks. That will only increase the addictive power cellular phones wield, as well as their usage.

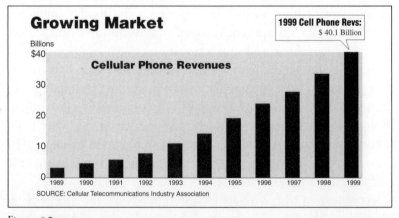

Figure 6.2

What think tanks, Wall Street analysts, and government regulators alike have dramatically underestimated is the money needed to bid for spectrum, build out new wireless networks, market services, and keep up with cutting-edge technology. They also badly misunderstood what the real impact of costs would be: a distinct edge to incumbent players with the hefty cash flows—mostly from the use of existing copper networks—needed to develop wireless systems.

After the original lotteries, there were literally thousands of potential wireless players in the United States, but it became obvious very quickly that only a handful would be able to develop their new licenses. Many license holders sold their interests for huge windfall profits. The ranks of new providers winnowed very quickly to the Baby Bells and a handful of upstarts, the most prominent of which was Lin Broadcasting.

Lin's rising expenses encouraged it to join forces with Craig McCaw, creating what then became the industry's biggest wireless company, McCaw Cellular. McCaw, in turn, remained independent until necessity drove it into the willing arms of AT&T, though it extracted a huge premium as the price of giving up its independence.

The sale of McCaw dramatically increased the stakes in the wireless wars. With AT&T controlling a near-national network, competition suddenly reached a new level. The players realized they had to bulk up quickly, or else leave the field to the majors. The result was a frenzy of merger activity, with most licenses and customers concentrating in the hands of a dozen or so majors, and territories' market values determined by POPs, or potential subscribers.

At this point in the game, the wireless industry was basically three-tier. At the top was AT&T, which now had by far the country's largest wireless network and the marketing and financial power to expand it. The second level included units of the seven Baby Bells, relative upstarts Sprint, Nextel Communications, and Alltel. On the third level were a host of far smaller companies such as Western Wireless and U.S. Cellular, which had established mostly niche markets.

The full-scale launch of the second generation of personal communication wireless systems, or PCSs, in the late 1990s fur-

ther upped the ante for cellular competition. The U.S. government auctioned off a whole new raft of spectrum, this time at far
higher prices reflecting the dramatic increase in value of wireless
franchises. As a result, far fewer companies were able to bid and
some who did, notably NextWave Communications, were forced
to relinquish their winnings for lack of funds. When NextWave's
properties were auctioned again, the field of bidders had nar-
rowed even further, with Alltel, Nextel, and Sprint all bowing out.
Though the courts have since overturned the reauction, it's
doubtful NextWave will have the needed funding to build a network. Rather, it will sell to the highest bidder.

The high cost of PCS auctions triggered yet another wave of
consolidation for the wireless industry. The ironic result: For the
first time since the original lottery, the Baby Bells—the old wireline incumbents who were supposed to be pulled down by a wireless revolution—emerged as the industry leaders.

Formed from the combination of cellular properties of Bell
Atlantic, GTE, NYNEX, Pacific Telesis, U.S. West, and other acquisitions, Verizon Communications' 55 percent–owned Verizon
Wireless unit has nearly twice as many wireless customers as the
old leader, AT&T Wireless. Sixty percent–owned by SBC Communications, Cingular Wireless is number two with half again as
many customers as Ma Bell's now spun-off subsidiary. Behind
these two giants, AT&T Wireless, Alltel, Nextel, and Sprint form a
distant second tier.

Much the same scenario has been played out overseas. Rising
costs of network buildout cut back the ranks of European
providers almost immediately following the initial launch of
wireless service. The high-priced auction of PCS spectrum in
2000 winnowed those numbers further by loading up the bidders
with nearly unmanageable debt loads.

The result has been a dramatic slashing of credit ratings, particularly for the formerly government-owned monopolies such as
British Telecom, France Telecom, and Deutsche Telekom, even
before they've begun to develop their new properties. That's
driven them to seek partners for their wireless units to meet the
extraordinary demand for capital. In Germany, for example, bit-

ter rivals Deutsche Telekom and British Telecom are sharing costs for the needed network buildout.

In South America, rising costs have enabled Spain's Telefonica to gain a hammerlock on the wireless industry. The company's 2001 merger of its Brazil operations with smaller Portugal Telecom's will help both companies meet the expense of building out their networks in that country. As they expand, it will become increasingly difficult for new entrants to compete with them as well.

As 3G hits the scene by mid-decade, the stakes will rise again. Costs will take another quantum leap forward as would-be competitors face the expenses of winning likely spectrum auctions, capital needs to finance building out networks, and higher operating and marketing costs for offering new services. That will further limit the number of companies who can compete, increasing the concentration of industry power.

PARADIGM VS. PROPHECY

Burdened by transmission lines and power plants that would be eligible for retirement pensions, America's energy grid is in dire need of a major technology overhaul. There's no shortage of new developments to fill the gap.

In the decade ahead, distributed generation sources from fuel cells and microgenerators to photovoltaics will proliferate. Superconductors will radically reduce voltage losses on power lines, and new communications technology will enable ever more efficient flows of electricity and natural gas from producers to consumers.

All of these technologies—particularly fuel cells—have been hyped in the energy industry as game breakers that will sink the giants and create a new generation of powerful upstarts. None of them, however, is nearly so revolutionary. In fact, not only will their developers fail to ascend to industry dominance, most will probably not even survive to mid-decade. Instead, these technologies will be absorbed by the ever evolving energy industry leaders, which will become far more profitable and dominant.

One reason for this is that there's already been a revolution in the energy industry. As recently as the mid-1990s, a potpourri of relatively small, highly regulated, local and regional fiefdoms produced and distributed the bulk of America's electricity and natural gas. Today, a handful of giants increasingly control the nation's generating capacity and gas throughput.

The change agent was the proliferation of advanced turbine technology that started in the mid-1990s. Developed by applying materials and designs used for jet engines, these advanced units use combustion gases directly—rather than the steam of traditional plant designs—to propel turbine blades. Combined cycle systems then use the exhaust to produce steam to run another turbine. The result: Something approaching 70 percent of the energy content of fuel is converted into electricity. In contrast, conventional power plants are able to extract just 30 to 35 percent.

When California became the first state to pass deregulation legislation in 1996, fear of the power of these new turbines ran deep throughout the industry. Speculation ran amuck that a wave of new entrants would build fleets of them, forcing price cuts and huge writedowns in the value of older, less efficient units. Utilities demanded recovery of these potential stranded costs up front as the price of peacefully going along with industry change.

As it turned out, stranded costs were a myth. The growing power shortage has dramatically increased the value of even the most inefficient plants, but advanced turbine technology has nonetheless worked a revolution in the industry.

Fearful of a competitive market, scores of electric utilities have exited the generating business altogether, selling their plants to the highest bidder (see Figure 6.3). The dozen or so remaining in the game have become aggressive global players, not only buying plants but building them wherever a profit can be made. Those opting out of generation have focused on building regional distribution empires via mergers with other distributors.

Volatile power prices have further tilted the balance of industry power toward the growing giants. Size has become essential as profits have been reinvested in more building and buying. With only a limited number of companies even making turbines, the

---

Companies Selling Power Plants

Bangor Hydro
CH Energy
Conectiv
Consolidated Edison
DQE Inc
Edison International*
EnergyEast
GPU Inc
Maine Public Service
National Grid USA
Niagara Mohawk
Northeast Utilities
NSTAR
PG&E*
Potomac Electric
RGS Energy
Sempra Energy*
Sierra Pacific
UIL Holdings
UNITIL
*Owns unregulated power plants.

Figure 6.3

giants have managed to corner the available supply for new power plants, at least to mid-decade.

In the postderegulation order, cash is more important than ever for facing down competition, reaching new markets, and staying ahead in the technology race. That's a major reason why the development of distributed generation, communications capability, and superconductors are evolutionary technologies—enhancing the leaders' power—rather than revolutionary ones. Only a handful of leaders have the cash to develop them to their full potential.

Like cellular phones in the 1980s, distributed generation's need for development cash is only beginning to be felt. Originally developed for the space program, today's fuel cell models convert the hydrogen in a fuel, such as natural gas, directly into electricity without burning it. There are two key components. A reformer converts the fuel into hydrogen. The fuel cell stack then combines the hydrogen with oxygen in the air to produce power. As a result, they create little pollution, require little space, and can theoretically be used for a wide range of applications, from generating power for homes off the grid to powering vehicles and portable electronic components.

The problem is there's still no uniform standard. Instead, several competing designs, each utilizing different elements and potential fuel sources, are competing for investment dollars. The models that appear to have the most economic potential run on natural gas, diesel, methane, or some derivative. There's little agreement among the developers as to which technology will ultimately become the standard, and glitches continue to arise with even the most promising.

Another problem is efficiency. Before advanced turbines hit the scene, fuel cells held a clear lead in potential efficiency over grid power plants. A design under development by startup FuelCell Energy Inc., for example, has demonstrated efficiency of better than 45 percent, 77 percent including steam output. Advanced turbines, however, are virtually as efficient, and they're in full commercial production as well.

With their efficiency advantage over new grid-generated power no longer a major factor, fuel cells' primary appeal is increased reliability. Even before the surge in demand for energy in recent years, the current grid of high-voltage lines criss-crossing the country has been in dire need of upgrades. Periodic outages, often triggered by events hundreds of miles from the spot, have become common and are a threat with every new surge in demand.

At the same time the grid's reliability has faded, the American economy is being driven by industries that have near-zero tolerance for power outages and require a higher quality of power. For these businesses, which include most e-commerce providers, data centers, and makers of sensitive electronics, power must not only keep flowing. It must do so at a steady rate with a minimum of fluctuation in frequency, power dips and, surges.

Power, in other words, must be "cleaner" than ever before. In addition, there's the challenge of adapting the grid's alternating current (AC) with the direct current (DC) devices used by many electronic components.

With demand surging and blackouts a fact of life, the grid is less and less capable of meeting this new demand. The result is a tremendous demand from industry to find new ways to ensure clean and reliable power. And users are willing to pay almost anything for it.

Because they create power at the source, fuel cells, microgenerators, photovoltaics, and other forms of distributed generation have been touted as a solution to the problem. Power-sensitive industries have also increasingly adopted a new generation of silicon-based power semiconductors, or powerchips.

Unlike the power switches that are found all over the modern grid, powerchips allow users to clean up power themselves. They do this by regulating power flows on an order of magnitude three to six times faster than the old electromagnetic switches. In addition, raw speed allows the power semiconductor to handle larger volumes of power, and it streamlines operations by eliminating peripheral electronics and hardware whose primary function was to clean up power.

Some have speculated that powerchips combined with a distributed generation source will someday displace the power grid. The preeminent maker of power semiconductors, PowerOne, for example, has already signed on a host of major tech companies as customers, including Cisco, Ericsson, Lucent, Nortel, and Teradyne, though demand for its products has fallen due to the end of the Nasdaq boom of the latter 1990s.

While its appeal will grow in the high-tech industry, the powerchip–distributed generation combo won't expand much beyond it, at least not this decade. The reason: The general public doesn't share the tech sector's overriding need and desire for clean power. Instead, most of us are focused on reliability, holding down costs, and simplicity. In other words, most of us don't want to be an electrical engineer to run the air conditioner.

Ironically, perceived reliability could prove to be the biggest problem for fuel cells and other forms of distributed generation. Electricity consumers in deregulated markets have been increasingly reluctant even to switch suppliers on the grid, especially after the spiking prices in California. The experience with other network industries that have deregulated—telecommunications, airlines, and the like—means even fewer will leave the certainty of the grid for the brave new world of fuel cells, despite the promised benefits.

As for actual reliability, fuel cells, are still years at best from real commercial development. Photovoltaics are in demand, but only for limited uses. Fuel cells face numerous technical problems, not the least of which is the lack of a common, interchangeable design among the makers, and leading developer Plug Power has been forced to delay its aggressive rollout plans as well.

Even the most advanced designs for distributed generation are nowhere near being cost-competitive. It's likely rapid advances will dramatically cut the cost of distributed generation in coming years. Progress will be accelerated if companies succeed in mass-producing them, but distributed generation will still fail miserably on cost and simplicity in the battle to win a mass market.

No matter how far costs fall, it will always cost more in time and money to buy, install, and power up a fuel cell than to call the power company to turn on an existing hookup. Buyers will have to weigh the upfront costs against any projected savings, which right now are nonexistent, in comparison with the advanced turbines now taking over the grid. Fuel cells should require minimum maintenance when they hit the market, but there's always the chance of trouble and the hassle involved with getting things fixed.

There's also the problem of what to power fuel cells and micro-generators with. The most promising models use natural gas, which wipes out whatever cost-efficiency advantage they have when energy prices spike. A fuel cell developed by IdaCorp includes a fuel reformer that's been tested, using methanol, at the World Methanol Conference in Copenhagen. That could give newer models the ability to switch fuels and avoid potentially disastrous dependence on a single fuel.

Even if such fuel switching becomes commonplace, fuel cell users will still be forced to make a whole new raft of complex decisions, ranging from what fuel to buy to whether to lock in the price. Fuel decisions will also be impacted by rising restrictions on air pollution, which are certain to come down harder on home generators than large, diversified power producers. No matter how exciting it sounds, home generation will always be far more complicated than plugging into the grid.

As a result, few outside of the tech industry are likely to cut the cord to the grid, even as advances are made. Those in the most power flow–sensitive sectors of the economy are also likely to think twice. Figure 6.4 shows the monetary impact outages can have on varying business sectors.

For one thing, the superior reliability of the powerchip–distributed generation combination is in large part due to the ability to switch back to the grid at opportune times, for example, when grid electricity is cheap or repairs are needed. For another, there's the growing promise of another evolutionary technology, superconductivity.

When cooled to cryogenic temperatures, superconductors lose all resistance to electrons and become perfect conductors of electricity. That enables superconducting wire to carry far more power than copper or aluminum conductors with very low losses.

Superconducting coils can store electricity almost indefinitely. Just as important, they can also discharge it to circuits and power grids on demand to maintain the consistent voltage needed by even the most power-sensitive industries. That, in turn, allows for far more compact transmission systems, which can be deployed with few environmental and public health concerns.

American Superconductor is one of the leading developers of superconductivity products. The company's two major products are superconducting magnetic energy storage (SMES) and cable (HTS). Its D-SMES system was successfully deployed on two utility systems, one in Wisconsin in July 2000 and the other in

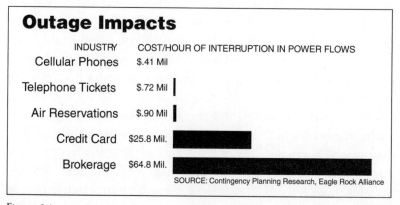

Figure 6.4

Houston in spring 2001. The storage devices are placed at strategic points on the power network and consist of a cryogenically cooled storage magnet, advanced line-monitoring equipment to detect voltage deviations, and a bank of inverters to inject real and reactive power to counteract them.

The company has also demonstrated its HTS superconducting cable system in Detroit. Developed with American's partner, Italy-based Pirelli Cables & Systems, the superconducting cable can carry three times more power than the copper cable it replaces. It's expected to be in heavy demand in urban areas, due to the social costs of disruption, the difficulty in locating new facilities, and its ability to limit the potential effect of electromagnetic fields.

The biggest problem for superconductors is investment. The deregulation of generation spurred a tidal wave of interest and allowed the advanced turbine revolution to unfold, but America's transmission system remains a regulated entity, with rates set according to the cost of service. As a result, incentives for investing in efficiency-rich technology like superconductors are unclear. The need for redundancies in networks, which superconductors could eliminate, is a further complication.

By 2003, almost all utilities will have turned their power transmission systems over to regional transmission operators (RTOs) jointly owned by several utilities. FERC's goal is to reduce the number of RTOs nationwide to four superregional entities, with the power to dramatically smooth the path to open markets. These RTOs will potentially have the ability to access capital at a low cost, as well as the financial incentive to deploy HTS to increase system throughput. That also will be a powerful incentive for both businesses and consumers to remain hooked up to the grid, rather than migrating to fuel cells, microturbines, or photovoltaics.

Distributed generation will remain an increasingly powerful niche market for both high tech and in areas where the grid isn't an option. Fuel cells, for example, could potentially dominate rural areas, where they may be fueled with propane. Photovoltaics, which convert sunlight directly into electricity, are emerging as especially popular alternatives in sunny rural areas, as well as for environmentally conscious grid users.

The real surprise to distributed generation's proponents is who it will chiefly benefit: the energy industry's leading companies. The more profitable the distributed generation business becomes, the greater the incentive will be for major power generators and distributors to increase their already-growing piece of the action; because they have far deeper pockets and control access to critical distribution networks, the big boys will be ideally placed to take control.

Dozens of utilities—both generators and distributors—have already invested heavily in the development of distributed generation. In fact, most developers are products of utility investment. Plug Power's biggest backer and 33 percent owner is Detroit-based electric and gas utility DTE Energy. Microturbine leader Capstone Turbine was grown from an investment fund formed by major utilities, several of which remain major distributors of its products. Utilities Avista, DQE, IdaCorp, and a score of others are now developing relationships with fuel cell companies or are building their own models.

For utilities that own and distribute natural gas, fuel cell sales promise a windfall. New Jersey Resources estimates it will double its gas deliveries to residential consumers convinced to buy fuel cells. Gas distribution companies nationwide could reap a similar windfall, as will gas producers who will profit from a new source of demand.

In photovoltaics, many of the leading players are either energy giants or allied with them. UniSource's Global Solar subsidiary has developed a thin-film-material photovoltaic that's now in use by the U.S. military. Enron has teamed with BP Amoco/Solarex to develop applications as well.

The bottom line is today's power technologies have tremendous appeal, and they'll likely become widespread in the decade ahead, even though they have little chance of upsetting the pecking order of the energy utility industry. Just as with cellular phones over the last 10 years, only a handful of major players have the capital to fully exploit the new technologies. Fundamentally, they're evolutionary, not revolutionary.

THE NEXT RE-EVOLUTION

Here in the early twenty-first century, there's no shortage of candidates for the next breakthrough technology. Biotech companies are using our knowledge of the human genome to develop cures for an ever-widening range of diseases. A new generation of automobiles is set to hit the streets using far less gasoline and creating far less pollution than ever. The Internet has become almost ubiquitous and, as the speed of communications networks is increased, more and more applications will be developed.

Energy, communications, and water also will enjoy their share of advances, as investment pours into their industries. Major players like Duke Energy, Dynegy, and Enron, for example, are using the Internet to grow trading businesses for energy. Enron's enrononline.com is already the largest and most profitable e-commerce site in the world, trading a wide range of commodities, including telecommunications bandwidth.

At this point, however, none of the new technologies looks likely to start a revolution. Instead, they'll only increase the ability of existing players to do their job more efficiently, cheaply, and profitably. That adds up to more growth and more opportunity. The growth of Enron's trading site, for example, simultaneously widened its lead in market share for trading electricity and natural gas in the late 1990s.

Even evolutionary technologies pose dangers for incumbents who are ill-prepared for them. Over the next decade, many companies will take wrong turns that could run them headlong into financial disasters, investing in technologies that prove obsolete. The key to circumventing these dangers is having management with the flexibility, organizational skills, and vision to use change to its advantage.

....

INDUSTRY PROFILE: JOHN HOWE

As Chairman of the Massachusetts Department of Public Utilities from 1995 to 1997, John Howe was a key architect of the state's now five-year-old deregulation plan. His wide-ranging resume includes three years at the department's gas oversight division, a tour of duty at a small in-state hydropower company, a year as a research assistant at the U.S. Department of Energy, and five years at J. Makowski, formerly the largest independent power developer in New England, which later became a unit of PG&E.

Now Vice President of Electric Industry Affairs at American Superconductor, Howe's key concern is the nation's decaying electric transmission infrastructure. His duties are twofold: providing strategic direction for the company, a developer of superconductor technology in an increasingly dynamic industry, and serving as liaison with the rest of the industry, including the electric utilities that are potentially American's biggest customers.

Q: WHAT'S THE MOST IMPORTANT CHANGE IN THE POWER INDUSTRY SINCE YOU CAME INTO THE BUSINESS?

A: The electric industry has become an incredibly dynamic place. There's a recognition and willingness to entertain new approaches that simply didn't exist 15 years ago. Personnel-wise, rotation has increased. The traditional utility employee has been downsized and there's been an influx of senior managers with finance, technology, trading, and entrepreneurial backgrounds. The downside is there's less of a premium on the fundamental principles of engineering among these industry leaders, so we've lost a tremendous amount of the historical knowledge base about what makes electric systems work. That's impeded our ability to find solutions to today's problems.

Q: WHAT'S THE BIGGEST PROBLEM AND OPPORTUNITY
  IN THE ELECTRIC INDUSTRY?

A: Fixing the brittleness of the transmission infrastructure. Huge amounts of capital have flowed into electric
power generation in response to deregulation, but
there's a critical need to find and implement new ways to
move power. I'm afraid we haven't yet adapted the
lessons learned in telecom and natural gas deregulation.
As I see it, the key lesson from the restructuring of those
industries is that deregulation led to the investment of
large amounts of capital in networks and transportation
infrastructure, not simply in the commodities moved
over those networks.

Outmoded regulation is the biggest hurdle to new
transmission investment. We have a dysfunctional, complex, and often self-contradictory overlay of federal and
state regulation. And while the Federal Energy Regulatory Commission has tried to introduce an open-access
interstate transmission network, states have been reluctant to give up control. In fact, several are actually
reversing deregulation to try to maintain control over
their transmission systems.

There are plenty of potential investors in transmission systems out there if conditions were right. For
example, Warren Buffett recently said he's ready to pour
in billions if there's sufficient regulatory change. But
you've got to change the system to reflect today's risks
and allow for enough returns to attract capital. I'm a
proponent of the idea that the power industry won't
reach a stable end state until transmission is made a
truly competitive function.

Q: HOW CAN SUPERCONDUCTORS HELP SOLVE THE
  TRANSMISSION SYSTEM'S PROBLEMS AND HOW WILL
  THEY IMPACT THE UTILITY INDUSTRY?

A: Superconductor technology can dramatically improve
the power grid's reliability by better regulating power
flows. It can also reduce the need for big, obtrusive, over-

head power lines, which are now viewed with suspicion by the public.

American Superconductor first introduced power quality applications of our SMES systems in the early 1990s. In 2000, we deployed this technology on utility grids for the first time in a new configuration we call D-SMES (distributed superconducting magnetic energy storage). Our partner Pirelli is introducing another key superconductor application, a high-capacity cable, in a pilot demonstration on a live grid in Detroit. Over the next five years, we can expect to see a steady, progressive rollout of a wide array of superconductor-based applications to increase the bandwidth and reliability of electric power grids.

New companies will be at the forefront of superconductors' development and use. But utilities are still the logical dominant users. The new technology will change the industry. But just as distributed generation has gone from competitive threat to opportunity for utilities in just a few years, I likewise expect that utilities will absorb superconductor technology and be changed by it in the process. In the telecommunications industry, for example, it was the upstarts like MCI and Sprint that introduced fiber-optic technology, but now traditional players like the Baby Bells are using it as well. Power utilities will change in the same way the communications companies have changed.

Incidentally, the debate between alternating current and direct current is raging again, a hundred years after AC's greater transformability and economies of scale won the day. The digital economy needs cleaner power and can actually run much better on DC, so we could see the development of a parallel DC grid in some areas, which could conceivably shake up the existing order.

Q: HAS REGULATION CHANGED SINCE YOU LEFT THE MASSACHUSETTS DEPARTMENT OF PUBLIC UTILITIES?

A: Not enough. For competition to succeed, regulators must ensure that workably competitive conditions exist, and then step away. I fear regulators have done too little to ensure competitive conditions and not enough to step away and allow competitive processes to unfold.

I have very little patience for the argument that deregulation is a failed experiment, because it's been done successfully in many countries around the world. We're the ones who have screwed it up in the United States! I believe the reason is we have not reconciled ourselves to the notion that regulation requires stepping away from micromanaging the market. We're supposed to be moving to lighter-handed oversight systems. Yet the industry is controlled by 50 state agencies as well as federal agencies, which often impose conflicting or inconsistent requirements. If anything, during this transition to supposed deregulation, regulation has become more complex and contradictory than ever before.

Unfortunately, we've seen a slowdown in the process of industry restructuring and a reversal of course in some states. I'm afraid where that leaves us is at the worst of all possible places—halfway across a stream where the water is rising. I believe we can't really turn back at this point. But the worst place to be from a reliability and competitive standpoint is right where we are.

The key lesson we should learn from other nations that have deregulated successfully is the need to move forward decisively. Given the steady growth in demand, the electrification of the economy, difficulties in siting, and environmental pressures on existing plants, if we freeze regulation in place we're only going to make matters worse. We've got to get to a stable place to encourage new investment in the T&D infrastructure, and we should encourage market forces to operate. We're just not there yet.

....

CHAPTER 7

Riding the Boom

It may be hard to believe but less than a century ago only wealthy neighborhoods had electricity. Phone service was rare in a world ruled by the telegraph. Clean, sanitary water systems were as unrealistic as spaceships.

Then, for nearly three decades, investment poured into all of these essential services, reaching a crescendo in the late 1920s (see Figure 7.1).

The money came from many sources. In energy, all the great families of the Industrial Revolution—Morgans, Mellons, Peabodys, Vanderbilts—anted up. J.P. Morgan wound up controlling an empire of systems stretching across the country. Thomas Edison's brainchild, General Electric, was transformed into a colossus overnight by creating systems nationwide to spur demand for its products. British-born entrepreneur Samuel Insull used foreign capital to build the massive Commonwealth Edison utility holding company, establishing many of today's accounting standards and business practices in the process.

Money was also the key to the success of Theodore Vail's AT&T as it built a nationwide, copper wire–based communications network, displacing the telegraph completely in a matter of a few decades. It was vital to building the gargantuan water and wastewater systems that are the heart of urban life.

A century later, electricity, natural gas, communications, and water are critical for survival in America. Yet the ability to meet demand for these services by utility providers is increasingly in

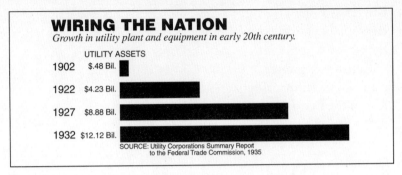

WIRING THE NATION
Growth in utility plant and equipment in early 20th century.

UTILITY ASSETS

1902	$.48 Bil.
1922	$4.23 Bil.
1927	$8.88 Bil.
1932	$12.12 Bil.

SOURCE: Utility Corporations Summary Report
to the Federal Trade Commission, 1935

Figure 7.1

doubt. Power outages, water safety scares, and communications breakdowns have become commonplace. The technology has advanced but the price of service has skyrocketed, creating a widening divide between those who can afford to live a twenty-first century life and those who may be forced into a late-nineteenth-century one.

The key to bridging this gap is a new investment boom. For nearly 20 years, almost no new capital has gone into building energy infrastructure, from power plants and gas pipelines to developing new reserves of oil and gas. Strapped municipalities and small rural systems increasingly lack the funds to ensure water supplies are safe enough to drink. Advancing technological needs and a crushing mountain of debt have dried up capital in the communications industry as well.

The new investment boom will bring better, smarter, and cheaper power, water, and communications to the average person in the early twenty-first century, just as the last boom did a century ago. Over the next decade, trillions of dollars will be deployed to build power plants, power lines, and water treatment plants, as well to finance new energy technology, oil and gas resource development, and the upgrade of communications networks.

SCAPEGOAT AND SAVIOR

Advancing deregulation has been the scapegoat for much of the trouble in the energy and communications industries. California

Governor Gray Davis, for example, has blamed his state's 1996 law for allowing major out-of-state generating companies to reap huge profits at the expense of consumers.

Consumer groups, officials in other states, and federal politicians like California Senator Dianne Feinstein have also voiced fear of the market power of a rising elite of industry giants. A bill to throw utility executives in jail if they allegedly gouge the public is making the rounds in the California state legislature and similar measures are drawing interest in New York.

Similarly, critics of the telecommunications industry are turning their fire on the Telecom Act of 1996, which opened all markets to all comers. Some have pointed to the ascendancy of the Baby Bell offspring of the old AT&T as evidence of deregulation's failure.

Large companies are using their muscle to crush smaller rivals, evidenced by the bankruptcy of numerous small communications companies and power producers. On the consumer level, big industrial and commercial users have gained buying power at the expense of formerly subsidized residential customers, and over 100 companies have merged with others in their respective industries to gain the heft needed to meet global competition.

The irony, however, is that deregulation is the best hope to close America's investment deficit in essential services. The lifting of controls has created a new breed of superutilities with access to the deep pools of low-cost capital necessary to invest anywhere, anytime. These emerging giants can deploy resources quickly and efficiently to where they're needed most. Unlike the utilities of yesteryear, they have every incentive to do so, since it will create the greatest profit.

Most important, they're increasingly large, publicly traded companies, making them a natural conduit for the teeming billions of dollars ready to pour into their industries. Major energy companies, for example, will all be in play for takeovers once the Public Utility Holding Company Act goes by the board. They're the natural candidates to ride the new investment boom.

Federal, state, and local governments are also theoretically capable of investing billions in essential service infrastructure. A history of high credit ratings and favorable tax privileges put the muni monopolies in the driver's seat when it came to building the nation's urban water and wastewater systems up until the 1970s. Agencies like the Tennessee Valley Authority played a critical role in electrifying once-impoverished areas of the country like the Southeast.

Unfortunately, any major infrastructure expense by a state, federal, or local entity today will come at the price of either higher taxes or a lower credit rating. As recently as the 1970s, state and local governments received billions of dollars in revenue sharing from the federal government, allowing them to fund myriad needed projects and services. The Reagan administration then did away with revenue sharing in the 80s. As a result, most state and local entities have been hard-pressed to finance even existing obligations, let alone major new investments in energy, communications, or water.

The attempt by California's Department of Water and Power beginning in early 2001 to buy power wholesale and sell it retail to defaulted utilities PG&E and Edison International is likely to rank among the greatest financial follies of all time. It will wind up costing the state's residents tens of billions in taxes and fees. Also, as it lowers the state's credit rating, it will make it more expensive to finance other worthy projects in the future. That's not likely to inspire any converts to the cause of government-financed infrastructure buildout.

Even the success stories of government investment in power infrastructure raise questions. The Tennessee Valley Authority (TVA) and Washington Water Power Authority invested billions of taxpayer-subsidized money in nuclear power plants in the 1970s and 80s, many of which were never opened. TVA's debt load is some $887 per kilowatt of capacity, far above the typical investor-owned utility.

Not only are investor-owned utilities less indebted, but they raise their own money. Their credit is not dependent on a government guarantee that can crowd out other worthy projects. The shareholders' and bondholders' dollars are at risk in projects, not the taxpayers'.

If utility projects' profits fall short, their investors—not ratepayers or taxpayers—suffer the consequences. The upshot:

The emerging utility giants are the only realistic hope of closing the investment deficit in essential services. Their shareholders are the primary beneficiaries of a trend that's only in its infancy.

The emerging giants' origins and business plans vary widely, but all have three things in common: access to the low-cost capital needed to grow in rapidly changing and investment-starved markets; management with the experience, skill, and vision to keep them moving in the right direction; and the right mix of physical and human assets to achieve their goals.

The energy, communications, and water companies profiled in this chapter all share those strengths. Note, however, that they're prototypes for success, not an all-inclusive list of winners. These are the best examples of utilities that have the strengths to be winners. Later chapters will explain how to find other companies worthy of considering as investment.

In addition, each of the companies highlighted here is a rapidly growing, increasingly powerful company, but some could stumble in coming years, and others will rise to take their place. While the rise of upstarts in these industries will continue to be rare, it's possible that five years from now a company currently unknown will rise to prominence. Furthermore, it's almost certain that an unforeseen megamerger will create a new powerhouse sometime in the next five years.

Even the stocks that do stay on course won't always be strong buys. In the stock market, value is a function of price. The best companies can be overpriced and the worst-run can be buys at the right price for aggressive investors betting on a comeback. Before you buy any of these stocks, read the investing tips in Chapters 10 and 11. You should refer to these rules periodically to judge your picks' progress.

ENERGY EFFICIENCIES

In 1900, electricity was a niche product used only in major cities by those who could afford it. By 1932, it was nearly ubiquitous. During that time, the number of utility companies shrank from thousands to effectively five massive holding companies, which together controlled almost the entire U.S. power and natural gas grid. Ultimately, all came under the power of one man, J.P. Morgan (see Figure 7.2).

These companies used a wide range of sources to finance their growth. Much came from overseas, where men like Insull and Germany's Henry Villard became adept at harnessing European institutions' and investors' lust for investing in America's growth.

Thomas Edison's General Electric was the driving force behind the creation of Electric Bond & Share, which eventually became the world's largest utility holding company with interests throughout the United States and overseas via its American & Foreign Power Company unit. As the leading manufacturer of generators, switches, and wires needed to build and run electric systems, GE essentially financed the building of utilities across the country for the purpose of selling its products.

As payment for the equipment, the company granted promissory notes, allowing it to book income from both the sale and interest on the notes. Deals were also financed with common stock. GE eventually spun off its holdings at EBS to survive a financial crisis, but not before its inside position, providing equipment, ensured it industry leadership that still exists today. GE, for example, was a driving force behind the move to nuclear power in the 1960s and 70s, and it's a leader in the advanced turbine revolution, as well as fuel cells.

Investment in utilities from outside the industry was sharply curtailed by the Public Utility Holding Company Act of 1935

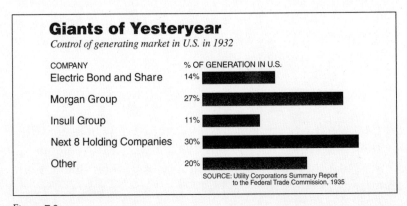

Giants of Yesteryear
Control of generating market in U.S. in 1932

COMPANY	% OF GENERATION IN U.S.
Electric Bond and Share	14%
Morgan Group	27%
Insull Group	11%
Next 8 Holding Companies	30%
Other	20%

SOURCE: Utility Corporations Summary Report to the Federal Trade Commission, 1935

Figure 7.2

(PUHCA). Not only did it largely cut off the flow of foreign money, it also limited potential ownership of utilities by American investors not registered as holding companies with the Securities and Exchange Commission to less than 5 percent of total stock outstanding.

The elimination of PUHCA in the next few years should ignite a new wave of investment in utilities. Like the Morgans and Mellons of the last century, billionaire Warren Buffett has emerged as a major potential investor.

In early 2000, Buffett's flagship Berkshire Hathaway completed the $1.6 billion takeover of MidAmerican Energy, the holding company of an Iowa-based electric and gas utility, as well as global power producer CalEnergy. The deal brought aggressive utility executive David Sokol aboard Berkshire, setting the stage for more acquisitions in the industry once PUHCA restrictions are removed.

Major companies outside the industry are also likely to join the investment wave. Big Oil's ExxonMobil, BP Amoco, and Chevron Texaco—which already owns 27 percent of energy marketer Dynegy—have a natural interest in investing heavily in electric power due to their position in natural gas. GE itself is likely to take a bigger interest, thanks to its stake in fuel cells.

The last investment boom in power and gas moved through the major holding companies that came to dominate the energy utility industry. Likewise, the twenty-first-century boom mostly will move through the emerging cadre of energy giants who are carving out a dominant industry position through unmatched access to low-cost capital and visionary management. (See Figure 7.3.)

Companies with expertise in the wholesale marketing of both electricity and natural gas—the dominant fuel to generate power—have the greatest potential in the boom. They'll be able to take advantage of the growth in both markets, as well as upward and downward price volatility.

Supply and demand for power and gas are intimately related. A summer spike in demand for electricity will create a corresponding surge in demand for natural gas, which is the fuel of choice for most power plants. Higher demand will push gas prices up, which in turn will further increase the price of electricity. A shortage of gas will push up power prices by making it more expensive to operate plants.

An unexpected drop in demand for power, on the other hand, also diminishes demand for natural gas, pushing down prices in both markets. The new breed of major marketers wins by owning assets at all ends of the deal—from gas production and power generation to energy storage and distribution—and by wielding their financial power to supply energy to areas of greatest need.

Enron was far and away the world's leading wholesale marketer of both electricity and natural gas up until mid-2001. Born from a merger of two pipeline companies in the mid-1980s, the company was among the first to recognize the potential of deregulation of gas and, later, electricity.

In the latter 1990s, Enron put its expertise on the Internet, creating an entirely new market for energy, as well as for a wide range of other commodities, including telecommunications bandwidth. EnronOnline has rapidly become the globe's largest and most profitable e-commerce site. The company has operations throughout the world and controls an estimated 20 percent of the U.S. wholesale market.

Enron's early strategy was to back its paper commitments— basically contracts to buy and sell energy—with assets like power plants, pipelines, and gas reserves. As its markets grew, however, Chairman Ken Lay moved closer to an optionality-based approach, where future profitability will be determined more on how management both anticipates the markets and uses others' assets to make profits.

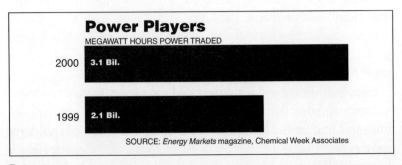

Power Players
MEGAWATT HOURS POWER TRADED

2000	3.1 Bil.
1999	2.1 Bil.

SOURCE: *Energy Markets* magazine, Chemical Week Associates

Figure 7.3

As a result, Enron was essentially its industry's leading financial house, relying on unmatched money power and human capital, and featuring a wide range of strategic assets, which were leveraged with debt to finance more growth in energy trading. In the end, it was the company's lack of assets, poor investments in unrelated businesses, and overly complex financial arrangements that brought it down by late 2001. That has opened the field to its rivals.

Duke Energy's strategy is decidedly more asset-based than Enron's, though it's also a top-five marketer of electricity and natural gas. Formed from the mid-1990s merger of Carolinas-based electric utility Duke Power with nationwide pipeline PanEnergy, the company runs power plants worldwide, is a major operator of pipelines, and owns the country's largest gas gathering and processing company in a venture with Phillips Petroleum.

CEO Richard Priory, however, is hardly sentimental about any of Duke's assets, routinely disposing of power plants and pipelines when management sees a better opportunity to put its capital to work. The 1999 sale of a major pipeline system to Michigan-based CMS Energy, for example, helped the company cut debt from the PanEnergy merger and fund generating plants in power-starved areas for 2000 and 2001.

The Carolinas-based utility unit is perhaps the most efficient in the country, featuring nuclear and coal-fired facilities built and run by Duke itself. Cash from these operations has gone a long way to cheaply finance growth elsewhere in the organization, and the company has put its building expertise to work in a venture with Fluor Corp to develop power plants globally. The company has built several large plants adjacent to its pipeline holdings, allowing for easy fueling and cost controls.

Duke has also pursued an asset-based strategy abroad, particularly in Latin America where it has become a leading player with targeted acquisitions in the past couple of years. Duke has continued to invest in new technologies as well.

AES was born from the opportunity unleashed by the Public Utility Regulatory Power Act of 1978 (PURPA), designed to reduce the country's reliance on non-OPEC sources of energy. The law essentially required utilities to buy all the power generated by renewable resources like hydropower, solar, geothermal, and wind at a premium price. As a result, hundreds of independent power producers (IPPs) sprang up, particularly in states like New York and California where regulators were even more aggressively supporting them.

AES was one of the most aggressive of the new breed. Unlike most of its IPP brethren, the company grew its business independently of PURPA-related opportunities. As a result, it's now the world's largest nongovernment power producer, even as volatile natural gas prices and deregulation have run all but a handful of IPPs out of business.

AES's basic rule is invest anywhere, as long as there's a need to be filled. Under the direction of Dennis Bakke and Roger Sant, the company has built an empire of 64,000 megawatts of power capacity stretching across 32 countries. It also owns distribution utilities serving some 18 million customers. Assets range from Indiana-based electric utility Ipalco and Illinois-based Cilcorp to three leading distribution companies in Kazakhstan and Brazil's biggest fiber-optic communications network.

Such far-flung assets expose the company to numerous political, regulatory, and currency risks, but it also makes AES the most diversified utility in the world, protecting it from the risks of a single country. The company's stated aim of hiring local talent for its projects and its goal of having its workers have fun are also unique, major factors in its ongoing success.

Control of natural gas production will also be a road to success in coming years. Dominion Resources produces, stores, transports, markets, and distributes the fuel, and also generates and distributes electricity throughout the Northeast and Midwest. As a result, it profits from greater natural gas usage, including its potential use in fuel cells: higher gas prices, rising demand for electricity, and rising power prices.

Up until the late 1990s, the company was essentially a Virginia-based electric utility saddled with mediocre-performing assets including Latin American power production and financial services. Then, in 1999, CEO Thomas Capps, who had emerged victorious in a brutal succession battle, took the company in a completely new direction, agreeing to merge with aggressive natural gas giant Consolidated Natural Gas. The company has since divested its noncore assets and is focused solely on expanding the profitability of its 20,000 megawatts of power plant capacity, gas reserves, pipelines, and other ventures.

Dominion has also become a leading national player in nuclear power, recently purchasing Connecticut's Millstone plant complex from Northeast Utilities. Operating nukes has long been Dominion's strong suit, with its four Virginia-based units consistently rated among the country's best since the 1980s. Political and regulatory risk and long lead times mean new nuclear plants aren't likely to be built in the United States anytime soon, despite the backing of the Bush administration. With natural gas prices so volatile, Dominion's operating nukes will only become more valuable in coming years. Figure 7.4 shows the stats of some leading energy companies.

Another company on the short list for emerging giants is gas and electric marketing powerhouse Dynegy. Like Duke, the company has built a thriving national energy marketing business including a thriving Internet presence, backed up with physical assets. It also enjoys steady cash flows from power and gas distribution operations, which it acquired in the Illinova merger. Fast-growing Dynegy's expertise makes it a likely takeover target after PUHCA is repealed, with 27 percent owner Chevron Texaco the almost certain suitor.

El Paso Energy is perhaps even more asset-focused than Duke. The company became the largest pipeline company in the United

Emerging Energy Giants

Company	Recent Market Value (Billions)	Assets (Billions)	Generating Capacity MW	Distribution Customers (Millions)	Revenues (Billions)	S&P Bond Rating
AES Corp	$24.41	$31.03	64,000	18.0	$6.69	B+ (positive)
Dominion Resources	16.44	29.40	19,000	3.8	9.26	BBB+ (stable)
Duke Energy	34.65	58.18	34,000	2.1	49.32	A+ (negative)
Dynegy	18.37	21.42	25,000	0.6	25.91	BBB+ (stable)
El Paso Energy	33.52	27.45	2,050	0.0	21.95	BBB+ (stable)
EnergyEast	2.34	7.00	0	2.0	2.96	A- (negative)
Enron Corp	45.79	65.50	4,500	0.6	100.79	BBB+ (stable)
Kinder Morgan	6.59	8.42	0	0.0	2.71	BBB (stable)

SOURCE: Utility Forecaster

Figure 7.4

States after its 2000 merger with Coastal Corp. Its postmerger asset mix also includes power plants, gas storage, processing and refining facilities, and production operations. As the general partner in El Paso Energy Partners, which owns a wealth of high-cash-flow pipeline assets, the company also enjoys a reliable cash-flow stream that enables it to expand in good times and bad.

Exelon Energy is the nation's premier bet on nuclear power. The company owns more than 20 percent of the nuclear power plant capacity in the United States, after forming from the 2000 merger of Philadelphia-based PECO Energy and Chicago-based Unicom. Exelon has also been aggressively buying nuclear power plants from smaller owners who lacked the economies of scale to make them competitive. The company has been able to control its costs even as its empire has expanded, and its greater size limits the risk for something going wrong at a single plant.

WIRES AND PIPES

Transmission & Distribution (T&D) is the wires-and-pipes side of the business, the transmission of energy from producers and marketers to consumers. T&D doesn't have the glamour of energy production, generation, and marketing. Providers still operate as monopolies, and returns are set according to so-called cost of service, even in states where customers now have a choice of marketers.

T&D companies, however, also have incredible promise for riding the investment boom. One of Warren Buffett's first forays was a small stake in GPU, a company that's completely divested its power plants.

At their core, T&D companies are gatekeepers. They collect a fee whenever a part of their systems is used, whether it be gas pipelines, power lines, or gas storage facilities. Their long-term profitability depends on finding new ways to increase the throughput of their systems. The best companies will be interfacing with customers to find new ways to boost sales, and they will enjoy virtually recession-proof cash flow.

The challenge of T&D companies in coming years will be to upgrade the country's increasingly overburdened high-voltage power lines, and get the allowed returns from regulators to pay for it. That will require some considerable changes in existing regulation, but it will almost certainly happen.

The transition to deregulation has created one major problem for some T&D companies. Several states stuck their former monopoly utilities with "providers of last resort" obligations under their competition plans. These essentially forced the former monopolies to continue providing electricity at a fixed rate to any customer who did not choose an alternative supplier.

When they sold their power plants, most T&D companies locked in the price of power for their expected last-resort customers for a period of several years. When power prices started rising in 2000, thousands of customers who had left for competitors switched back to them as last-resort suppliers to get the lower fixed rate. As a result, T&D's were suddenly forced to serve an influx of unexpected customers by buying power at expensive market rates and selling it for a steep loss at locked-in prices.

One of the victims was GPU, which rang up more than $300 million in losses serving its returning last-resort customers. Pennsylvania regulators' willingness to compensate the company for its losses, however, has since limited this risk to GPU's health. More important, the Keystone State's decision promises that other states will allow T&D companies relief from this impediment to their development.

Ultimately, T&D companies will have no real commodity risk. Instead, they'll simply draw a fee when their systems are used, based on returns set by regulators. As a result, they'll ultimately be the lowest-risk stocks in the energy industry.

One of the more interesting T&D players is EnergyEast, which controls a network of natural gas and electric distribution companies in upstate New York and New England. The company has divested all of its power plant interests, but it's also limited near-term exposure to higher purchased power costs by locking in future supplies. The utility is now focused on boosting throughput of its system and acquiring other T&D companies. Finances are very strong and opportunity for more expansion is great, so it's a takeover target.

On a slightly different track is Kinder Morgan, the brainchild of former Enron executive Richard Kinder. The company owns a network of pipelines and storage facilities for a wide range of energy-related commodities across the country. Management has focused on buying assets that generate large and growing cash flows, which it can use to create more growth. It also has no supplier-of-last-resort obligations, since it was never an electric utility.

WIRED FOR GROWTH

Wall Street threw billions at the telecommunications industry in the latter 1990s. Given the failure of many of its targets—competitive local exchange carriers, direct subscriber line companies, and cellular and satellite upstarts—investors are unlikely to be so indiscriminate in the future. That leaves the big boys, the companies with access to low-cost capital even in bad times, in control of the game.

When it comes to size and financial power, the Baby Bell offspring of the 1984 AT&T breakup have no peer. Since spring 2000, their industry has imploded. Profit margins have collapsed in long distance and are on the way down in everything from wireless to high-speed data. Through it all, however, the Bells' profits have held steady, thanks to dominance over the most stable communications revenue generator, local phone service.

Despite regulators' best efforts to dilute their power, the Bells' control over the local loop has remained rock-solid. Coupled with savings realized in a series of mergers, the Bells have unmatched financial power. Even as others have rung up billions in debt, building state-of-the-art networks, the Bells have used revenue from their antiquated but long-since-paid-for copper phone networks to cheaply finance their own upgrades. They now have competitive technology without the debt.

Since the breakup, the Bells' primary risks have always been regulatory. Anxious to prevent the creation of a new Ma Bell, federal and state officials have repeatedly tried to curtail Bell power, with little understanding that competitive phone markets would favor size over the long haul.

Now that the Bells are trouncing their cash-starved rivals, they've won new allies in Bush administration appointees to the Federal

Communications Commission. FCC Chairman Michael Powell has made it clear he favors letting market players battle it out for dominance and has publicly excoriated his predecessor William Kennard for allegedly trying to ensure competition by attaching conditions to merger approvals and other policy decisions.

By late 2002, the Bells will have won their long-sought entry into most states' long-distance telephone and high-speed data markets. Subsidies to help competitors will be scaled back or axed completely. The phone industry will have wholly returned to its true state of nature, with the best of the biggest battling it out to become the second Ma Bell.

Of the Bells, Verizon is in perhaps the best position for future dominance (see Figure 7.5). The company's primary area of operations is the data business–rich Northeast, which it dominates. But it also has operations nationwide via local phone franchises acquired from the 2000 GTE merger and 55 percent–owned Verizon Wireless, the country's biggest wireless company.

Verizon has had no problem converting its local phone customers into users of its wireless services, and it's had huge success grabbing market share in the long-distance business—in New York, Connecticut, and Massachusetts—from AT&T and others. Once it wins entry into long distance in its other core states, it will snap up a massive chunk of its region's data market as well. Verizon could also launch a takeover effort for a major long-distance provider, a move that would all but create a second Ma Bell.

SBC Communications' CEO Edward Whitacre has been no less prescient in reading the future of communications. Thanks to a series of aggressive acquisitions, the company controls a third of

Contenders for the Throne

Company Market	Value (Billions)	Assets (Billions)	Customers (Millions)	S&P Bond Rating
Qwest Communications	$65.96	$73.50	29	BBB+ (stable)
SBC Communications	142.60	98.65	80	AA- (stable)
Telefonica	56.52	50.00	62	A+ (stable)
Verizon Communications	152.90	164.74	100	A+ (stable)
Vodafone	167.30	220.75	50	A (stable)

SOURCE: Utility Forecaster

Figure 7.5

America's local phone connections via ownership of three former Baby Bells—Midwest-based Ameritech, PacTel, and Southwestern Bell—as well as virtual Bell clone, Southern New England Telecom.

SBC has also made a huge effort to grow its cellular phone service business, last year forging Cingular Wireless, the country's second-largest provider, in an alliance with BellSouth. It has speeded the technological development of its network even as it methodically wins entry to the long-distance and high-speed data business throughout its territory.

The company is more internationally inclined than Verizon, with high-growth operations in Latin America and a share of myriad European telecoms via its 42 percent stake in TeleDanmark. Its future, however, will be determined in the United States where, like Verizon, there's little to stop its rise.

Qwest Communications is the third great candidate for the next Ma Bell. Alone of all the upstart telecoms that hit the scene during the financing boom of the 1990s, Qwest is a sure bet to survive as well as thrive. In fact, it's used the collapse in telecom capital markets to increase its dominance.

The key is Qwest's merger with Baby Bell US West, which gave it a near monopoly on local phone connections in 11 states and a recession-proof stream of cash flow. Engineered by CEO Joseph Nacchio, a former AT&T executive, the deal came under heavy fire from all sides when it was announced.

Regulators and consumers worried that basic service would erode under the aggressive Qwest, while Wall Streeters fretted that the company's theretofore rapid growth would screech to a halt under the burden of stodgy, problem-plagued US West. Others were concerned the purchase price was too high.

As it turned out, all of the critics were wrong. Even as capital markets have dried up for other rivals, the company has been able to use the US West cash flows to fund further growth in its core competency: the high-speed data market. The potential of these properties will explode further as the company wins entry into the long-distance and high-speed data market throughout US West's Rocky Mountain territory.

Future acquisition targets include BellSouth, which would take the company into another high-growth region, the Southeast, and give it 40 percent of Cingular Wireless, filling the cellular hole in its business strategy. Until then, however, the company will be hard to knock off course in expanding its power.

Since it was formed in 1924 as Spain's monopoly telecom, Telefonica has enjoyed powerful, Bells-like cash flows. Since the late 1980s, freed of its regulatory shackles, it's put its financial muscle to work building a global empire. The company has already achieved dominance throughout Latin America, acquiring privatized former monopolies in a half dozen countries and leveraging their assets, undreamed of even by the prebreakup AT&T.

Formed from its combined Latin American and European cellular assets, the company's Moviles subsidiary is rapidly emerging as the dominant wireless provider in the Spanish- and Portuguese-speaking world. Telefonica has built a sizable presence in southern Europe as well. Similarly, its Terra Networks subsidiary is the world's dominant Internet presence for those speaking Iberian-based languages. Telefonica remains dominant in local and long-distance service throughout Spain and Latin America, and it's made a major move into the entertainment business.

A decade ago, Vodafone was a fledgling spinoff from Britain's Racal. Today, the company has not only eclipsed its parent, it's become the world's biggest provider of wireless services, dwarfing its homeland's former leader British Telecom.

Vodafone's assets feature operations in every high-growth corner of the world. Its primary U.S. asset is a 45 percent share of Verizon Wireless, by far the biggest cellular company in the United States. European assets are anchored by the 2000 purchase of Germany's Mannesmann, achieved after a drawn-out hostile takeover battle. Besides establishing Vodafone as the dominant Euro wireless company, the deal also included nontelecom assets that it was able to sell to reduce debt.

As a result, despite one of the most aggressive expansion plans in its industry, Vodafone has been able to maintain a steady credit rating. It has been able to easily finance deals for more assets as well, including major cellular providers in Australia and Japan. Concluded in early 2001, these deals were wrapped up at prices far below those prevailing just a few months earlier.

The idea for WorldCom was allegedly dreamed up by its founder Bernard Ebbers on the back of a napkin in a Mississippi diner. Ebbers' ability to move his ambitious plan forward is no less legendary. Until his attempt to merge with Sprint failed in mid-2000, Ebbers successfully acquired and absorbed 100 businesses, most with state-of-the-art technologies. The crowning glory was the takeover of MCI, which he snatched right out from under far larger players British Telecom—which actually owned 20 percent of MCI—and GTE.

WorldCom was hit hard by the slowdown in telecommunications investment in 2000. While the MCI long-distance business has been a big loser, in the business-to-business area the company continues to build a dominant global position. It has spun off MCI's consumer long-distance business as a tracking stock, which will limit its downward impact on overall operations. WorldCom is also likely to prove very attractive as a merger partner.

WATER WORKS

With state and federal funding a dry hole, despite efforts to revive it, investor-owned water utilities are the solution to the industry's investment deficit. The biggest players in this country, American Water Works and Philadelphia Suburban, are becoming increasingly adept at raising capital to finance takeovers of smaller, weak, water systems, fueling their own growth.

A large chunk of that future financing is likely to come from overseas. The effect on U.S. water stocks is certain to be breathtaking. Even the largest U.S. water services provider—American Water Works—is a minnow compared to the European behemoths likely to pour investment into the industry over the next 10 years.

For example, France's Vivendi Environment, itself a spinoff of huge conglomerate Vivendi Universal, has assets of $35 billion, compared to American's $6.1 billion. It's nearly 25 times the size of the country's second-largest water utility, Philadelphia Suburban, of which it owns 17 percent, and 17 times the size of the next five largest U.S. water utes combined. Figure 7.6 shows the asset size of the largest U.S. water utilities.

This size disparity means the behemoths have created a quantum move in water company shares every time they've invested in the United States. The buyout of E-Town Water by Thames Water, for example, was at a 50 percent premium to the predeal price, and it set off a stampede into water shares in 1999. Neighboring Middlesex Water stock, for example, soared 30 percent in one day, only to give it all up the next.

Any deals for the remaining U.S. water utes are certain to be even more explosive. In the meantime, they continue to grow in size and strength as they move industry power away from the old muni monopolies.

Run by the Ware family for generations, American Water Works is still the country's premier water utility, serving 10 million people in 23 states. The company's primary strategy continues to be to pursue growth through acquisitions of smaller systems at the right price, but it has also beefed up its water system management operations. In this business, which involves managing municipal systems for a fee, profits are unregulated, affording opportunities for rapid growth. AWW has already gained business from 1,300 communities nationwide. In addition, all of these systems are candidates for future takeovers, as they become comfortable with American's high level of service.

Philadelphia Suburban is a smaller company, with just over 600,000 accounts, giving it the ability to turn smaller deals into much faster growth. CEO Nick DeBenedictis has more than doubled the utility's size in the past decade simply by acquiring small,

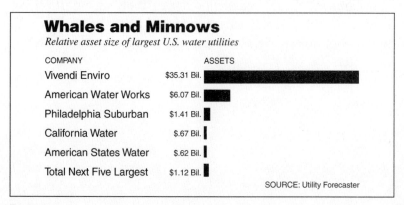

Whales and Minnows
Relative asset size of largest U.S. water utilities

COMPANY	ASSETS	
Vivendi Enviro	$35.31 Bil.	
American Water Works	$6.07 Bil.	
Philadelphia Suburban	$1.41 Bil.	
California Water	$.67 Bil.	
American States Water	$.62 Bil.	
Total Next Five Largest	$1.12 Bil.	

SOURCE: Utility Forecaster

Figure 7.6

financially challenged, neighboring systems and adding them to the company's system.

The utility has expanded its strategy over the past three years to five other states outside its home of Pennsylvania, including the 2001 foray into fast-growing North Carolina. With numerous small systems nearby ready to be acquired, there are many more deals ahead to fuel growth.

Globally, the best bet in water is Vivendi Environment. Aside from a 17 percent stake in Philadelphia Suburban, the company's operations include management of more than one-third of the waste of Paris, and ownership of America's largest water treatment company, U.S. Filter, which owns numerous processes for cleaning up water. The company has water and waste treatment operations worldwide, with a huge presence in its home market of Europe.

Vivendi is still majority-owned by parent Vivendi Universal, which has used its stable cash flows to finance its massive growth in the entertainment industry, notably the purchase of Seagram. It continues to be aggressive in pursuing new growth opportunities, the financing of which was a major reason for the unit's initial public offering.

THE WINNERS' CIRCLE

Based on the trends discussed in this book, these companies are right now the best bets for survivors and thrivers in these increasingly competitive and volatile industries. Building a portfolio of them, using the advice in Chapters 10 and 11, is the surest way to capitalize on the changes now gripping energy, communications, and water.

INDUSTRY PROFILE: NICK DEBENEDICTIS

In his own words, Nick DeBenedictis took a "circuitous route" to becoming CEO of Philadelphia Suburban, America's second-largest water utility. After starting his career with the U.S. Army Corps of Engineers, Nick left in 1972 to become one of the first employees of the Environmental Protection Agency, which was then writing the nation's water quality standards.

In the early 1980s, he took a turn in politics, joining the Thornburgh administration in Pennsylvania as a cabinet secretary, drawing up the state's drinking water law and gaining expertise in a wide range of political/environmental issues, including energy and water disposal. That led to a job a few years later as vice president in charge of environment and public policy at then-embattled Philadelphia Electric.

When he returned to the water industry at the helm of Philadelphia Suburban in 1992, Nick put his unique blend of regulatory, legislative, and public policy experience to work, launching the utility's wildly successful growth-through-acquisitions strategy. In the past eight years, Philadelphia Suburban has completed 64 acquisitions, more than doubling its customer rolls and putting profits on track for 10 percent–plus annual growth long-term.

Q: TELL ME ABOUT PHILADELPHIA SUBURBAN'S
   GROWTH STRATEGY.

A: When I joined this company it was widely respected for its technical expertise and financial strength. But it was not at all aggressive in its growth pattern. I decided to leverage our core strength—efficiently operating water utility systems—to tackle the biggest problem I saw as a regulator: the growing inability of small water systems to meet even a minimum of water quality standards.

At the time, everyone knew about small systems' problems with inadequate filtration and unsafe dams.

The legislature's response was that these small systems couldn't afford to do anything. We thought they really couldn't afford not to. PSC saw the opportunity to grow by acquiring these troubled systems and absorbing them into our own.

Basically, as the energy and telephone industries have already found out, size counts. The water business in the U.S. is still fragmented into nearly 60,000 different systems, largely because the industry has been perceived as a social/health responsibility of municipalities. The problem is this has prevented the development of economies of scale, and therefore the ability of systems to raise enough capital to make the needed investment in new technologies and infrastructure rehabilitation to ensure water quality. In contrast, a larger company can do those things.

We're basically talking about a win-win situation for all concerned. Shareholders get high returns on investment, since absorbing the new systems increases sales and economies of scale, driving down unit costs. Customers get better water quality and lower rates than they would otherwise have paid, since we're spreading out the cost to provide clean water over more people.

We call our growth model 4-7-10-5. Our target is to grow our customer base 4 percent a year, mostly through acquisitions and some internal growth. Coupled with rate increases for infrastructure, that will produce revenue growth of about 7 percent. Factoring in cost-cutting—much of which will result from growing economies of scale—our target from that is 10 percent earnings growth, which in turn easily allows dividend growth of 5 percent.

Q: HOW SUPPORTIVE HAVE REGULATORS BEEN OF YOUR EFFORTS?

A: Very. As the last monopoly, water utilities like ours depend on regulators to grant us an adequate return on our investment. Fortunately, Pennsylvania has recognized the importance of economies of scale to the industry and supported our efforts to build infrastructure as well as make acquisitions. We've now expanded our growth-through-acquisitions strategy to other states—particularly Illinois, New Jersey, North Carolina, and Ohio—and it's been well received.

Regulation is important in another way: Enforcement of environmental regulation drives smaller municipal and investor-owned utility systems into a sell mode. That makes it far easier for us to do deals. My view is in the next few years, regulations are only going to get tougher. And that it's going to get harder for small municipalities to hide from EPA enforcement.

Q: WHO IS YOUR MAIN COMPETITION?

A: As monopolies, we have no basic business competition, and that's not going to change. For one thing, it would be extremely expensive to move water around in a national network of pipes. The electricity costs alone would overwhelm you. Second, water is the only utility service that's ingested—and because of cleanliness issues, no one wants other people's water moving through their pipes. Also the California debacle has slowed down the whole deregulation movement.

Where we have faced competition is in making acquisitions. But that's cooled off as well. Basically, there are four business models in the global water utility business. The French—who really dominate the industry—the British, the Americans, and ROW, or the rest of the world.

Under the French model, which is also the ROW model, municipalities own the water systems themselves, and they contract out operations to service providers under very-long-term contracts. For example, two of the largest French companies—Vivendi and Suez—received their charters from Napoleon. Both have based their growth on finding new munis to manage worldwide under long-lived contracts, most recently in the United States.

Up until about 40 years ago, the British water industry was nearly as fragmented as our own. The government nationalized it into seven river basin regional companies to increase economies of scale but failed to improve performance. That prompted the Thatcher government to privatize it in the 1980s and for a brief time, the British water companies were very profitable and among the most influential businesses. Then Tony Blair came in and maimed the industry with rate cuts. As a result, they're now pulling money out of Britain to make acquisitions in the United States.

The French and British buying has consolidated the number of U.S. water companies which serve over 100,000 customers down to four. And only one, American Water Works, competes with us in the East.

A few years ago, it looked like electric utilities were going to get into the water business to protect their customer bases and as part of the utility services convergence strategies that were then popular. Minnesota P&L (now Allete), GPU, DQE, NiSource, and Southern Company all made a move. DQE's AquaSource was the most aggressive in acquiring small systems, but without much profitability to date. Even more dangerous was Enron's spinoff Azurix, whose stock dropped over 50 percent after unsuccessfully trying to compete globally with the big French firms.

The result is the electrics are pulling out and there are a wealth of small systems for sale now, without many buyers. Strategic acquisitions have enabled Philadelphia Suburban to consistently return almost 20 cents on every dollar of revenue—in a regulated industry with no competitive operating risk.

Q: WHAT INVOLVEMENT DOES VIVENDI HAVE IN THE
COMPANY?

A: They own 17 percent of our stock, have two seats on our board, and are very supportive of our efforts. They let us tap into their research and development, which is the best in the world. And we team up with their subsidiary, U.S. Filter, in the contract management business, where our expertise dealing with municipalities and other entities is important to them. Our goal, when we do contract management on our own, is to sign contracts as a prelude to a later purchase.

On top of that, we've been a very good investment for Vivendi, and they obviously want us to succeed. Incidentally, Vivendi is prevented from increasing its stake in us above 20 percent by Pennsylvania's anti-greenmail law, unless they buy all the stock.

Q: WHAT'S YOUR COMPANY REALLY WORTH?

A: What would you pay for a vintage Packard? There are really only four companies in our industry big enough to buy. That makes buying us like buying a collector car.

As long as our earnings are growing 10 percent a year or better, I think there's a lot of merit for shareholders to stay independent. Of course, we've had suitors before and we'll look at any offers as they come—that is our fiduciary responsibility.

This is a long-term 20-year game. One year, the acquisitions will knock your socks off. The next year it could be slower. But there are a lot of companies out there, and that means a lot of growth for us.

CHAPTER 8

···

Morgan, Mergers, and Money

More than 100 energy, communications, and water utilities have merged since the early 1990s. If history is any guide, there will be at least that many deals in the next 10 years.

As the financial press has repeatedly highlighted, there are plenty of ways for a merged company to fail. Corporate cultures often clash. Turf battles between top executives can escalate. The cost of making deals—particularly debt—may put management under an inordinate amount of pressure to meet unrealistic goals, and the very economic and market assumptions on which a merger is based may prove flawed.

Every utility merger completed over the past decade, however, has created a more powerful company that has been better able to compete. This has been true even with unions between relatively weak companies, such as the late-1990s deal between Ohio-based Centerior Energy and Ohio Edison to form First Energy.

Utility executives have plenty of incentive to do deals. Pulling off a merger usually means a hefty bonus in the short run. Long-term, doing deals increases the industry stature of managers, smoothing the way for still more acquisitions.

Shareholders of targeted companies usually do even better, scoring windfall gains of anywhere from 20 to 50 percent when mergers are completed, and gaining a stake in bigger, stronger companies thereafter. Even owners of the acquiring company, which can be hurt if the Street believes it's paying too great a price, generally cash in over the long haul, as deals boost sales and profits.

Critics of utility deregulation have held up the recent merger wave as clear evidence of corporate greed run amuck. Mergers mean fewer providers and potential competitors, which theoretically reduces the choices for consumers promised by deregulation's proponents. In addition, the larger utilities have become, the more difficult it's been for smaller rivals to compete with them. That's a major reason most CLECs and IPPs are now history.

The irony is, over the long pull, industry consolidation is the surest way for companies to cut costs and improve industry efficiency. Big, financially powerful companies have a far easier time raising capital than smaller, weaker ones, and they're far more attractive as targets for investment from outside forces as well. Consequently, they're much more likely to spur the investment boom needed in these industries.

Only an investment boom will ensure reliable, low-cost, energy, communications, and water service for the greatest number of users in the years ahead. The larger and more efficient utilities can become, the better they'll deliver the promised benefits of deregulation—lower rates and better service—to consumers.

During most of the Clinton administration, there was a clear recognition that utilities needed to get bigger to meet their growing challenges. The Federal Communications Commission and Federal Energy Regulatory Commission routinely approved every deal that crossed their desks, and the Justice Department rarely interfered. Most state governments were also eager to approve mergers.

By late 1999, regulators on both the state and federal levels had become considerably more skeptical of industry consolidation, partly because of the sheer size of deals being proposed. Regulators, particularly at the FCC, began to scrutinize deals much more closely, taking the extraordinary step of rejecting the proposed merger of WorldCom and Sprint in 2000.

Under the George W. Bush administration, regulators are again looking at utility mergers favorably, even large ones. Even if they wind up taking a harder line, however, the consolidation of energy, communications, and water remains inevitable.

EMPIRE BUILDERS

Why are utility mergers so successful? The answer lies in the last major wave of utility consolidation, which occurred in the early twentieth century. At that time, energy, water, and communications were also reaping the benefits of a massive investment boom that was intimately connected with industry consolidation.

In the early days of electricity, utility system ownership was extremely fragmented. Most industry players took for granted that electricity would never be more than a niche product, provided by isolated plants set up for a specified purpose such as running a factory. Only Thomas Edison saw differently, doggedly pursuing his vision of a world where central stations produced low-cost power for everyone. With the financial backing of banking magnate J.P. Morgan, Edison completed his Pearl Street Station power plant in New York City on September 4, 1882, and a new age of electricity was born.

Despite Pearl's success, however, Edison's concept proved extremely difficult to duplicate. In spring of 1883, there were 334 isolated plants in operation, but only Pearl Street as a central station. As Pearl continued to lose money, even Morgan began to lose faith that Edison's dream would work. As the company's financial troubles mounted, Morgan began to exert his influence to take it in another direction.

Edison's concept, however, had another champion in his 22-year-old apprentice, Samuel Insull. While most of Edison's associates joined Morgan in advocating an approach including isolated plants, Insull stuck to his belief that the central station held the best chance of bringing power to the people, and big profits to the family of Edison companies. Over the next 40 years, he used his organizational genius to make the inventor's dream a reality.

Despite the opposition of Morgan and his allies, Edison appointed Insull the head of a new unit—Thomas A. Edison Construction Department—charged to sell and build central stations around the country. Over the next 18 months, Insull traversed the country, selling plants in Massachusetts, New York, Ohio, and Pennsylvania. His success forced a showdown with the Morgan faction in October 1884, which Insull won by using

Edison's popularity with shareholders to install a pro–central station president and directors.

Unfortunately, just at his moment of triumph, Edison suffered the death of his wife and largely lost his creative wind. His concept of central stations, however, was off and running. The killer application was the advent of the electric streetcar in American cities. By the end of 1889, there were 154 such railway systems in cities, and central stations became the way to run them.

At the same time, alternating current won its longstanding battle with direct current as the electricity of choice. Edison himself had been a tireless proponent of DC, for safety reasons. Technical reasons, however, prevented DC from being transmitted for more than a mile. Thanks to George Westinghouse and William Stanley's invention of the transformer, AC could be transmitted cheaply for hundreds of miles. The rise of AC made possible a whole new scale of central station. No longer would every city block need a power plant. Instead, much bigger plants could provide energy to many city blocks.

Insull was quick to grasp the implications. From 1887 to 1888, he dramatically increased the company's production capacity at its Schenectady plant, quadrupling sales and boosting return on investment by 30 percent while continuing to increase the plant's productive capacity. Figure 8.1 displays Edison Inc.'s enterprise structure pre-1889.

Despite the enterprise's rapid growth, Morgan was largely

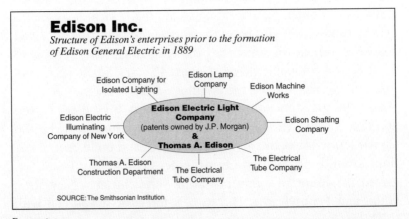

Edison Inc.
Structure of Edison's enterprises prior to the formation of Edison General Electric in 1889

Edison Company for Isolated Lighting

Edison Lamp Company

Edison Machine Works

Edison Electric Illuminating Company of New York

Edison Electric Light Company
(patents owned by J.P. Morgan)
&
Thomas A. Edison

Edison Shafting Company

Thomas A. Edison Construction Department

The Electrical Tube Company

The Electrical Tube Company

SOURCE: The Smithsonian Institution

Figure 8.1

unwilling to open his coffers, so Insull turned to foreign capital markets, hooking up with German financier Henry Villard in 1889. The two soon launched a proposal to consolidate all of Edison's empire for the first time under one organization. They reached a deal with Morgan, and Edison General Electric was born.

As Edison's personal business manager and effective champion, Insull began to establish a set of principles that ultimately became a model for American manufacturers as well as utilities. The first rule was to always expand: by raising new capital, plowing profits back into the business, and borrowing heavily when possible. The second was to spread fixed costs as thinly as possible among operations. The third rule was to sell electricity as cheaply as possible to increase sales, which in turn would lower unit costs of production, yielding greater profits.

In the years that followed, this radical approach took the nation by storm. Insull's efforts cut the price of Edison's electric lamps by more than 56 percent from 1886 to 1891, while boosting profits. By dramatically increasing the company's economies of scale, he had set the electric industry on course for breakneck growth.

Villard's financing approach, however, was deeply flawed. When the company sold a central station in a new town, it essentially set up a utility to be its customer. Villard's approach, however, was to take stock in the utility, rather than be paid with cash-generating bonds. This gave Edison equity control over the entity, but it provided little capital to plow back into operations.

As a result, Insull had to continue borrowing heavily to expand, and the company remained dependent on financiers like Morgan for growth. Growth was also hampered by Edison's continued hostility to AC, which prevented Insull from fully exploiting his strategy of increasing economies of scale for building central stations.

The situation blew up in 1892. Morgan and the Vanderbilts—also major Edison shareholders—engineered the takeover of Edison General Electric by rival Thomson-Houston, which Villard had been attempting to acquire. Thomas Edison himself was profitably but effectively retired from the business and Villard was also bought out at a handsome price.

Insull was offered a high post in the new organization. Instead, he took his approach to Chicago and created an empire built on his principles of building economies of scale. Beginning as president of Chicago Edison, he bought utilities and built power plants throughout the Midwest over the next 40 years, always raising capital and always expanding to bring electricity to the largest numbers of people at the lowest possible price.

Recognizing fixed costs as the primary hurdle to bringing down prices, Insull became the driving force in the industry for building ever-larger power plants that maximized investment leverage and spread costs over the greatest numbers of people. Opportunities for expansion exploded in 1893, when the new General Electric's financial woes forced it to divest its portfolio of utilities at one-fourth their face value. Insull was able to buy equipment on the cheap and use it to create the largest power station in the world at Harrison Street, Chicago, in 1894.

Insull had just begun. As his company's plants grew in size and costs fell, he gave marching orders to his sales force: Sell at whatever price it takes to get the business. The results were nothing short of revolutionary. Despite an ongoing major economic depression, Chicago Edison quadrupled its connected load and nearly quintupled annual sales by 1895. The company's total revenue was greater than its total capitalization had been three years earlier.

Insull's model for success was copied all over the country. Cities coast-to-coast demanded power as cheap and reliable as that of Insull's Chicago Edison. As the municipalization movement failed in the financial crisis of 1907, entrepreneurs coast-to-coast worked to follow his example. Figure 8.2 shows the components of the Insull empire.

Insull himself stuck to his Midwest territory, but nonetheless became a stockholder, officer, and director of utilities in California, Indiana, Kentucky, Louisiana, Pennsylvania, and Wisconsin. He continued to spread his gospel of economies of scale as chairman of the National Electric Light Association, launching a movement to electrify farms in the Midwest. Ultimately, he formed the Middle West Utilities Company as a holding company to cover his investments outside his core region, which included systems from upper New England to Oklahoma.

As his policies brought more and more power to the people, Insull's own profits and power grew. By 1927, his empire con-

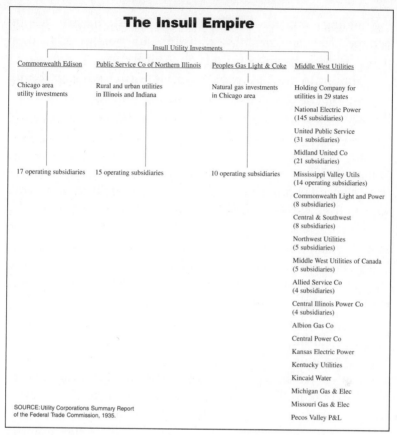

The Insull Empire

Insull Utility Investments

Commonwealth Edison	Public Service Co of Northern Illinois	Peoples Gas Light & Coke	Middle West Utilities
Chicago area utility investments	Rural and urban utilities in Illinois and Indiana	Natural gas investments in Chicago area	Holding Company for utilities in 29 states
			National Electric Power (145 subsidiaries)
			United Public Service (31 subsidiaries)
			Midland United Co (21 subsidiaries)
17 operating subsidiaries	15 operating subsidiaries	10 operating subsidiaries	Mississippi Valley Utils (14 operating subsidiaries)
			Commonwealth Light and Power (8 subsidiaries)
			Central & Southwest (8 subsidiaries)
			Northwest Utilities (5 subsidiaries)
			Middle West Utilities of Canada (5 subsidiaries)
			Allied Service Co (4 subsidiaries)
			Central Illinois Power Co (4 subsidiaries)
			Albion Gas Co
			Central Power Co
			Kansas Electric Power
			Kentucky Utilities
			Kincaid Water
			Michigan Gas & Elec
			Missouri Gas & Elec
			Pecos Valley P&L

SOURCE: Utility Corporations Summary Report of the Federal Trade Commission, 1935.

Figure 8.2

trolled nearly 12 percent of all electricity produced in the United States, as well as a fair chunk of the nation's natural gas grid.

Success, however, emboldened Insull's enemies, particularly his archnemesis J.P. Morgan, who had come to dominate huge segments of the American economy since the Edison days. In 1927, Morgan launched a plan that was as audacious as it was aggressive: to establish his United Corporation holding company as the AT&T of the electric and natural gas industry, ruling an unbroken coast-to-coast monopoly.

Almost immediately, most of the major New York–based holding company groups came under his control. By 1928, only the Insull group remained to challenge Morgan's power. Insull fought fiercely, throwing down the gauntlet by buying two of the remaining holding companies with systems in 14 eastern states. It soon became clear, however, that Morgan's superior access to deep pools of low-cost capital would win the day.

Beginning in 1927, Morgan associates began buying up chunks of Insull-operated companies including Commonwealth Edison, the flagship and successor company to Chicago Edison. Forced to defend control of key assets, Insull aggressively turned to the capital markets. The initial launch of Insull Utility Investments in January 1929—a holding company created to take over and control Insull's far-flung operations—was a monumental success, soaring from $25 at its initial offering to $150 by August.

Unfortunately, the price of Insull's operating companies also soared, making it extremely expensive for him to buy them up. When the Depression hit, he had shored up his power base, but he was saddled with a huge amount of debt. The stocks of his empire held up well initially after the crash, and his operating companies' profits reached all-time highs in the first six months of 1931. In fact, even during the worst of times none of the operating companies went into bankruptcy.

Insull's need for capital to expand and hold his own, however, was the chink in the armor Morgan was looking for. Using every means at his disposal, he brought Insull to his knees by mid-1932, becoming the unchallenged titan of the energy utility industry (see Figure 8.3).

Morgan's dream of creating an electric and gas AT&T, however, was never realized. The election of Franklin Delano Roosevelt as U.S. president brought a return of the trustbusters to Washington. Within three years, the Public Utility Holding Company Act of 1935 (PUHCA), the Glass-Steagall Banking Act, the Corporation Bankruptcy Act, the Wagner-Connery Labor Act, and acts creating the Tennessee Valley Authority, the Securities and Exchange Commission, and the Rural Electrification Administration, had transformed American business and broken his power forever.

In the utility industry, the great holding companies—including Morgan's United Corporation—were given a death sentence to break up into regional and local monopolies. Each utility was to operate under a franchise granted by the local government and was to be run largely independent of its neighbors. Any future

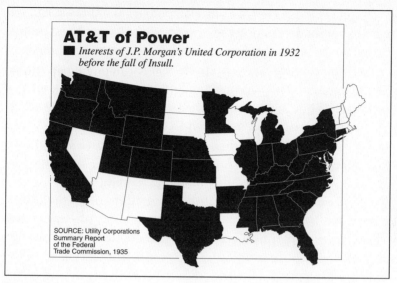

AT&T of Power
Interests of J.P. Morgan's United Corporation in 1932 before the fall of Insull.

SOURCE: Utility Corporations
Summary Report
of the Federal
Trade Commission, 1935

Figure 8.3

change in control over a utility system was to be strictly regulated by state and federal officials, as were company profits and investment in new facilities.

After the 1935 Act, it took another quarter century for the holding companies to completely unwind. The last meeting of the Electric Bond & Share Company—created from the spun-off systems of General Electric and once dominated by Morgan—was held in 1959, after which the last of its foreign and domestic assets were dispersed.

BACK TO THE FUTURE

PUHCA and the destruction of Morgan's energy AT&T ended the age of holding companies. To prevent the rise of another Morgan, the Act placed strict limits on utility investment from outside the industry, restricting foreign ownership of companies as well.

Companies that still owned several operating utilities were forced to register as holding companies with the newly formed Securities and Exchange Commission, which was charged with ensuring against uncompetitive behavior. Mergers between holding companies were generally discouraged.

Despite PUHCA's restrictions, electric and gas utilities still found ways to consolidate in order to bring down costs and boost profits. In a few decades, the hundreds of local operating companies around the country were effectively merged into regional operators, streamlining management and increasing their economies of scale. In addition, a number of smaller holding companies, such as Southern Company and American Electric Power—both of which had been part of Morgan's budding empire—were allowed to continue operating under the jurisdiction of the SEC, as outlined by PUHCA, and consolidated their holdings as well.

By the early 1980s, the negative connotations of holding companies had been all but forgotten. The victories of Reagan and Thatcher brought a new breed of regulators that were considerably more receptive to utility mergers as a necessary part of the industry deregulation they desired.

With government no longer acting to stop them, deals again began to pop up. One of the first was the 1988 union of Pacific Power and Utah Power & Light to form PacifiCorp, and other companies soon followed with their own deals. By the mid-1990s, the trickle of mergers had become a flood as states began to consider deregulation. More and more utilities came to the conclusion that Insull's precepts were on target: Only by getting bigger could they bring down their costs, increase their reach, and access the capital they needed to win in the age of cutthroat competition that lay ahead.

The very restrictions imposed by PUHCA in 1935 left numerous opportunities for better economies of scale through mergers in the energy industry. Transmission and distribution (T&D) companies stuck to the letter of Insull's rule to cut their costs by increasing their customer rolls. The first wave of T&D consolidation includes NSTAR's creation from the merger of Boston Edison and Commonwealth Energy; National Grid's buyout of adjoining New England Electric, Eastern Utilities, and Niagara Mohawk; EnergyEast's absorption of Connecticut Energy, CTG Resources, Central Maine Public Service, and RGS Energy; and KeySpan's buy of Eastern Enterprises and EnergyNorth.

The industry's biggest players are the product of the ongoing convergence of the electric and gas industries, including Dominion Resources, Duke Energy, Enron, and Reliant Energy. Mergers of small to mid-tier companies are joining the two businesses as well, including DTE Energy/MCN, SCANA/Public Service of North Carolina, and SIGCORP/Indiana Energy.

The most dramatic consolidation thus far has occurred in the communications industry. Facing competition in the local phone industry for the first time, Baby Bells Bell Atlantic and NYNEX dramatically cut their costs by merging first with each other and then with GTE to create Verizon Communications. SBC Communications' series of mergers with Pacific Telesis, Ameritech, and Southern New England Telecom had a similar impact. These deals increased the Bells' ability to access capital with their scale, scope, and market share. Both Verizon and SBC are already nearly as powerful as the former AT&T monopoly.

Bernie Ebbers understood the power of capital and reach when he engineered the creation of WorldCom through 100-plus mergers and acquisitions. So did Joseph Nacchio when he catapulted Qwest into the big time by buying Baby Bell U.S. West. In contrast, telecoms that have mismanaged their acquisition policy, like AT&T, or have refused to merge, like BellSouth, are already dropping well behind the industry leaders.

Pollution and the financial decline of municipal utilities have created a similar need to get big in the water industry, which still has nearly 60,000 very small systems ripe for purchase. The acquisitions have fueled the growth of the industry's biggest companies, American Water Works and Philadelphia Suburban, which took a giant leap forward with the 1989 buyout of Consumers Water. Acquisitions of smaller systems have also increased growth at numerous second-tier companies, such as Connecticut Water and New Jersey–based Middlesex Water.

Mergers over the next 10 years will continue to be fueled by the same compelling logic: Bigger utilities have the economies of scale and access to capital to do things more cheaply than small ones. This time around, however, there are two more major forces at work as well.

One is globalization, the other the likelihood of PUHCA repeal. Globalization has allowed industry giants to move capital across borders, with much of it flowing to the United States. European utilities such as Deutsche Telekom, National Grid,

Scottish Power, and Vivendi have been extremely active already in the U.S. merger market. In coming years, they'll be joined by other giants, such as Germany's RWE and E.ON.

Potentially, the biggest spur to future mergers will be the repeal of PUHCA. The act was designed to break the power of the old system and prevent the rise of another empire by limiting the degree to which the industry could consolidate. One way was by restricting the level of investment from outside the industry, thereby preventing a cash-rich power from a larger industry from taking over.

Superior access to capital was the reason J.P. Morgan's United Corporation was able to defeat Insull and the other empire builders for control of the energy utility industry in the 1930s. The power industry magnates were well-capitalized, but Morgan's resources were on a wholly different scale. His deep pockets simply overwhelmed the resources of those operating entirely within the industry, like Insull.

Big oil companies like ExxonMobil, BP Amoco, and Chevron-Texaco are several times larger than even the largest utilities. They could easily swallow a large chunk of the industry; the attractions are myriad. These companies already dominate the production of gas, making them a natural fit with the power plant assets of major generating companies. Big oils have also long coveted the power-trading expertise of energy utilities.

Repealing PUHCA would allow a wave of investment into utilities from the big oil companies, dramatically fueling mergers. While no one is likely to try a complete takeover of the industry a la Morgan, Warren Buffett and other independent investors are ready to pour in billions of dollars.

There are two ways for less capitalized investors to profit: Buy companies likely to be taken over and those already involved in a takeover, on a bet that the merger will be successfully closed.

PICKING TARGETS

Choosing takeover targets is the most lucrative way to bet on mergers. The premium—the difference between the offer and the predeal share price of the target—has averaged 25 to 30 percent in most deals. Those who own a takeover stock consequently realize a windfall short-term gain, as well as the opportunity to be part of a bigger, stronger company.

Picking likely takeover targets is straightforward. The ideal candidate is relatively small, low-priced, and owns valuable assets to attract a suitor. Picking who will merge with whom is far more complicated. Great companies can go begging for years, while weak ones get snapped up. Much depends on factors not easily discernable from a balance sheet, such as management's temperament and willingness to sell.

That's why any stock you buy for takeover appeal should be one you wouldn't mind owning for months and years, or as long as it takes to get a deal. Even if a good company isn't taken over, your investment will still be solid. Betting on a weak company to be taken over can be a disaster if you're wrong and no deal materializes. Use the five rules in Chapter 10 for a quality yardstick.

The second rule of picking merger candidates is to look at areas where deals are likely. Over the next decade, the 50 or so gas and electric T&D companies should shrink by half, as T&D's work to cut their unit costs by expanding their customer bases. Larger T&D companies can also provide a wider variety of services and have greater access to low-cost capital.

T&D companies are the most natural merger candidates among utilities. Their businesses are the most similar; they own networks of wires and pipes connecting customers, which means they can be combined with fewer complications. T&D utilities also own no power plants, so they have little or no long-term exposure to the commoditization of power and gas.

The first region of the country to fully deregulate, New England has hosted the largest number of T&D mergers to date, and it's likely to be the site of several more. No utility in the region is close to gaining the estimated 5 million customers needed to be competitive long-term in T&D. Everyone is potentially everyone else's target.

One of the most likely candidates is NSTAR, itself the product of a merger between neighboring utilities Boston Edison and Commonwealth Energy. In accordance with Massachusetts' deregulation, the company has sold all of its power plants and is now a pure wires-and-pipes distributor of electricity and natural gas. Energy marketers sell energy to customers, who pay a fee for the use of NSTAR's system. As a result, profits depend solely on throughput, rather than on the price of energy.

NSTAR's territory in the Boston environs is one of the most attractive in New England. That makes the company a natural target for any of the region's would-be empire builders, including Consolidated Edison, EnergyEast, and National Grid.

Another top-quality T&D company is AGL Resources, the natural gas distribution company for Georgia and parts of Tennessee and Virginia. The Georgia gas market is now completely deregulated. As with NSTAR in Massachusetts, marketers compete to sell gas to customers, who pay a fee to use the utility's systems. AGL participates to a limited degree in marketing as well as propane sales, but its profit also depends mostly on increasing throughput.

The Southeast's electricity market has yet to be deregulated. As it does open up, AGL will become increasingly attractive as a low-risk way to tap into one of the nation's highest-growth energy markets. Both NSTAR and AGL are high-quality companies with solid balance sheets and proven operating records. They'll be great investments even if no takeover offer appears (see Figure 8.4).

Smaller electric utilities in key markets are also prime takeover material. Tampa, Florida–based TECO Energy is an obvious choice in this group. The company has been a low-cost generator in the state of Florida for years and is now leveraging its expertise by building and operating unregulated plants around the country. Thanks to its small size, each successful project has a very positive impact on profits. Other assets include a low-sulfur-coal mining and transportation division, which should prove increasingly valuable as the energy investment boom kicks in.

Takeover Targets

Company (Exchange: Symbol)	Assets (bil $)	Key Asset	S&P Bond Rating
AGL Resources (NYSE: ATG)	2.02	gas distribution system, 3 states	A- (stable)
Connecticut Water (NSDQ: CTWS)	0.22	water distribution system, 2 states	none
Middlesex Water (NSDQ: MSEX)	0.22	water distribution system, 2 states	A (stable)
Mirant Corp (NYSE: MIR)	24.14	global power plant, marketing operation	BBB- (stable)
NSTAR (NYSE: NST)	5.57	Boston area electric/gas distribution	A- (stable)
Orion Holdings (NYSE: ORN)	3.87	U.S. power plant operation	BB (stable)
TECO Energy (NYSE: TE)	5.68	Florida energy generation, distribution	A (negative)

SOURCE: Utility Forecaster

Figure 8.4

TECO's primary appeal as a takeover target is its extensive energy infrastructure throughout the state of Florida. The Sunshine State has yet to open its doors to competition, but once it does, buying TECO will be one of the easiest ways to get a firm foothold.

Merchant generators are also ripe for takeovers, particularly companies that are independent or have spun off completely from utility parents. The two most likely candidates are Mirant Corp. and Orion Holdings. Mirant was spun off completely from parent Southern Company in April of 2001. The company has a thriving global and U.S. base of power plants, and is a major marketer of both electricity and natural gas. Formed from a venture between Constellation Energy and Goldman Sachs, and on track to be spun off from both, Orion owns power plants primarily in the Middle Atlantic states.

Both Mirant and Orion continue to build new plants aggressively, making them more attractive to suitors. The most likely acquirers are other power producers and big oil companies. The latter are effectively prohibited from buying utilities and their subsidiaries, but, with these merchant generators spun off from their parents, those restrictions are becoming less relevant. If PUHCA is repealed, there will be a rush from big oil to go on a shopping spree, particularly for utes that generate electricity, in order to gain expertise in all forms of energy. Big oils' expertise in natural gas—the fuel of nearly all new power plants—will also mesh well with electricity companies.

In telecommunications, the most attractive takeover targets have long been considered to be midsized companies like Alltel, BellSouth, Nextel, and Sprint. All four of these telecoms are attractive both for growth on their own and as potential buyout picks.

The most attractive communications assets over the next few years are likely to be the consumer long-distance units of AT&T and MCI (WorldCom). Both companies are deemphasizing their long-distance units by creating tracking stocks for them. This will have the effect of limiting the units' impact on overall results, which has been sharply negative over the past few years.

The units, however, could be extremely attractive to the Baby Bells as they win approval to offer long-distance service in their

home states. Buying MCI, for example, would give a Bell an
instant nationwide reach, making it a major player in consumer
long distance as well as giving it needed infrastructure. Such a
merger would have been considered unthinkable just a few years
ago. Today, opposition would likely delay regulatory approval
even under a Bush FCC, but given the low value Wall Street has
assigned long-distance telephone stocks, there's little risk to
potential buyers as they become available.

Poor takeover candidates include any company that's taken on
a considerable amount of debt to grow over the past few years.
Most of the competitive local exchange carriers, or CLECs, won't
make it back because of an inability to pay off debt. Rapidly growing wireless players with high debt levels and low credit ratings
should also be avoided.

Every U.S. water utility is a takeover target for one reason: Even
the biggest is small enough to be easily acquired by a European
giant such as RWE, Vivendi, or Suez Lyonnaise des Eaux. Over the
next few years, Euro giants will continue to add to their holdings
in the U.S. water industry, both as a way of diversifying out of
their own slow-growth markets and taking advantage of the dramatic transformation of this country's water industry from
extremely fragmented to consolidated.

Thus far, the Europeans have paid a huge premium to invest in
the United States. The takeover of E-Town by Thames Water was
negotiated at a price nearly 50 percent above the former's predeal
price. What's more, Thames paid all cash for its purchase; ditto
Kelda's buyout of Aquarion in early 2000.

One likely takeover candidate is Connecticut Water Service,
now the largest independent water utility in New England. The
company continues to grow in its home state by acquiring
smaller, weaker utilities and absorbing them into its lower-cost
system. It's also pushed across the border into Massachusetts.

Middlesex Water in New Jersey is often mentioned for its
takeover potential. The company has operations in Delaware as
well and is expanding its customer base at a rapid pace. The utility has faced considerable financial pressure as a result of hooking
up so many new connections, and the Garden State has been slow
to allow recovery of costs from consumers. A financially strong

parent would quickly solve those problems. Meanwhile, owning the ute would be a terrific platform for further growth in the eastern part of the country.

HIGH PERCENTAGE BETS

Betting on the success of utility mergers that have already been announced is one of the highest percentage wagers on Wall Street. Not only have more than 90 percent of proposed mergers been consummated, but those that failed were due to a fallout among the parties themselves. Regulators almost always went along. With the Bush administration in charge, the environment has become even more receptive.

The collapse of the Empire District/UtiliCorp, Entergy/FPL, Consolidated Edison/Northeast Utilities, and SJW/American Water Works mergers in early 2001 occurred because at least one of the partners pulled the plug. The Con Ed deal had won all needed regulatory approvals, but management got cold feet at the last minute due to concern about Northeast's purchase power costs. The Empire/UtiliCorp merger collapsed because UtiliCorp saw there would be delays for approving the deal in Arkansas, and was troubled by Missouri regulators' inability to grasp the merger's benefits. American's failed effort to buy California's SJW was also due to its frustration with regulatory delays.

Even the biggest example of regulatory rejection in recent years—WorldCom's bid for Sprint—is the exception that proves the rule. Regulators in the United States and the European Union threatened to reject the deal on the grounds there weren't enough safeguards. They might have changed their tune had the two companies been willing to bend a bit more.

As a result, there are few real regulatory risks to deals in progress. That's especially true of mergers between smaller utilities, which are simply too small to invite regulatory attention. That makes betting on them almost a sure-thing.

Investors can profit in three ways. First, unlike most industries, regulatory approvals take time to complete for utilities. Therefore, takeover stocks can trade at steep discounts to their stated takeover values for months after a merger is first announced.

Investors who buy before the deal is completed, and hold on until consummation, pocket this discount. Second, buyers also get any dividends paid during the time they hold the stock.

The third way to profit is from an increase in the takeover value itself. When a deal is negotiated at a fixed value—particularly when the offer is all cash—buying the target carries no market risk. Even if the stock of the acquiring company drops 50 percent, the acquired stock's takeover value will stay the same. As long as the deal is completed, the return is locked in.

Most deals, however, are negotiated at a target price that's not fixed per se, but rather is protected by a *collar*. As long as the acquiring company's stock stays within the collar, the takeover value will be equal to the target. If the acquirer's stock rises above the collar, the takeover value will rise. Investors will pocket the original premium, dividends, and a bonus from the higher takeover value.

One great example of just how high profits can go is the early 2000 takeover of Germany's Mannesmann by Britain's Vodafone. The latter launched a hostile takeover for Mannesmann, which the company's CEO Klaus Esser staunchly resisted until he secured a very favorable ratio of 5.896 Vodafone ADRs (American Depositors Receipts, the unit of the company's stock traded in the United States). By the time the merger won approval of German regulators, Mannesmann's value had doubled from its pre-takeover-battle levels, from the higher ratio and from a steady rise in Vodafone shares.

The downside of collars is when an acquirer's stock falls below the collar, it takes its target down with it. Consequently, capitalizing on these deals depends on the health of the overall market as well as that of the acquiring company. Happily, utilities tend to be relatively stable stocks, particularly water and T&D gas and electric utilities. When a stock trades in the midrange of its collar, odds are it will hold and quite possibly beat the target value.

Successfully betting on deals in progress—whether the takeover value is fixed, collared, or simply tied directly to the price of the acquirer's stock—is also a matter of timing. Even if you're right about a deal, if you buy in when the takeover stock's discount-to-takeover value is too small, your return will be paltry.

Likewise, a widening discount can be a sign that a deal is coming apart and that investors should steer clear (see Figure 8.5).

The best time to bet on a deal in progress is when another merger has failed either within or without the utility industry. In that case, the professional arbitrageurs who bet on the success of mergers will be short of capital and unable to place sufficient bets to close the spreads on other deals.

A disaster in a particularly big merger can have a particularly powerful effect on discounts. Arbs typically buy the acquired company and sell-short the acquirer to lock in the spread, so they generally lose in two positions when a big deal fails, forcing them to bail out all the more quickly.

There are five vital details needed to make any intelligent wager on a merger in progress. These are: (1) the offer in stock or cash for the company; (2) the discount between takeover price and the stock's current price; (3) the valuation of the stock absent the merger; (4) the principal hurdles to the deal, both regulatory and between the would-be merger partners; and (5) the projected return if and when the merger succeeds. Numbers 1 and 4 are relatively constant. Numbers 2, 3, and 5 are constantly changing with the price of the takeover target, and very often with the price of the acquirer.

The key is to find deals that offer the right balance between these five factors at a given time. For example, if Conectiv fell to just $20, it would be 20 percent below its $25 takeover value. The potential reward would be well worth the risk of Maryland or District of Columbia regulators giving the deal the thumbs down,

Playing the Percentages

Company (Exchange: Symbol)	Acquirer	Terms of Deal
Conectiv (NYSE: CIV)	Potomac Electric	$25 a share if Potomac stock trades between $19.50 and $24.50 at closing.
Niagara Mohawk (NYSE: NMK)	National Grid	$19 in stock or cash if Nat'l Grid trades between $32 and $51 at closing.
RGS Energy (NYSE: RGS)	EnergyEast	$39.50 a share if EnergyEast trades between $16.57 and $22.41 at closing.

SOURCE: Utility Forecaster

Figure 8.5

given the wide discount and the fact that Conectiv had a price/earnings ratio well below that of the average stock.

If, on the other hand, Conectiv rallied to $24, the discount would be only a few percentage points. In that case, the potential reward would not compensate investors for the risk of failure. It would be time to look for another deal to bet on.

Each of the takeover plays on the table, therefore, should be closely scrutinized prior to investing at all. In fact, it's likely several of these deals will be completed before this book is published. The good news is there will be plenty more where these came from in coming years. Provided you run your selections through these five criteria, you'll have a golden opportunity to profit from one of Wall Street's most overlooked but highest percentage wagers.

CONSOLIDATION'S LIMITS

Like the merger wave that ended in 1935, the curtain will ulti- mately come down on this round of utility consolidation. The end will come when state and federal regulators move to block new deals on a massive scale, as well as question the size of exist- ing companies. That's what happened during the administration of Franklin Roosevelt.

In some quarters, opposition is already building to new deals, particularly larger ones. Some states, notably Missouri, have become so problematic that utilities have given up, at least tem- porarily, trying to expand there. UtiliCorp, for example, is now moving more capital overseas rather than pursuing more merger opportunities in-state.

These troublespots are still isolated cases, but with more than 100 electric and gas utilities, 30 or so major U.S. communications companies, and literally thousands of small water providers, we're nowhere near the degree of industry consolidation that prevailed in the 1920s and 30s. That leaves plenty of room for more deals nationally before regulators really act to put on the brakes.

Until they do, Insull's principles of economies of scale and deep pockets will induce more and more utes to join forces. Others will be snapped up as outside money pours into the industry from investors who, like Morgan in the late 1920s, see an opportunity to reap a fortune by acquiring market power in an investment-needy industry.

We've already seen the first leveraged buyout of a utility since the Great Depression: the early 2000 takeover of little TNP Enterprises—holding company of Texas–New Mexico Power—by an investor group led by former Long Island Lighting boss William Catacosinos. Shareholders of TNP reaped a hefty premium for the deal. Warren Buffett's buyout of Mid-American Energy soon afterward was the second. They won't be the last.

Buying merger candidates and betting on deals in progress will be very profitable roads to success in utility investing for at least the next three to five years. The next chapter looks at the flip side of the merger wave: spinoffs of heretofore hidden assets that allow companies to focus their operations strategically, while handing shareholders windfall short-term profits.

. . . .

INDUSTRY PROFILE: ROBERT FAGAN

Like many utility executives, Robert Fagan began his career with a masters in engineering. The rest has been anything but typical. After serving in the 1960s with the U.S. Navy's legendary Admiral Rickover, Bob moved to General Electric where he soon jumped from systems engineering to business development. In 1980, he joined the company's nascent cogeneration unit, set up to take advantage of opportunities from the Public Utility Regulatory Power Act. In 1985, he left for Combustion Engineering, where he ultimately became Vice President of Business Development for Power Projects.

Though CE later left the power-production business, Fagan's experience made him a natural recruit for utility-backed independent power producers (IPPs). In the late 1980s, he was hired by SCE Corp.'s Mission Energy subsidiary to launch its East Coast operations and ultimately to oversee all the company's IPPs in the Americas. His success made him PP&L's top choice to launch its global IPP unit, which he built in five years from a $50 million bank account into a multibillion-dollar global powerhouse.

Bob's current tenure as Chairman and CEO of Florida-based TECO Energy began in late 1999. Since then, he's used his leadership to revive the company's earnings growth and his knowledge of the IPP business to create one of the fastest-growing generating businesses in North America.

Q: HOW DOES TECO ENERGY DEVELOP POWER
     PROJECTS?

A: To make our first cut, a project must be located in an area with an open wholesale market, robust demand for energy, and good growth prospects. That's why most of our projects are in the Sunbelt. Next, we look for a niche that offers us unique advantages to be a first-mover in that market, preferably where others can't take advantage.

Our plant in Virginia, for example, is at the end of the Delmarva Peninsula. That's at the end of the line as far as transmission goes, which virtually locks in our market and provides a lot of ancillary support. Our plant in Arizona is expected to be a prime beneficiary of restrictions on water usage that the state recently introduced. That's because it is being built under the old rules and it was grandfathered in, while future plants must adhere to much tougher conditions. Another good example of a niche plant is our proposed gasification project that will run on waste petroleum coke from a refinery in Louisiana and will produce steam, hydrogen, and sulfur, as well as electricity.

Gasification technology provides us with a unique niche because we have the first large-scale, commercially integrated, gasification combined-cycle plant in the country at our Tampa Electric utility subsidiary. With natural gas prices rising, this type of design is becoming more attractive and we have a head start as the first to operate one. We've entered a joint venture with Chevron Texaco to take the technology to a number of areas.

Combined with our utility operations, we have the potential to have 20,000 megawatts of capacity available over the next five years. That's enough to put us in the top ranks of power generators in the country.

Q: WHAT ADVANTAGES DOES HAVING AN ENGINEERING BACKGROUND GIVE YOU IN THIS INDUSTRY?

A: To be a successful power plant developer, you've got to learn the three sides of the business: engineering, finance, and the law. Coming from my engineering background, I had to learn the financial and legal side when I began developing projects, as well as how to become more of a generalist.

When people come in with various backgrounds, we give them the technical training to round them out. Not to be biased, but in my opinion engineers' background in numbers makes it much easier for them to pick up finance than it is for generalists to pick up engineers' technical knowledge. And almost all engineers have had finance and accounting as part of their training. The best developers I know of, however, started out as financial analysts. They really understand the numbers inside and out.

One unique advantage being an engineer has given me over the years is personal knowledge of a great many power projects now in operation. I've literally developed projects all over the world with GE, CE, Mission, PP&L, and now TECO. And I suspect I'll wind up owning at TECO some of the projects I worked on earlier in my career. All these projects become like your kids, you don't forget.

Q: WHAT DO YOU FORESEE FOR COAL-BASED ELECTRICITY IN GENERAL AND TECO'S COAL ASSETS IN PARTICULAR?

A: TECO has strong coal assets, including power plants, mines, and a shipping operation. The trouble is we're too small in both mining and shipping to generate the kind of growth numbers we can get from the IPP business. Expanding barge capacity, for example, is basically a one-shot deal. Recently we were able to buy a 40,000-ton oceangoing carrier in a government auction for 10 percent of new construction costs, which gave us a big lift. But you don't see those kinds of opportunities every day.

In Florida, most of our capacity is coal-based and our largest facility, Big Bend, has state-of-the-art flue-gas clean-up systems. In addition, we are very well positioned to expand our capacity by repowering our other old coal plants with clean, highly efficient gas turbines. In fact, we should be able to significantly increase our capacity in the state over the next five years, putting us in superb shape for deregulation. Incidentally, in my mind it's just a question of when not whether that will happen. The commission set up by Governor Bush is slated to make its recommendation by the end of 2001.

Q: WHAT'S THE BIGGEST CHALLENGE YOU AND YOUR INDUSTRY FACE TODAY?

A: To transform from regulated electric and gas utilities into providers of competitive services. We expect to have more than half of our profits from unregulated sources by 2003, up from 30 percent now. In this sense, I have an advantage coming from the independent power side of the business, which was competitive from day one. Unfortunately, a lot of companies are trying to transform themselves with managers stuck in a traditional industry mindset. Their CEOs can be an obstacle to their adjustment.

That's one reason why I didn't want to merge TECO with another utility when I came on board, as many on Wall Street suggested. My thought was that when you merge two utilities, you just get a huge utility. The way to build shareholder value is to transform your company and get the price/earnings multiple up before you start to look at mergers.

Incidentally, I believe very strongly that the way to solve the energy crisis is through free enterprise, not price caps. If you look at the more open markets like Britain, they've achieved amazing cost reductions and efficiencies. Unfortunately, the California situation has gotten so bad that companies are treating investing there like they would a foreign country. That's going to be the state's demise because when you go offshore, the required returns rise along with the risk.

CHAPTER 9

....

Hidden Treasure

You may never find a baseball card, poster, or rare coin in your attic that's worth more than your whole house, but that's exactly the kind of hidden treasure that's buried in the books of well-managed utilities.

Energy, communications, and water companies have historically been high-volume investors because they generate so much cash. When there are power plants, pipelines, water mains, or fiber networks to build, most of the money is plowed back into their core businesses. When there have been no major capital projects, investments have ranged from thrift stores to aircraft.

Most of these ventures have remained only small parts of their parents' overall operations, but others have become significant profit generators in their own rights.

The beauty is that Wall Street favors the pure play, not a profitable unit attached to a utility. As a result, analysts rarely take the time to find out about them, much less reward their owners for them. They remain hidden assets until the owning company takes the step of uncovering them, via an initial public offering (IPO) or direct spinoff to shareholders.

If they're well-timed, IPOs and spinoffs of hidden assets can trigger windfall profits for their parents' shareholders. Before its great fall in 2000, AT&T's initial public offering and eventual spinoff, Lucent Technologies, rose more than tenfold from its initial IPO price. Energy-related IPOs of utility assets in early 2001 were similarly enriching.

Buying a utility with a valuable hidden asset—and holding on until the eventual IPO or spinoff—is thus another smart path to energy, communications, and water industry profits in the decade ahead. For patient investors, it will be no less profitable than following the other two simple investment strategies: buying the industry's best and betting on mergers.

Unfortunately, not every utility diversification effort is a hidden treasure ready to be uncovered. Some are closer to being hidden landmines. The key is the operation itself: how well run it is, how potentially valuable it could be as a growth vehicle, and how savvy the parent is to maximize its value for shareholders.

THE STORY OF DIVERSIFICATION

The parable about not putting all of your eggs in one basket is standard fare for any grade-schooler; the wisdom is self-evident every time you invest for retirement, apply for a job or college, or buy a house. If you diversify your efforts—not pin all your hopes on one possible outcome—you won't be vulnerable to a single misstep or unexpected setback. That often spells the difference between ultimate success and failure.

In the 1950s and 60s, utilities enjoyed solid growth as Americans migrated from rural areas, where communications, water, and energy services weren't used heavily, to urban areas where they're an absolute necessity. Utilities invested heavily to meet new demand.

By the 1980s, most of the spending had wound down and utilities went to work winning rate increases from regulators to pay for the new capacity. With rising inflation and high interest rates pushing up costs, rate hike requests were considerably higher than most had projected. This triggered considerable disallowances from regulators, forcing utilities to write off billions of dollars in already capitalized costs. More than a few companies suffered dividend cuts, and half a dozen were forced either into or to the point of bankruptcy.

By the mid-1980s, however, the companies that emerged relatively healthy had rising cash-flow streams to invest. Given the experience with regulators in the 70s and 80s—and the generally low returns set on their core businesses—they chose to take most of it out of the utility industry altogether in search of higher returns.

Thus was born the great era of utility diversification. Following the foremost business theory of the day, companies explored a wide range of options. The thinking was that diversification would not only generate higher returns, but would protect them from business failures by enabling them to avoid the cardinal sin of putting all their eggs in one basket.

How wrong they were. In fact, the further afield utilities strayed from their core businesses, the more disastrous the results. The example of Pacific Enterprises—which has since been merged into Sempra Energy—is a case in point.

Flush with cash in the mid-1980s, the company invested in industries not even remotely related to its core business of delivering natural gas to southern California. The most visible was Thrifty Drug, but there were also considerable outlays in real estate and other enterprises.

Pacific's management reasoned these were high-cash-flow businesses. Instead, the lack of prior experience triggered a financial disaster that almost drove the company into bankruptcy, despite the unmatched operating strength of its gas utility operations.

After a few years of floundering, it became obvious Thrifty wasn't going to be worth the high purchase price. Meanwhile, the company's debt load had become unmanageable. Finally, Pacific was forced to take a huge writeoff of its investment—as well as some of its other ill-conceived ventures—cutting its dividend and recovering only after merging with Enova, parent of San Diego G&E, in 1998 to form Sempra.

In the 1980s, Arizona's biggest electric utility, Pinnacle West, then known as AZP Corp., worked itself to the point of bankruptcy by purchasing a local savings and loan, Merabank, and investing heavily in local real estate development.

Management figured it had learned about the rapid development of the Phoenix area from hooking up new customers to its lines. It wanted to make a more leveraged bet on a trend it thought would continue for years.

As it turned out, it was right about the ultimate growth of the Valley of the Sun, which has exceeded even the most optimistic forecasts over the past 20 years. However, it didn't recognize the normal building cycle that accompanies such growth, that is, sometimes even the fastest-growing area takes a break due to temporary overbuilding.

As it turned out, that's exactly what happened in Phoenix. A decade of rapid building temporarily exhausted the market, setting off a downturn soon after AZP paid a record price for Merabank. Just as the company's increased debt load started to take a bite out of profits, Merabank was discovered to be entwined with the savings and loan crisis.

For a few months in early 1990, it looked like AZP/Pinnacle might not make it. Despite a solid outlook at the utility—which was winding up construction at the giant Palo Verde nuclear plant—the stock sank into single-digits as Merabank and its real estate investments went bust. Only a timely rescue from Washington saved the day, freeing the company from its Merabank commitments. It was years before the utility, renamed Pinnacle West, was able to pay a dividend again.

Dozens of utilities from coast to coast had similar experiences with their diversification efforts. In the early 1990s, Baltimore G&E's commitment to its widely diversified investment portfolio nearly caused it to lose its biggest source of cash flow, the Calvert Cliffs nuclear plant, to poor performance and a threatened, regulator-ordered shutdown.

Potomac Electric spent half a decade trying to extricate itself from its portfolio of aircraft leases, condemning shareholders to mediocre returns for years. FPL's foray into the insurance industry by buying Colonial Penn was also a fiasco, and a major reason it cut its dividend in 1994.

Water and communications companies, too, have had their share of diversification disasters. In the late 1980s, Aquarion, Consumers Water, and several other water utilities nearly brought themselves to the brink with ill-timed outlays in the water quality testing business.

Though intimately related to their core operations, the business was subject to several other factors management lacked the experience to foresee, such as the deemphasizing of environmental issues in the last half of the first Bush administration. In addition, there were some far better established, larger players in the business with whom the tiny utility subsidiaries simply lacked the economies of scales to compete.

The worst diversification effort made by communications utilities was the interactive craze of the early to mid-1990s. Worried about losing market share to upstarts after deregulation, phone companies of all stripes began feverishly searching for other sources of revenue. Several chose to stake their futures on the potential of interactive media.

The U.S. West/Time Warner venture in July 1993 was the first grand scheme to marry the switching capabilities of phone companies with the entertainment banks and connection capacity of the cable companies. It was followed by Bell Atlantic's ultimately failed attempt to merge with the nation's largest cable service provider, John Malone's Tele-Communications (TCI), in November 1993. Most ambitious of all was the acquisition spree launched by C. Michael Armstrong when he became CEO of AT&T in 1997, resulting in the successful takeovers of TCI and MediaOne, the former cable unit of U.S. West.

As it turned out, Bell Atlantic—now Verizon Communications—got out the luckiest. The money it saved not buying TCI allowed it to make the far more sensible acquisitions of neighboring Baby Bell NYNEX and later GTE, both of which it's been able to merge with seamlessly to create the nation's premier communications company. The U.S. West/Time Warner venture—now owned jointly by AT&T and AOL—has never amounted to much more than a headache for its owners, though both original owners fared well when they were bought out.

In contrast, AT&T's plans to dominate communications by controlling the marriage of telephone and cable television have all but cinched its ultimate destruction. High debt has driven down the company's credit rating, and growth in the cable business has failed to offset the rapid erosion of its long-distance business. Any plans to marry cable and telephone have been a huge disappointment.

The company's breakup into at least three separate parts is a tacit admission its plans have failed. Given the size of its component parts relative to their emerging competitors, it's unlikely AT&T will even exist as we know it by the end of the decade.

The failure of these far-flung diversification efforts, coupled with new opportunities presented by deregulation, has triggered a dramatic shift in utility investment back to core businesses. Even here, companies haven't been immune to potentially life-threatening woes, but their odds of success have been much greater.

In 1992, Tucson Electric avoided Chapter 11 only by some fast financial footwork, after overbuilding power plants in its capacity-saturated region through an unregulated subsidiary. Now organized as UniSource Energy, the former Tucson is realizing explosive profits from the same power plant investments that nearly drove it out of business a decade ago.

The herd of companies who invested overseas in the early to mid-1990s provide another good example. By focusing on core businesses about which they knew everything, managers were confident they would avoid the operating traps they had so often stepped into by diversifying elsewhere. Unfortunately, many were investing in countries they knew nothing about, and the cultural and language mistakes were just as disastrous, as Chapter 5 points out.

SUCCESS STORIES

Happily, the history of utility diversification isn't one of complete failure. Many companies avoided the troublespots by focusing on ventures well within their realms of expertise, or by keeping their investments small until they knew the business well.

For successfully diversifying electric and gas utilities, the prime areas of investment are intimately related to what they did as regulated monopolies. These include unregulated or merchant power generation, natural gas pipeline and storage services, the relatively new business of energy marketing, and a wide range of customer-focused energy services.

Energy utilities have also historically been involved with the exploration and production of fossil fuels to power their own plants and service their customers. As a result, several have successfully created such energy-producing units.

In water, the primary avenue to successful diversification has been in contract management and other related services. These involve essentially the same functions as running a water utility system, without the capital outlay. As a result, companies know exactly how to gauge their successes and failures.

Cellular phones are by far the most successful communications company diversification in the past 20 years. Here the technology was slightly different for providers to master, but the basic economics of phone calls was almost identical. Many of the providers were well-versed in necessary marketing as well. As a result, the transition was extremely smooth and the diversified operations were quickly integrated into businesses.

Utility subsidiaries have a huge advantage over their rivals when they first enter an industry: a parent with deep pockets. Until the new units grow large enough to have a significant impact on growth, management can afford to make mistakes as a necessary learning process.

In the best cases, parent companies have consciously nurtured their new operations until they were big enough to stand on their own. Some, however, have been supportive in spite of themselves. At these companies—which included most utilities involved with diversification—the unregulated unit was commonly treated with little respect from the parent's upper management.

Sometimes the snobbery went on even after the subsidiary's managers had proven the unit's value as a profit generator. As a result, the units never got big enough to hurt the parent until they were strong enough to survive without it.

The new breed of managers running America's energy, communications, and water companies have a far different appreciation for the value of all assets, including unregulated units that never got much attention in the past. The result has been an emphasis on growing these operations and on realizing shareholder value through IPOs and spinoffs.

During the late 1990s, the most successful IPOs of hidden assets were in telecommunications. Starting with the blockbuster Lucent offering by AT&T, a series of explosive offerings hit the Street over the next couple of years. BCE's spinoff of its equipment operation Nortel was every bit as successful as Lucent's IPO, and has held its value better.

Telefonica's well-timed IPO of its Internet operations Terra Networks—formed by joining the web units of all of its Latin American holdings—allowed it to build a world-class company in a very short amount of time. AT&T's launch of AT&T Wireless is by far the most successful part of that company and the most potentially enriching move made by management over the past several years. Sprint's tracking stock PCS also enjoyed an explosive debut, as did energy player Williams Companies' offering of its fiber-optic operations in Williams Communications.

By mid-2000, the attention had shifted to energy. The first effort was the successful IPO of NRG Energy—Northern States Power's unregulated power-generation unit—on the eve of the parent's merger with New Century Energies.

The offering of nearly 20 percent of NRG stock was a smash hit. The company used the proceeds to expand further by buying and building power plants across the country, and accelerated its expansion after the merger was completed. NRG's steady appreciation went on to boost its parent—now dubbed Xcel Energy—close to 50 percent from its pre-IPO days (see Figure 9.1).

The most significant unleashing of shareholder value in 2000 was Southern Company's IPO of its unregulated global energy marketing and power production arm Southern Energy (SEI). The initial offering held its own, but then steadily rose in value as SEI's profits began to surge. The unit continued to expand rapidly, attracting more attention from investors during the California crisis.

Finally, in April 2001, Southern spun off its unit to shareholders as Mirant Corp. By that time, the unit, which had been buried away in the company's books prior to its mid-2000 IPO, had increased the value of its parent's shares by 50 percent. It also won Southern management new respect for its ability to raise capital and fuel growth in new, though related, businesses.

Southern—which now consists of the company's regulated utilities in Alabama, Florida, Georgia, and Mississippi—plans to use what it learned at Mirant to launch a similar business in the Southeast. And it should have no trouble raising the capital to do so.

The Southern/Mirant example has since been repeated several times in the energy industry, with equally explosive results. UtiliCorp

Energy IPOs

Company	Parent	First Month Performance
Aquila Energy	UtiliCorp	37.3%
Mirant Corp	Southern Co	6.3
NRG Energy	Xcel Energy	21.0
Orion Energy	Constellation	8.2
Reliant Resources	Reliant Corp	11.7

SOURCE: Utility Forecaster

Figure 9.1

United's IPO of its merchant energy unit, Aquila Energy, was one of the most successful in industry history, all the more remarkable considering it was completed at a solid premium in a period when other IPOs were going begging. In fact, several IPOs planned about the same time had to be canceled for lack of interest.

FINDING ASSETS

More than two dozen energy, water, and communications utilities today derive 20 percent or more of their revenues from such hidden operations. Some are involved in multiple ventures, others in a single, highly focused effort. All are great candidates for finding hidden treasure.

The key is to look for operations that are closely related to their parents' core businesses, which are involved in growing markets and have a track record of success. It's also important that the parent be in solid financial shape to ensure the spinoff's operations have a chance to grow.

In addition, the only way to buy a hidden asset—that is, a unit that has yet to be IPO'd and spun off—is to first buy stock in the parent company. This means the parent must be a good long-term investment for the hidden asset to be worth buying into, and also applies to companies that have had their initial IPO but which are still majority-owned by the parent.

In the case of units that have been IPO'd but not fully spun off, the parent is almost always the better bet than the unit. That's because you usually get both pieces of the company at a discount; if they ever do completely separate, you'll reap a windfall gain.

That was the case with Southern Company's spinoff of its Mirant subsidiary to its shareholders in 1998. It's likely to be the case if UtiliCorp elects to completely spin off its Aquila merchant energy unit, which it IPO'd in April 2001. Aquila has emerged as one of the largest marketers of both electricity and natural gas by building a trading talent pool second to none and expanding aggressively as its knowledge of the market grew.

Despite gangbuster growth beginning in the early 1990s, Utili-Corp shares got little credit for the company's surging unit until management decided to launch the IPO. Suddenly the stock was catapulted 50 percent above its pre-IPO price.

If UtiliCorp elects to spin off its remaining 80 percent stake in Aquila to shareholders, the stock should take another leap ahead. If not, Aquila's growth will continue to propel the parent's earnings. UtiliCorp also has considerable investments overseas that are very profitable and could be spun off in the future.

Unlike UtiliCorp, IdaCorp still hasn't given investors a chance to participate directly in its most important hidden asset: its rapidly growing, fuel cells production and research unit. The company has patented a fuel reformer that could someday limit fuel cells' current dangerous dependence on natural gas. It has also marketed its designs in Japan, throughout the Northwest, and in Europe.

The fuel cells unit is a cash hog, but unlike its rivals in the industry—such as Plug Power—it's only a small part of a financially powerful parent. That means, unlike its rivals, it's assured of the cash to keep expanding. For its part, IdaCorp's utility operations are very healthy, controlling some of the West's least-cost hydroelectric power supplies.

Producing natural gas, coal, and oil has long been a specialty of many utilities. Several have now turned these operations into major profit centers, using the steady cash-flow stream from the regulated utilities to finance aggressive expansion of producing energy reserves.

Two of the best in this category are Dakotas-based MDU Resources and Alabama/Gulf Coast operator Energen. Both companies are solidly grounded in highly efficient, financially strong gas distribution utilities, with MDU also controlling an electric utility. Also, both operate in states where retail deregulation isn't likely at least for several years.

Both companies have had the cash to expand rapidly in energy production. Energen's focus is on adding to its reserves of producing properties when the price is right, while locking in the highest price possible to keep growth going, through an aggressive hedging program. MDU's Fidelity oil and gas unit has a similar approach, and has also built a substantial business in mining aggregates.

Rising commodity prices, efficient management, and aggressive expansion have catapulted both companies' earnings sharply higher in recent years. While their stocks have benefited, they're only about half as expensive, relative to their earnings, as big oils and other energy stocks. A well-timed IPO of hidden energy-producing assets would remedy that in short order. Meanwhile, both are among the lowest-risk plays around in energy.

Communications company spinoffs were the rage of the late 1990s. Virtually any offering was snatched up at prices far exceeding even the most optimistic projections. In the early part of this decade, most of these IPOs crashed and burned; Wall Street won't go near anything that smells like them. The upshot is there are once again hidden assets that will one day reward their parents' patient owners.

The two biggest are Verizon Wireless, 55 percent owned by Verizon Communications and 45 percent by Vodafone, and Cingular Wireless, jointly owned by SBC Communications (60 percent) and BellSouth (40 percent).

As the country's largest and second-largest wireless providers, respectively, these units represent extraordinary market power in an increasingly consolidating industry. Verizon's system is composed of the territories of the former Bell Atlantic, NYNEX, and GTE, as well as U.S. West and the Airtouch spinoff of Pacific Telesis. As such, its network reaches completely across the country, giving it unmatched economies of scale. Cingular's network is nearly as extensive, including the systems of the former Southwestern Bell, Pacific Telesis, Ameritech, Southern New England Telecom, CellularOne, and BellSouth.

Both wireless companies continue to enjoy strong customer growth and are increasing profitability as well with more conservative targets; both are now far larger than the number three U.S. wireless provider, AT&T Wireless; and they're extremely strong financially in an industry now overloaded by debt.

Despite these strengths, however, both Verizon Wireless and Cingular were forced to postpone IPOs in late 2000 and early 2001 due to poor market conditions. That sets up a tremendous profit opportunity in both the short and long term when the IPOs eventually do come off. In the meantime, the value of these hidden assets is incalculable to their financially powerful parents, particularly Verizon, Vodafone, and SBC.

In the water arena, Southwest Water's robust growth from its contract management division is the industry's best-kept secret. The unit now contributes well over half of the utility's revenues, fueling its 20 percent–plus average earnings growth over the past five years.

Southwest falls off Wall Street's radar screen for two reasons. First, few are aware of the growth in the contract management sector, and fewer are aware of the players, outside French giants Vivendi and Suez. Second, Southwest competes in the U.S. hinterland, while the giants are focused on big cities, attracting most of the attention. Third, the company itself is small, too small in fact for large institutions to buy.

Ultimately, however, such rapid growth will be noticed, particularly as Southwest gains heft through acquisitions and new contracts. The next time the water industry captures the investment public's imagination—as it did during the merger wave in 1998—this hidden asset will start to produce some real returns for shareholders of this overlooked gem.

HIDDEN MINEFIELDS

Unfortunately, some of the most attractive hidden assets are buried too deeply. In these cases, the parents' problems are simply too great to buy the assets in hopes of a spinoff. In fact, their woes could ultimately cripple the attractive asset's value.

A case in point is Edison International's Mission Energy unit. One of the first IPPs, or independent power producers, Mission has built a solid portfolio of power generation and marketing assets in the United States and around the world. Since being hurt by the collapse of a project in Mexico in the early 1990s, the unit has enjoyed strong, uninterrupted growth, despite occasional missteps and adverse events.

Edison itself, however, is severely hampered by the troubles at its Southern California Edison unit, which is near default on several billion dollars of debt due to the Golden State's power crisis. Rather than immediately follow neighboring utility PG&E into bankruptcy, the company instead elected to negotiate a deal with Governor Davis for its financial recovery. Its ability to avoid ultimate Chapter 11 depends on the success of the plan, which is by no means assured.

Wall Street has long considered Mission Energy an ideal candidate for an IPO and possible spinoff from parent Edison. If so, it would be a strong takeover target for another generator or possibly a major oil company. The unit has been ring-fenced, or legally shielded, from the woes of its parent, which has kept its credit rating stable. Its preferred stocks should be safe, even if the parent is forced to declare bankruptcy.

Unfortunately, an IPO now could create considerable rancor over who should benefit from the proceeds. Consequently, it's unlikely we'll see one for at least several more years. Until then, Edison will be primarily a play on a financial recovery, with Mission's fortunes having little or no effect on its share price.

Another group of hidden-asset plays to avoid are companies that have strayed too far from the core utility business. Not only is the track record for such unfocused diversification extremely poor, but these utilities are likely to be considered far too diffuse for a pure-play IPO to have much impact on the parent's price.

One example is Hawaiian Electric, which in the past decade has dodged disasters in shipping, insurance, and foreign power plant development. The company currently operates two units, a utility that's frighteningly dependent on imported oil to run its power plants and a generally well-run bank (see Figure 9.2).

Leave it Buried

Company	Primary Unrelated Asset	% Hidden Asset Revenues
Allete	auto auctions,water utilities	58
Citizens Utilities	CLEC	20
Hawaiian Electric	banking,miscellaneous	26
Otter Tail Power	healthcare,plastics	56
Western Resources	home security	27

SOURCE: Utility Forecaster

Figure 9.2

Otter Tail Power's nonutility businesses are not only over half its revenues, there are more of them than you can shake a stick at, ranging from electronics to health care. The company has enjoyed steady profitability at most of these units, and is likely to continue to. One reason is a policy of generally letting all the members of its family of companies run themselves.

Unfortunately, this is a company no one really understands anymore, outside of management. As a result, though there are undoubtedly some fabulous hidden-asset possibilities, particularly for an acquirer, investor (and acquirer) confusion will likely limit their impact.

One of the benefits of buying a company for the value of its assets is, no matter how poorly it performs, there's always a potential attraction for a suitor. As a result, even if a profitable spinoff doesn't appear, you can get bailed out of a bad bet.

That doesn't always happen, however, and even a cheap investment can get a lot cheaper. In late 2000, AT&T had emerged as a big-time value. Wall Street was skeptical about the company's freshly completed mergers with MediaOne and Tele-Communications to form the country's largest cable television empire. AT&T's plan to be a full-service provider seemed closer than ever.

Then management dropped a bombshell: Because of the high level of debt it had taken on to finance the deals—and lagging long-distance phone operations—it was abandoning its plans to be a one-stop communications shop. Instead, it would divide into at least three separate units, each of which would take its chances on the market. This management about-face shattered whatever confidence anyone had left in Ma Bell's management, and the stock plummeted nearly 50 percent, despite the potential value of some of the underlying units.

For the most part, however, buying utilities for their hidden assets is a low-risk way to earn an uncommon return. The next chapter shows how to put the three strategies together: buying emerging giants, picking takeover targets, and betting on mergers in progress and prospecting hidden assets.

· ·

INDUSTRY PROFILE: RICK GREEN

UtiliCorp United CEO Rick Green took an unusual route to the top of his thriving global energy company. He and his brother Robert are the fourth generation in their family business. Rick's experience began at age 13, when he worked summers and holidays at a power plant to save money for a car. After college, he returned to the company as assistant superintendent of a coal-fired plant, quickly moved up through the ranks, and reached the top spot in the mid-1980s, while only in his mid-thirties.

Since taking the helm, Green has transformed his company from sleepy little electric and gas utility Missouri Public Service into a multinational powerhouse, with assets ranging from a major global marketer of energy to operating the largest utility network in New Zealand. Rick has consistently done what Wall Street loves best, setting aggressive profit targets and achieving them.

Q: WHAT EXPERIENCE PREPARED YOU BEST FOR
   RUNNING UTILICORP?

A: It has to be having had the opportunity to work with utility crews early in my career, in both power plants and on power lines out in the field. I gained valuable experience dealing with power plant outages, tornadoes, ice storms, and the like. And I gained firsthand knowledge of how to work with people on the front line in this industry. That's been at least as valuable to me as my academic education.

Incidentally, all of these experiences were great fun for me as a teenager. No one in the family was telling me I had to work at the company. My entering the business just progressed in a very natural way. The same is true for my brother Robert.

I don't think I could be any luckier. I live in interesting times. This is a rare opportunity to be with the right company at the right time, and to work in global markets as they go through massive change.

Q: WHAT IS UTILICORP'S LONG-TERM STRATEGY FOR
    GROWTH?

A: Since 1994, we've deployed a twofold strategy. We've
built an extensive network business, which consists of
owning basic wires, pipes, and fiber-optic distribution
systems globally. Also, we have developed a highly disci-
plined strategy to manage, market, and trade energy.
These skills reside in our now publicly traded Aquila
subsidiary, which is one of North America's largest
energy marketers.

Aquila also has developed major initiatives in e-
commerce and bandwidth capacity trading to help fuel
its rapid growth. Aquila's 2000 EBIT jumped 140 percent
over 1999, with annual sales of more than $26 billion
and assets of nearly $8 billion.

These strategies actually took root in the 70s and early
80s. In those days, utilities like ours were spending
nearly all of our time with regulatory commissions,
seeking rate increases to keep up with rising inflation
and interest rates. So we decided our profitability was
too dependent on the politics of regulation and the
unpredictability of summer and winter temperature
extremes.

In 1984, we moved to diversify the risk profile of our
operations. We changed the company name to UtiliCorp
United and began to acquire midsized electric and gas
systems across the country. In doing so, we spread our
risks across a more diverse regulatory and climate base.

Last year's acquisition of St. Joseph Light & Power in
Missouri was a continuation of that strategy, although
we've now shifted our focus overseas because asset prices
are lower and the regulatory environment is more receptive. In that regard, since the mid-1990s our strategy has
focused more on buying utility networks—the basic
wires and pipes—in overseas markets having stable
economies and governments, and where deregulation
has progressed sufficiently to have clear rules.

At present, we have extensive investments in Australia, Canada, and New Zealand, and the U.K. and Europe are on our watch list if market conditions there improve. Going abroad is an extension of the strategy we applied domestically—diminishing our operating risk by spreading it around the world. Accomplishing that is a relatively smooth process, thanks to the globalization of the industry.

Q: WHAT IS THE FUTURE OF AQUILA?

A: Aquila was born in 1986 from our desire to participate in what we saw as a huge change in the energy utility industry: the conversion of electricity and natural gas into commodities from monopoly-priced services. We figured we needed to participate and learn—and lead— if we were going to compete.

Since then, Aquila has far exceeded our expectations as a profit center. It's also helped educate our entire workforce to understand and manage the risks associated with commodities. And it's yielded profits beyond energy marketing and trading as well. For example, Aquila today is a leading provider of risk management products around the industry.

Now that we've completed a partial IPO, a big part of Aquila's strategy will be to acquire power generation capacity to back up its high-growth marketing and energy products business. It's already made some purchases, such as last year's buyout of GPU's unregulated generation. We're also looking at the potential to expand in Western Europe as that market progresses.

We'd love to spin our regulated U.S. generation into Aquila and run our utilities as pure network businesses. Unfortunately, this country's retail market is making little progress toward competition, and our state regulators haven't shown an interest in taking that step. We do, however, continue to disaggregate our network assets outside the U.S. Recently, for example, we reached an agreement to sell the hydro plants at our British Columbia unit.

Q: IS UTILICORP PURSUING ANY OTHER AVENUES FOR
   GROWTH?

A: For now, our emphasis is on developing market share in our two key areas of strategic focus—networks and Aquila's merchant energy activities. And there are, of course, some opportunities to leverage our expertise in both units.

In Aquila's case, our risk management products have been very successful, selling the expertise that has evolved from the execution of our strategy. In networks, we were aggressive about laying fiber-optic cable beginning in Australia in 1997, and that enabled us to hook up with Quanta Services in the U.S., of which we now own about 35 percent.

Quanta, which is in the business of network construction and maintenance, is a strategic investment that allows us to capitalize on the need to improve U.S. networks in coming years, as well as the looming buildout of broadband capacity across the country. It also puts us first in line at a highly effective firm whenever our own networks need upgrades and repairs.

We may also once again become more active in acquisitions. But buying regulated U.S. utilities has become extremely pricey and the pace of regulatory approvals hasn't gotten any better. Our acquisition of St. Joseph represented an uncommon ability to extract synergies. But it's a unique occurrence. Until we see some change in the domestic market cycle, most of our capital dollars for network business are going to flow out of the United States.

....

CHAPTER 10

···

Five Rules for
Investing Success

For most of the twentieth century, Wall Street pitched utilities as stocks for "widows and orphans"—the choice for people who couldn't afford to lose a penny of principal.

Energy, communications, and water companies are still uniquely secure. If anything, the services they provide are more essential than ever. You can cancel a trip, postpone buying a new car or house, or even put off a medical operation, but when the thermometer's hugging zero outside, home heating is essential. Likewise, unrestricted clean water isn't a luxury. And can you imagine living without a telephone?

Regardless of the state of the markets or the economy, you're going to pay to keep the energy, communications, and water flowing. That translates into unmatched revenue security for the companies, which, barring extraordinary circumstances, means remarkably steady earnings. Utility stocks still weather bear markets and recessions more effectively than any other industry. Only rarely will their stocks be subject to the kind of volatility other sectors experience.

The rules of investing in utility stocks, however, have changed dramatically since the widows-and-orphans days. As recently as the early 1990s, it made little difference which electric, natural gas, communications, or water stock you bought. With few exceptions, all shared the strength of remarkable revenue security, along with very steady profits. Utility dividends were considered sacred by management, to be reduced or eliminated only under the gravest possible circumstances.

Utility stocks typically marched in lockstep. Some, such as Duke Power, sold at premium valuations to their rivals, but all followed a basic trading rule: When interest rates fell, their dividends gained appeal and their stocks rose. When rates rose, their dividends lost appeal and their stocks fell. The key to success in utilities was to buy when rates had risen for a time and stocks were cheap. You could then lock them away and collect the dividends while waiting for the inevitable rebound.

Today, such a nondiscriminating investment strategy is a formula for disaster. PG&E was among the largest and most successful energy companies in the country as recently as the late 1990s. Then, the electricity market in its home state of California imploded and it was driven into bankruptcy in a matter of months.

With global competition rising in energy and communications, today's utilities face more challenges than ever before. Future risks will take many shapes, from volatile energy prices to the impact of both evolutionary and revolutionary technologies. Rising debt loads and unforeseen negative shifts in regulation will also take their toll.

On the bright side, the opportunities for growth in utility investing are unprecedented. As the dominance of the best companies has increased, so has their earnings growth. The more investment flows to energy, communications, and water, the faster these companies will grow. At the same time, their stocks will close the steep discount at which they've historically traded to the overall stock market.

For investors who buy the winners, the potent combination of sizable capital gains, generous dividends, and unrivaled safety will be hard to match anywhere on Wall Street. Realizing the profit opportunities and avoiding the pitfalls, however, depends on following a series of simple, yet critical rules.

Following, I outline five that I've developed over the past 13-plus years in my newsletter *Utility Forecaster*. There's nothing fancy about these trading rules. There are no complex charts you need a doctorate in alchemy or hieroglyphics to decipher.

Each is a time-tested, commonsense rule for getting the most out of utility stocks. No matter how much or how little experience you've had investing in utilities, by the time you finish reading this, you'll know more than the average banker or broker about making money in this unique industry. You'll be able to take advantage of what are truly once-in-a-lifetime opportunities in some of the most overlooked and surprisingly rewarding stocks in the world.

RULE #1: BUY FOR THE LONG HAUL

Utility stocks are, first and foremost, long-term investments. In general it makes sense to sell only if something goes wrong with the company's long-term fundamentals.

There are three reasons for this approach. First, all of the trends I've outlined in this book are essentially long-term in nature. Bull and bear markets on Wall Street come and go, the economy will boom and bust, but the investment boom in energy, communications, and water is only beginning. The only way to really take advantage is to place your bets and let them ride.

Second, though most utilities are now investing in growth, they still pay dividends up to four times those of the average stock. And they're increasing them at above-average rates. The only way to collect those dividends is to hold the stocks for years, not months.

One thing many investors don't realize is that half of Standard & Poor's 500 stock index's long-term return comes from reinvested dividends. Traders are only playing for half the market's long-run return. That applies to most utility mutual funds as well, which tend to trade frequently to maximize quarterly returns.

Third, small investors who try to play peaks and valleys in utility stock prices get burned more often than not. Wall Street buys and sells sectors. Consequently, when things are perceived to be bad for utilities, even the best companies can take a dive. Again, that's because many money managers are concerned solely about quarterly performance and sell in packs.

When small investors try to do the same thing, they often wind up buying high and selling low. The potential reward for being right just isn't worth playing for. Suppose you buy a utility stock paying an annual yield of 6 percent. Over the next six months, the stock gives you a total return (capital gains plus dividends) of 30 percent. Worried it's near a top, you then sell.

Assuming you're in the 28 percent tax bracket, you forfeit 28 percent of your return to Uncle Sam. The resulting 21.6 percent gain, not including brokerage commissions, is still not bad. And let's say your fears prove right about the stock and it falls 15 percent (a substantial drop for a utility) over the next six months. Factoring in the tax on the 6 percent dividend, your return for the year would be less than 14 percent. By selling, you saved almost 8 percent, but you now have the headache of deciding where to reinvest. Your timing doesn't have to be off by much to wipe out the 8 percent saving.

The utility bear market of 1993–1994 proved this point. From the time utes peaked in mid-September 1993 to when they bottomed in November 1994, the Dow Utility Average fell by some 30 percent. That bone-crushing drop jarred many investors out of their utes—a tragic mistake. Barely six months later, the best companies had fully recovered their lost ground, and within a year so had most of the rest. Those who stayed put through the drop and recovery continued to draw high dividends, while avoiding taxes (except on their dividends), commissions, and the worry of deciding when to get back in (see Figure 10.1).

The same thing happened in 1999. Concerns about interest rates and fascination with technology made utilities wallflowers during Wall Street's bull-market party. The more the stocks underperformed, the less investors wanted to own them. Few bought anywhere near the bottom and, as a result, most missed out on the historic rebound of 2000.

Long-term investors must recognize that their priorities differ from those of big fund managers. Rather than try to play the trend, the best idea is to buy when managers are selling. Plan to hold at least three to five years, unless a company's long-run prospects diminish. You'll have to swim upstream from time to time, but your dividends will keep flowing. If you've chosen well, your picks will be at higher levels three years down the road, no matter what the short term brings.

Utility Bulls and Bears

Duration of Bear Market	S&P Utilities Loss %	Duration (Months)	Recovery %
May-December 1950	-11.1	7	80.4
May-November 1957	-10.7	6	121.1
Nov 1961-June 1962	-20.6	7	45.3
May 1965-Sept 1966	-18.6	16	13.6
April 1967-March 1968	-12.7	11	12.7
Nov 1968-June 1970	-30.3	19	28.9
Jan 1971-July 1972	-15.7	17	15.4
Dec 1972-Sept 1974	-49.9	21	84.1
July 1977-March 1980	-20.3	32	164.5
Jan 1987-Dec 1987	-14.7	11	48.6
Dec 1989-Sept 1990	-14.4	9	43.3
Sept 1993-Oct 1994	-22.5	13	121.5
June 1999-Mar 2000	-10.0	10	45.0

SOURCE: Utility Forecaster

Figure 10.1

RULE #2: BE YOUR OWN ANALYST

The total return potential of the best energy, communications, and water stocks is staggering, but you won't reach it by throwing a dart at a list of utilities or by buying shares in the company you write your monthly checks to. In fact, because their priorities are decidedly not long-term, Wall Street's best and brightest won't always show you the way, either.

The only way to really be certain you're on the right track is to do what the pros do themselves: Size up the risks and long-term growth potential of each company you buy, preferably before you invest.

At first blush, that may sound like a pretty tall order. Any analyst worth his or her salt spends days poring over financial statements, visiting companies' facilities, and talking to management, even after they recommend a stock. That's a lot of hours most investors don't have to spare.

The good news, however, is you don't have to. In fact, by using readily available information, you can size up the essential facts of a company inside of an hour.

Three Criteria

There are three basic types of criteria for sizing up utilities: regulatory, financial, and operating. Companies scoring highly in all three areas are well positioned for growth with relatively few risks. Long-term investors should avoid those that score poorly.

In the days before deregulation, regulators enjoyed make-or-break power over utilities' profits. Officials set customer rates according to the "cost of service." Regulators decided whether expenditures should be part of the cost of service, as well as the return that companies were allowed to earn on them.

Here in the deregulation era, cost of service–style regulation is out. As the chief arbiters of change, though, officials' power has arguably increased. Consequently, how a utility gets along with the state and federal regulators who oversee its operations is more critical than ever.

In an age when access to low-cost capital determines industry winners and losers, utilities' financial strength is equally vital. Rising debt by itself isn't necessarily a sign of trouble ahead. If unchecked, however, it will hurt companies' credit ratings and their ability to access low-cost capital. In contrast, big companies with rising cash flow face no such challenges.

Rating a company's operations boils down to two factors: how valuable and well positioned its assets are, and how well they're managed. This can be assessed by conventional measurements: how efficiently the business is run, and how well management is achieving its strategic aims.

In my newsletter, *Utility Forecaster,* I've developed an eight-point rating system measuring these three areas, which I list for each group below. Companies meeting the most criteria are the best bets for the next three to five years. Note that because energy, communications, and water companies operate somewhat differently, criteria vary slightly from group to group.

Energy Utilities

Regulatory Criteria—I ask three questions when assessing the tenor of relations for energy distributors and producers. Is the company's primary national or regional market in the process of deregulation, and have the rules been set to allow it to compete without one hand tied behind its back? Is the company's service territory economically healthy? Healthy regions/countries generally enjoy better regulator/utility relations. Does the company operate in several states or countries, thereby diversifying regulatory risk?

A yes answer to all three questions indicates good regulatory relations. A no answer to the first question means a company is in danger of regulatory strife, though the risk is limited if the answer to questions two and three is yes. Companies answering no to all three questions are not good long-term investments.

Financial Criteria—Nothing summarizes a company's financial strength like its bond rating. Because of their forward-looking and generally very conservative analysis, I prefer Standard & Poor's ratings, which can be found in most libraries, of a company's senior debt. An investment grade rating (BBB– or higher) indicates the company enjoys access to low-cost capital. A rating of A– or better is preferable, giving it more flexibility to acquire or build assets.

Not even S&P has a perfect record in forecasting. Consequently, I use two other measurements of financial strength. The company's payout ratio measures the percentage of its annual earnings that it pays out in annual dividends to shareholders. A lower ratio—under 70 percent—generally means the dividend is safer. It also means the company is plowing back more money into its growth. Payout ratio information can be found in numerous sources, including annual reports. Online services such as Yahoo! provide it for free.

The company's cash-flow coverage of capital costs provides a warning of heavy borrowing needs. I look for projected coverage of at least 70 percent over the next three to five years. The best sources of this information are the 10-K and 10-Q documents that companies must file with the Securities and Exchange Commission. They can be accessed online for free with Yahoo! and other online services, or by contacting the companies themselves.

Taken together, the bond rating, payout ratio, and cash-flow coverage of capital costs provide a pretty clear picture of a company's financial power. Utilities meeting all three criteria are best. Those failing on all three counts are best avoided as long-term investments.

Operating Criteria—When it comes to measuring the efficiency of an energy utility, there's no better gauge than what it charges its most profitable customers, industry. The lower a company's industrial rates, the more efficiently it's being run and the less it has to fear competition. Rates in the era of deregulation are determined by how well plants are run, the fuels used to run them (coal and nuclear are the most stable-priced), and overhead at the rest of the business. In general, companies charging their largest customers less than 5 cents per kilowatt hour will have the easiest time keeping them.

Managerial skill plays a major role in companies' cost structure, financial strength, and regulatory relations. It's most important for setting companies' strategic direction. I look at where a utility is putting its cash, how well its investments are paying off, and the prospects for growing them. Most important, I analyze the job that management has done meeting its own internal growth goals. Consistent performance means there's less chance for the kind of earnings warnings and disappointments that have crippled so many stocks in recent years.

Water Utilities

Regulatory Criteria—Water utilities' rates are still set according to the cost of service. Regulators in some states regularly peer over the shoulders of executives to ensure expenditures were prudent for new facilities and for purchasing water for resale. Other states, notably Pennsylvania, back big utilities' efforts to absorb smaller, cash-strapped ones with rate increases and swift approvals.

I assess water utilities' relations with regulators by asking three questions. Have companies been treated fairly in recent regulatory rulings, including requests to recover the cost of building new water treatment facilities and the rising cost of purchased water. Is the service territory economically healthy? Do companies operate in several state or national regulatory environments to lessen their risk to a single group of officials?

Companies answering yes to all three questions are in good shape. Those answering no to the first question could be headed for a lot of trouble and are best avoided. A yes answer to question one ensures there's little immediate problem, but investors should keep an eye out for trouble ahead.

Financial Criteria—My financial criteria for water companies are identical to those for energy utilities. The fact that many small water utilities aren't rated by S&P means they lack the financial power to capitalize on many growth opportunities.

Operating Criteria—Water utilities face no competition, but profitability can be severely impacted by the cost of water they must purchase on the open market. Companies that own the source of at least 90 percent of the water they sell aren't vulnerable to changes in wholesale water rates. Those that must buy from other sources can face spiking costs, particularly as the nation's pollution problems grow.

Water company managements' worth is summed up by how they've pursued the two avenues to growth in the industry: buying adjoining water systems and managing systems under contract. The best proof is in how fast companies have grown their customer rolls, sales, and profits.

Communications Utilities

Regulatory Criteria—With even the former monopolistic, local phone business now open to competition, regulatory criteria are less important to communications companies than to energy and water utilities. Nonetheless, state and particular federal officials still wield enormous power over industry combatants.

I look at just one criterion in this area: the degree to which regulators can hamper a company's growth under current law. The most impacted are the four remaining Baby Bells that must win state and federal approval to enter the long-distance telephone and data business. Cable companies are basically unregulated monopolies, but there are restrictions on ownership that can retard growth.

Financial Criteria—With companies piling on debt in the late 1990s for expansion and acquisitions, balance sheet strength is more important than ever for communications companies. The strong will be able to expand rapidly, even while their debt-burdened rivals slide into potential bankruptcy.

I use the same three criteria as for water and energy utilities: Payout ratio, cash-flow coverage of capital costs, and S&P bond rating. Most communications companies are more indebted than they were five years ago, but those meeting these simple and easy-to-access criteria will prove the most fit for the future.

Operating Criteria—I use four operating criteria (outlined below) to assess communications companies' long-run staying power. It's no coincidence that each is intimately connected with financial strength.

First, companies that own a last-mile network—the local phone and cable television linkups that run directly into residences and businesses—have an enormous advantage over their rivals in the industry in controlling costs. Second, companies that derive a significant portion of revenue (40 percent or more) from steady services like local phone and cable service enjoy steady cash flows, enabling them to grow, regardless of how tough it is to raise capital. Third, last-mile networks in rural areas provide the safest of all cash-flow streams due to lack of potential competition.

Fourth, having an operating margin—operating expenses as a percentage of revenue—over 20 percent indicates efficient and profitable overall corporate operations, as well as growing financial power for growth in the industry. Management should be piloting the company in the direction of financial power and growth.

How do you tell if a utility is Grade A? Simply add up the number of criteria a firm meets. Stocks meeting at least six of the eight criteria in their sector are very well positioned. Those meeting four or five have a few potential worries to keep an eye on. Those meeting three or less are probably best avoided, at least as part of a long-term strategy. The table in Appendix 1 shows how more than 200 utilities stack up according to these criteria.

RULE #3: DIVERSIFY

Over the long pull, recession and inflation are the two greatest enemies of the long-term investor. The only way to beat them is to bet on companies that can consistently grow at a rapid rate, and whose prospects the market hasn't fully recognized.

If you follow Rule #2, you'll be way ahead of the game picking the utilities with the best prospects for growth. You can fine-tune your performance for even better returns by diversifying two ways. First, spread your investment among at least 7 or 8 different companies. Second, make sure you own several stocks from each of the major utility sectors: energy, communications, and water.

The rationale for spreading your investment among several stocks is simple. If you put all your funds into one stock—no matter how strong it looks—you run the risk of losing everything if something unexpectedly goes wrong internally. The untimely passing of a key executive, negative regulatory developments, a power plant explosion, and a thousand other factors can derail you. By owning several different companies of equal strength, you take that kind of risk out of the equation.

The reasoning for diversifying among the different utility sectors is similar. Though all of the best stocks in these sectors are sharply undervalued relative to their long-run prospects, they behave differently in varying market environments.

Energy and water utilities, for example, have historically performed very well in a slow-growth economy. Investors view them as safe havens and flock to them when fear is in the air. In contrast, telecommunications is widely viewed as one of the growth engines of the economy. These stocks perform best when bullish passions on Wall Street are running high.

A brief look at the market history of the past few years confirms this paradigm. In early 1997, the collapse of the Thai market and economy set off a chain reaction around the developing world. Growth screeched to a halt as panic-stricken foreign investors fled all markets Latin, Asian, or African.

Eventually, fear spread to most of the developed world, including the United States, where growth industries like technology and telecom crashed and burned. The bright spots were energy and water utilities, where recession-resistant income streams were viewed as safe havens from the market's terrifying storms.

Some fancy footwork by then–Treasury Secretary Robert Rubin, Federal Reserve Chairman Alan Greenspan, and President Bill Clinton headed off disaster by pumping the U.S. economy and markets with money until the rest of the world began bouncing back. The next year, the NASDAQ doubled and telecom stocks exploded to the upside. In contrast, energy and water utilities entered a 10-month bear market, which left them among the world's worst-performing stock groups.

The tables turned again in early 2000. Energy and water utilities began a powerful recovery in which their growth potential gathered attention on Wall Street. Telecom meanwhile began to head south as the economy slowed and the Internet boom died (see Figure 10.2).

Through it all, owning a basket of the best growers in each group produced consistent overall returns year after year. You could have done better had you presciently switched from group to group at the right time. On the other hand, you could have fared as did the average utility mutual fund, many of which jumped ship from energy utilities just in time to ride down the telecom stock bust.

There are a couple of caveats to this strategy. First, as I pointed out in Chapter 7, energy utilities are becoming an increasingly diverse group. Companies that have focused on producing natural gas and electricity in the postderegulation world are now much more tied to economic growth. Their growth rates are better than ever and they're likely to do far better in a bull market than in the past, but they're also more vulnerable to a prolonged recession than before.

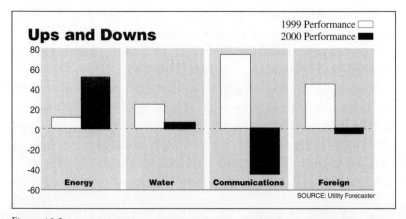

Figure 10.2

In direct contrast is the growing list of companies that have sold their power plants to focus on the distribution of energy over power lines and gas pipelines. Once the transition to deregulation is complete, these wires-and-pipes companies will be network services providers, with no direct commodity price risk. As regulated monopolies, they're likely to trade as utilities have historically, rising when interest rates fall and falling when rates rise. They'll also be safe havens when times are tough, due to their ultraconsistent revenue and profit streams. In addition, dividends will be high, due to the cash-generating nature of their business.

In coming years, foreign-based utilities will buy several more high-quality U.S. utilities. All else equal, the combinations will be treated as riskier than the premerger U.S. companies. For example, despite the solid nature of its core energy businesses in the United States and Britain, National Grid hasn't been treated with nearly the degree of safe-haven reverence as its New England Electric subsidiary was before its merger. Equally, foreign telecoms that buy a U.S. Baby Bell will be considered a good deal riskier than the Bell alone, despite the combination's enhanced financial power.

Some companies do a combination of two or more essential services. Several energy companies have invested heavily in fiber-optic cable–based, high-speed communications networks. In such cases, the stocks will likely follow the group to which they're most closely identified, probably energy, but it will be largely up to the whims of the market.

In 2000, for example, the stock of energy powerhouse Williams Companies was hurt by concerns about its communications unit, despite its robust overall profit picture and the relatively small size of the unit. In early 2001, Enron shares were battered, partly because of concerns about its broadband investments.

Over time, misperceptions of risk will fade away in the face of superior, consistent growth. Great utilities will rise to their full value. By maintaining a balance among great stocks that perform well in different environments, you can smooth out your returns year to year. At the least, that will make it a lot easier to hold powerful stocks in a slumping sector as long as it takes.

RULE #4: NEVER SELL ON BAD NEWS

Wall Street traders have a saying: Don't fight the tape. That means simply not to be short or sell stocks—that is, bet on a drop in the market—unless there's clear evidence of a downtrend. It also means don't buy or even hold stocks unless there's a clear uptrend.

For traders, not fighting the tape is the difference between keeping and losing a very well-paying job. For the long-term investor, though, it's actually pretty lousy advice.

For one thing, by the time everyone thinks "the tape" is going one way, it's usually far too late to sell. Battered stocks could go lower as those afraid to fight the tape sell out, and stocks with serious fundamental problems could go a lot lower. Investors whose time horizon stretches beyond the current season should be thinking of buying, not selling. In fact, it's just when the crowd is most panicked that the best bargains appear.

Utility stocks' market history is rich with examples why well-publicized threats are never good reasons to sell. Back in 1984, utilities were at the end of a nearly 20-year slump, which had seen them transform from high multiple growth stocks to high dividend plays. *Business Week* unintentionally called the bottom with its cover headline, "Are Utilities Obsolete?"

The infamous article's premise was that electric utilities would be displaced by other power sources. By that time, investors' pessimism was so great all the selling was over. The industry has since undergone a growth renaissance and has been among the top-performing sectors over that time.

Business Week's article is a clear example of just how wrong-headed consensus thinking often is. By the time some issue is plastered all over the local papers, most of the buying or selling related to it has been done. As far as the stock market is concerned, it's a nonissue.

Another example came with the controversy over acid rain. Throughout his 1988 presidential campaign, George Bush promised tougher regulations to combat utility emissions. When he won, the market punished stocks of polluting utilities. The consensus was big coal-burning utilities would face billions in cleanup costs. As usual, the conventional wisdom proved disastrously wrong. In fact, the Clean Air Act of 1990 held down costs by giving polluters plenty of time to clean up emissions; many are doing better than ever.

Perhaps the greatest example of crowd-following folly was in 1993–1994, when deregulation first became an industrywide topic. Panicked by the so-called experts that industry change would bankrupt scores of companies, investors dumped their energy utilities. Some called it the beginning of the end for the industry, envisioning a system where third parties cherry-pick utilities' best customers.

As the years have proven, reality was far more benign. In fact, deregulation has opened the door to explosive growth for the entire sector, particularly the emerging group of boom riders profiled in Chapter 7. Aside from the teetering California utilities, there have been no bankruptcies, and even shareholders of many of the worst-run companies have been rescued by takeovers. Contrary to the experts, deregulation has proceeded slowly and beneficially for most utilities. The only real losers were those misguided souls who sold out at the height of the 1993–1994 panic.

Communications companies in the wake of the NASDAQ meltdown of 2000–2001 are likely to prove the next great examples of why it never pays to sell into bad news. CNBC and the other financial media have been relentlessly reporting bad news about the group, just as they were irrepressibly bullish at the peak in early 2000.

If you're a trader—that is, have a time horizon lasting weeks if not days—every panic can be a major event. Selling before the damage gets bad and buying as the recovery gets under way can yield stupendous profits for those who time the market correctly, and who don't mind the whole thing blowing up in their faces every once in a while.

For long-term investors, it's absolutely critical not to get knocked off your game by market events. Bear markets will follow bull market runs for stocks. Recessions will occur, and the short-run damage can be catastrophic. Any number of factors can panic the market out of a sector at any time, and given the impact of television, the effect can be as sudden and dramatic as it is irrational.

It happened again in early 2001. America's most dominant electric utilities were riding high as earnings soared from power sales into electricity-starved markets. The sector, however, was hit hard by a growing panic that California's woes would roll back deregulation nationwide. There was no evidence that this would happen, but investors sold heavily, even companies that had little or no exposure to the Golden State. Their folly was demonstrated by the subsequent rebound.

While events like these can shake your confidence, it's critical to stick to your long-term plan. As long as you own good stocks that are still on track for strong growth—stocks that score highly on the safety ratings test in Rule #2—turn off your television. Better yet, use the opportunity to buy more of your favorites at rock-bottom prices that won't be around long, once the crowd is led in another direction.

RULE #5: REINVEST DIVIDENDS

Even more than the average stock, utilities owe their value as wealth-builders to the power of the payout. Unless you need the income, reinvest your dividends; use them to buy additional shares of your favorite companies.

More than any other industry, utilities encourage reinvestment. Under a dividend reinvestment plan, or DRIP, your shares are held with the company itself, rather than with a broker. Per request, the company automatically uses your dividends to buy additional shares for your account.

DRIPs confer several advantages over holding utilities in a conventional brokerage account. They charge little or no commission for purchases, which are often made at a discount to the stock's market price. You can make additional cash investments in shares, also at little or no commission. And you can buy and hold fractional shares of a company, just as you would a mutual fund. Brokerages typically do not allow you to hold fractional shares.

The ability to buy fractional shares means you can effectively dollar cost average into your utilities as well, always buying more stock when the price is lowest. Most plans give you the flexibility to take part of your dividend in cash—even wired directly to your bank account—while reinvesting the rest.

Most DRIPs still require you to buy your initial shares from your broker before signing up for the plan, but a growing number of companies now allow investors to buy their first shares directly, completely bypassing the broker. These plans offer the best of all worlds: direct ownership in great companies with the ability to invest as much or as little as you want with little or no fees or expenses. You'll also receive financial reports directly from the companies themselves, rather than indirectly though a broker (see Figure 10.3).

There are a few drawbacks to DRIPs. For one thing, you'll still owe taxes on the dividends, even if you reinvest them. Many people shelter DRIPs in self-directed IRAs to avoid this hassle.

DRIPs have also been known to be tough to cash out of, though most plans allow you to sell by the next day. Also, once you send

Buy Direct

Company	Phone	Initial Minimum Investment
CMS Energy	517-788-1868	$500
Dominion Resources	800-552-4034	250
Duke Energy	800-488-3853	250
Energen	800-654-3206	250
Enron	800-662-7662	250
Entergy	800-333-4368	1000
ExxonMobil	800-252-1800	250
KeySpan Energy	800-482-3638	250
MDU Resources	800-813-3324	50
Philadelphia Suburban	800-205-8314	500
SBC Communications	800-351-7221	500
Southern Company	800-565-2577	250
Chevron Texaco	800-283-9785	250
UtiliCorp United	800-487-6661	250
Verizon Communications	800-631-2355	1000

SOURCE: Utility Forecaster

Figure 10.3

in your check for shares, you're at the mercy of the plan's date for entering new investment. In contrast, brokerages allow you to control your entry and exit prices by almost instant execution and confirmation.

For this reason, DRIPs should be viewed solely as long-term investments. The model stocks to buy through them are the winners profiled in Chapter 7, or the stocks listed in the model portfolios in Appendix 4.

To start a DRIP, simply call the utility in question and ask for a prospectus. The table lists several first-rate companies offering direct purchase of initial shares of stock. As you buy, be sure to follow the other rules in this chapter. They are:

- Buy with the intention of holding for at least the next three to five years.

- Analyze your stocks carefully using regulatory, financial, and operating criteria.

- Diversify between individual companies as well as between utility groups that perform well in different environments.

- Never sell into bad news, buy into it when opportunity arises.

....

INDUSTRY PROFILE: LOWELL MILLER

Lowell Miller isn't your typical money manager. He's never worked for a Wall Street firm or bank. His $500 million firm, Miller/Howard Investments, operates two hours from Manhattan in Woodstock, New York, what he jokingly refers to as "the heart of the Catskills financial district." His specialty in utilities is almost unheard-of.

Miller's long-term performance is equally uncommon. His firm earned the top ranking among mid-cap money managers for the five years ended in 2000 according to Money Manager Reports. *In addition, his Flex Funds Total Return Utilities Fund draws a five-star rating from mutual fund rater Morningstar. That's turning heads, even in an investment specialty known more for trend-following than individual thinking.*

Q: WHY DO YOU SPECIALIZE IN UTILITIES?

A: Because energy, water, and communications service is more important than the government. No other business can claim that. Think about it. If the government collapsed today, it wouldn't have nearly the impact on your daily life as not being able to turn on the lights.

From an investment point of view, that makes this industry the most reliable around, despite deregulation. Then there are the dividends. When we first started Miller/Howard in the early 1980s, we were a research boutique. We were basically concerned with doing something quantitatively based that we could sell to institutions.

At the time, several of our clients wanted to get involved in fixed income. We looked through all the data from Ibbotsen, starting in the 1940s, and it looked to us that fixed income was a bad idea. For most time periods, bonds earned little or nothing, adjusted for inflation; many times the return was negative.

Then we discovered that the Dow Utility Average actually outperformed bonds after inflation by 8.5-to-1 from 1945 through 1990, and with less volatility. Most of the reason was continuous compounding of dividends. Utility stocks, in other words, provided strong growth as well as high income, and they compared favorably to the rest of the stock market as well. Amazingly, there's been no comprehensive, published study on these stocks.

Q: WHAT'S THE MOST IMPORTANT STRENGTH YOU
   LOOK FOR IN A UTILITY STOCK?

A: Strong, consistent dividend growth is the most reliable indicator of quality for utilities. When management increases a company's payout over time, it's sending investors a signal that sales, cash flow, and profits are on an upward track, and that it expects the good times to continue. In addition, rising dividends push up a security's value by making it worth more to income seekers.

Incidentally, the biggest dividend growers in the utility industry are also the highest-quality stocks; they've performed the best over time. So you can literally expect to get the biggest returns overall by buying the safest stocks. That's the opposite from the bond market, where lower-rated, high-yielding junk offers by far the highest potential returns, but with considerably greater risks than high-quality bonds.

Q: WHAT'S CHANGED ABOUT YOUR APPROACH OVER
   THE PAST 20 YEARS?

A: When we first started focusing on utilities, we thought we'd tapped into a nice, quiet, gentleman's industry, with few disruptions. Since deregulation hit we've had to move a bit faster, but the opportunities have been greater as well.

My overriding focus is still to pick the highest-quality stocks I can find, particularly by looking at dividend growth. The original principles of quality haven't changed. But I now also try to pick out the winners from deregulation in all the various sectors.

By the way, I believe a balanced utilities portfolio has got to include representatives from all the various sectors. My clients own some of the generating and marketing companies that are making headlines today, but we also hold electric and gas T&D companies, gas pipelines, local and long-distance telephone companies, resource companies, and water utilities.

Not specializing in any one sector helps us avoid the bumps that inevitably affect any single group of stocks. And it keeps us focused on buying quality companies wherever they turn up.

Q: HOW DOES YOUR APPROACH DIFFER FROM MORE MAINSTREAM FIRMS?

A: For one thing, very few Wall Streeters specialize in utilities and even fewer understand them. Among those that do focus on them, most buy only the big capitalization companies, such as those listed in the Dow Utility Average. Mutual funds in particular must stick to the most liquid utilities. The reason is they must have the ability to sell quickly to deal with unexpected shareholder redemptions.

Our firm serves 400-plus individuals. Because they rarely move at the same time, we can afford to take our time building as well as liquidating positions. That allows us to buy utilities in the mid-cap range, as well as big blue chips. Mid-cap is often where the real value lies. In contrast, the big caps that the funds and most institutions buy can be very volatile. The mid-cap advantage is one reason I've been able to consistently outperform industry benchmarks over the years.

Q: ARE UTILITIES STILL SAFE INVESTMENTS?

A: In a word, yes. In fact, in my opinion they offer the best of all possible worlds. Provided you stick to quality and don't invest in troubled companies, such as those in California or with a lot of nuclear power risk, utilities' dividends are among the most effective and lowest-risk ways to build wealth around.

Now that we have deregulation, the best utilities are also growth companies. And then there's the consolidation of the industry. Warren Buffett and apparently a host of other concerns will be buying utilities once Congress repeals the Public Utility Holding Company Act. That will make the sector much more attractive for buying takeover targets.

. . . .

CHAPTER 11

The Surest Return

Before the great Nasdaq crackup of 2000–2001, investing for yield was derided as yesterday's strategy. More than a few money-hungry brokers encouraged people dependent on investment income to sell their dividend-paying stocks and bonds and buy growth stocks. The rationale: Investors could sell a piece of their soaring stock portfolio when they needed money.

Today, the folly of that advice has been exposed. Many investors who couldn't afford to lose have seen their portfolios drop 50 percent and more. Worse, like a farmer in famine times, they've had to sell their seed corn—the battered stocks themselves—for dimes on the dollar in order to pay their expenses.

Tragically, most will never come close to recovering their lost wealth. Their experience is a critical lesson: Never, ever count on a rising stock market to pay your bills. If you need investment income to live, buy something that throws off a yield in cold, hard cash—the surest return on Wall Street.

Income-paying stocks, bonds, and other securities have the added advantage of outperforming the average growth stock by a mile when the market is floundering. In fact, because they're viewed as safe havens, money flows into them during bear markets, driving up their value. While they tend to lag behind in bull markets, they keep paying you to hold on.

Investing for yield is essentially a long-term game. You have to buy and hold on long enough to collect a steady stream of income. Sticking around limits the impact of market volatility, but it does carry two major risks: credit risk, including the possibility of default, and inflation risk, which erodes the value of principal and interest.

Since the 1960s, cash-rich, steady-growth energy, communications, and water utilities have earned a well-deserved reputation for dishing out high yields while protecting against credit and inflation risk. These companies are still Wall Street's premier income-investment vehicles.

Despite immense changes, communications and water companies offer a compelling strength other sectors can only envy: revenue security in even the worst of times. No matter what's going on with the economy and markets, demand for essential services like energy, communications, and water will remain solid. Utility companies will keep earning the money to pay their obligations, including debt interest and dividends.

Deregulation has raised some operating risks. Aggressive expansion plans at home and abroad, mergers and acquisitions, and extensive borrowing have pressured traditional measures of financial strength, such as credit ratings. Even the emerging global powerhouses have slowed payout growth to plow more money back into their businesses, and some could stumble in coming years.

Many weaker utilities have cut or eliminated dividends since the mid-1980s. Some will be driven out of business, as were heavily indebted competitive local exchange carriers in early 2001. You can't count on a takeover to bail out a bad investment.

Burned by events in California and elsewhere, ratings agencies like Standard & Poor's and Moody's have grown hypervigilant for the next great potential threat. Cuts in utility credit ratings, once rare events, have become almost commonplace, and often it's been the former AAA credits that have suffered the most. In 2000, for example, ratings for AT&T, British Telecom, and Deutsche Telekom were cut to the single A range due to heavy borrowing to fund acquisitions.

Happily, competition, consolidation, and globalization have also enriched the growth potential of strong utilities. Many of their income-generating securities now have the ability to meet and beat inflation over the long pull.

If you believe the media, inflation hasn't been much of a threat for more than a decade. If you've shopped for groceries, bought a stamp, gassed up your car, bought a house, paid property taxes, gone out to a restaurant, or purchased insurance lately, you know differently. Despite the official low levels, inflation is very much alive and kicking. In fact, it's likely to become even more of a threat in coming years, partly due to rising energy prices.

The key for income investors: Make sure any yield-paying investment can at least match but preferably beat inflation. Utilities offer a wide variety of income-generating securities that can do that *and* guard against credit risk. In Figure 11.1, I highlight the best of these, some of which are widely known and some of which are not. Each type is represented in the Income Portfolio of my newsletter *Utility Forecaster,* a recent installment of which is shown Appendix 4.

These investments range widely in terms of risk and potential reward. The graph illustrates this by presenting each investment on a risk-reward continuum. In general, the more conservative have fewer credit risks, money market–beating yields, little inflation risk, and some opportunity to grow. The further you move to the aggressive end of the continuum, the higher the yields and

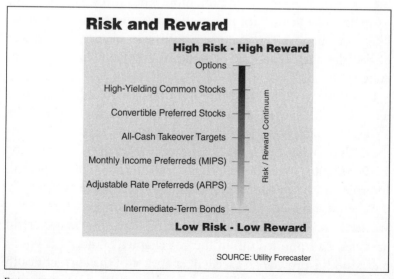

Figure 11.1

growth potential will be, but the greater the credit and/or inflation risk.

You can assess utility income investments with the safety criteria described under Rule #2 in the previous chapter. As a rule of thumb, you should buy only the preferred stocks or bonds of companies whose common stocks you wouldn't mind owning. Only companies that can grow are assured to keep paying the dividends and interest on their other securities.

The side of the continuum you emphasize depends on how much risk you can live with. In reality, most income investors' objectives fall somewhere in between conservative and aggressive. Most are better off with a well-diversified combination of both.

SAFETY FIRST

The hallmarks of all conservative income investments are protection against inflation and low credit risks. The tradeoff is limited potential for growth.

On the far conservative side of the risk-reward continuum are intermediate-term bonds of utilities with medium investment grade credit quality. These securities pay a fixed yield and mature within 5 to 10 years. The relatively short time to maturity protects their principal against rising inflation, since investors can count on getting par value back in a matter of a few years. In contrast, long-term bonds—particularly Treasuries—mature in a matter of decades. Any economic or political event can cause them to crater.

Intermediate-term bonds are not only less volatile than long-term bonds, they've actually outperformed them since the 1920s. One reason: Long-term Treasury bonds lost an average of more than 4 percent a year, adjusted for inflation, during the 1970s, despite paying double-digit yields for much of the period. Intermediate-term paper held its ground (see Figure 11.2).

When it comes to judging credit quality, most investors' analysis starts and stops with the bond ratings issued by major credit agencies. As I pointed out in the last chapter, Standard & Poor's and Moody's provide an excellent snapshot of the current health of a company. In general, bonds rated from BBB– to A+ are con-

Rating Maturity

Type of Security	Years to Redemption	Inflation Risk	Potential Reward
Treasury Bills	0 to 90 days	none	low
Short-term Notes	90 days to 3 years	low	low
Intermediate-term Bonds	3 to 10 years	low	moderate
Long-term Bonds	10 to 30 years	high	high*
Ordinary Preferred Stocks	Indefinite	high	moderate
New Breed Preferreds	up to 40 years	moderate	moderate

Using market timing, not investing.

SOURCE: Utility Forecaster

Figure 11.2

sidered medium- to low-investment grade. They yield more than the top-rated AAA or AA fare, with little real additional risk.

The best test of a bond's credit risk, however, is whether or not you would want to own the common stock for the long haul. Unless you can answer yes, steer clear, no matter how attractive the yield looks or how high the rating is. An exception would be bonds purchased as a bet on a particularly battered company's survival; these should be viewed as more aggressive income investments, far out on the risk-reward spectrum.

To rate an issuing company's worthiness as a long-run investment, see how it matches up to the regulatory, financial, and operating criteria described in Chapter 10. The more criteria met, the lower the credit risk of the company's bonds and preferred stocks.

There are several things to be aware of when buying a bond. First of all, you're almost always better off using a full-service broker. Specific individual bond issues are often difficult, if not impossible, to locate on your own, and quotes are difficult to get from on-line services like Yahoo!

Bond prices are quoted as a percentage of par value. For example, a $1,000 bond selling for $900 will be listed as selling for 90. Bonds are typically quoted two ways. The *ask* price is the price at which a bond may be purchased. The *bid* price is the price at which you can sell a bond.

Depending on how frequently traded a particular bond is, the ask price can be quite a bit higher than the bid price. A good broker can help to favorably navigate such spreads; when a particular bond you want is not available, he or she can point out an alternative that's just as solid and higher-yielding to boot. Consequently, hiring a broker is generally well worth whatever higher commission or fee you have to pay, provided of course that they're familiar with bonds.

Most utilities' bonds are listed on the New York Stock Exchange. However, they lack symbols in a conventional sense. Instead, the best way to locate them is the way the professional brokers do, by using a standardized numerical identification system. The most common of these is the Cusip number. Bonds can also be tracked down through their BB number or ISIN, their international security identification number. The latter is particularly useful when hunting down a foreign bond.

Many bonds are callable, which means the issuer can redeem them on or after a specified date (call date) at a specified price (call price). Some bonds reduce their call price over time until it ultimately reaches par value when they mature.

The call price comes into play only when a bond has rallied sharply above its par value, usually as a result of falling interest rates. Call provisions are designed to protect the issuer from paying well above market rates on their debt. The easiest way to avoid their impact is to buy only bonds trading well below their call prices.

It's also acceptable to buy a bond trading above its call price, if the interest payment is high enough. In that case, you'll be compensated for the principal you'll lose if it's called at a price below what you paid for it. Figure 11.3 shows a shorthand way to calculate a bond's yield-to-maturity, the annual total return to expect, based on the purchase price.

The same formula can also be used to tabulate a yield-to-call, what the return will be if you buy a bond that's called. Substitute the call price for the purchase price and subtract from the current price. Divide the difference by the years left to maturity to get the annual premium. To get the yield-to-call, subtract the annual premium from the annual interest payment and divide by the average of the par value and current price.

Using this formula, the same bond trading at 110 and callable in

Yield to Maturity Shorthand

Par Value = $1,000

Current Price = $800

Coupon Yield = 8 percent, or $80 per year.

Years to Maturity = 10

Annual Discount (Premium) = (Par Value - Current Price) / Years to Maturity

Current Yield = Coupon Yield / Current Price

10% Current Yield = $80 / $800

Yield to Maturity = (Annual Discount (Premium) + Annual Interest) / (Average of Par Value and Current Price)

20 = (1,000 - 800) / 10

9% Yield to Maturity = (20 + 80) / 900

SOURCE: *Beating the Dow with Bonds* by Michael B. O'Higgins
and John McCarty, HarperCollins (reprinted by permission)

Figure 11.3

ten years at 100 would have a yield-to-call of 6.7 percent. That's an annual premium of $10 [(1100 − 1000)/10], subtracted from annual interest of $80, for an annual return of $70. You then divide the result by the average between the call price and current price, which in this case is 1050, to get a yield-to-call of 6.7 percent.

You can get virtually the same result by using any multifunction calculator. Both yield-to-maturity and yield-to-call fluctuate to reflect changes in interest rates.

Bonds vary in seniority. In the event of a bankruptcy, the most senior bonds would be paid off first, the least senior and subordinated paper last. Bonds secured by an asset or sinking fund—a pool of money set up separately to pay them off—enjoy the most bankruptcy protection. First-mortgage bonds hold a senior claim to all assets.

Barring bankruptcy, there's little practical difference between the risks of senior and less-senior bonds; if there is a default, however, senior bonds' prices will hold up the best. The senior first-mortgage bonds of defaulted Edison International and PG&E, for example, traded at around 80 cents on the dollar in 2001, despite the fact that the companies had stopped paying interest. In contrast, less-senior paper sold for barely 60 percent of par value. Consequently, the most conservative investors will want to stick with seniors, though yields are typically lower than for less-senior bonds.

All utility bonds—even medium investment grade intermediate-term selections—share one more important risk to be mindful of. If their issuers are unexpectedly taken over by a company with a lower credit rating, they can take a spill due to increased perceived credit risk, no matter how solid the acquirer. Some mergers have been known to spark ratings cuts because of reliance on debt financing.

Other than to say almost every energy, communications, and water utility is potentially another's takeover target, specific mergers are virtually impossible to predict. The important thing is, though a merger may cause some short-term pain to bond-holders, most deals ultimately create more powerful companies.

Credit ratings may be cut in the short run. That was the case when tiny but highly rated Ipalco Enterprises merged with lower-rated but infinitely more powerful AES Corp. in early 2001. In the long term, the combined company's greater strength makes it considerably safer than the acquired utility alone.

When entering an order, instruct your broker to look for the bond you've chosen using the Cusip or other identification number. If it's not available, ask for bonds issued by the same company with roughly the same 5- to 10-year maturities. If that fails, have the broker seek intermediate-term bonds issued by other compa-nies that stack up well on the safety criteria, and whose common stocks you wouldn't mind owning.

PREFERRED OPTION

Preferred stocks are the next step out on the credit risk-reward continuum. These are junior obligations to bonds. In the event of a default, they'd be paid off only after all bondholders are fully compensated, at which point there may be little left.

In the early 1990s, Tucson Electric dished out dramatically devalued common stock to its preferred shareholders, in lieu of cash, under its bankruptcy avoidance plan. Preferred holders of Public Service of New Hampshire received similar treatment when Northeast Utilities' acquisition brought that company out of bankruptcy. On the other hand, there are cases of full recovery by preferred shareholders, such as when Long Island Lighting avoided Chapter 11 by selling itself to KeySpan Energy and the Long Island Power Authority.

Barring a default, owning preferreds entails few risks that owning bonds does not. Few companies' preferred credit ratings are ever cut without commensurate reductions in their bond ratings, to which California utilities' defaults of early 2001 attest. Fewer utilities default on their preferreds without suspending interest payments on their bonds.

As a result, preferreds pose little real additional credit risk to bonds. They do, however, offer several huge advantages. Yields in some cases are up to 2 to 3 percentage points more. They're far more liquid or heavily traded than bonds. Most are listed on major stock exchanges like the NYSE and have designated trading symbols. Preferreds' prices are posted daily in the financial press and can be accessed on Yahoo! Bid/ask spreads are seldom very wide.

Until the mid-1990s, preferred stocks were an afterthought to most utilities' plans to raise capital. With common stocks paying high yields, and bond issues satisfying the risk-averse, the market for preferred stocks was mostly corporations, which, thanks to a tax loophole, can shelter from taxes 70 percent of the interest from preferred stocks.

The need to plow cash back into growth slowed the prolific dividend increases of the 1980s and early 90s. At the same time, deregulation has increased investor scrutiny whenever utilities issue bonds. Companies have become more cautious about issuing debt.

Enter the new breed of capital preferred securities. Born from a loophole in the tax code, these are actually issued by separate capital corporations set up by utilities solely for that purpose. The parent company then borrows the proceeds from the capital corporation. In so doing, it can count the dividends paid as debt interest, paying them from pretax, rather than posttax, profits. The savings allow them to push yields higher for capital preferreds than for ordinary preferreds and common stocks.

As Figure 11.4 shows, there are several species of the new breed of preferreds, ranging from the monthly income (MIPs) to the adjustable-rate (ARPs) and convertibles. Each has different investment features, as well as a lot in common.

Capital Preferreds

Type of Preferred	Dividend Acronym	Frequency	Convertible?	Maturity Callable?	(Years)
Adjustable Rate Preferred Securities	ARPS	monthly, quarterly	no	yes	40
Canadian Originated Preferred Securities	COPrS	quarterly	no	yes	50
Feline Preferred Redeemable Increased Dividend Securities	PRIDES	semi-annually	yes	yes	3 to 5
Monthly Income Preferred Securities	MIPS	monthly	no	yes	40
Preferred Equity Income Securities	PIES	quarterly	yes	yes	3 to 5
Preferred Equity Participating Securities	PEPS	semi-annually	yes	yes	3 to 5
Quarterly Income Preferred Securities	QUIPS	quarterly	no	yes	50
Perpetual Trust Originated Preferred Securities	TOPrS	quarterly	no	yes	40
Trust Convertible Preferred Securities	EPPICS	quarterly	yes	no	n/a

Maturity measured from issue date.

SOURCE: Utility Forecaster

Figure 11.4

Because of their official status as debt, the tax loophole mandates that capital preferreds have a set maturity, usually 40 to 50 years from their issue date. Most were issued at their call prices, with call dates set about five years in the future. This has limited their ability to profit from falling interest rates, but it also limits their exposure to rising interest rates and inflation. The reason: Such low call prices keep their yields far higher than they would were they ordinary fixed-income securities. So when rates rise, they've got to rise a long way before capital preferreds' already high yields will become uncompetitive.

Since the mid-1990s, prices of capital preferred securities—especially the monthly income-paying MIPs—have remained remarkably stable, despite ups and downs in interest rates. As a result, in a practical sense they limit inflation risk as much as or more than most intermediate-term bonds.

Even more immune to rate swings, and therefore more conservative, are Adjustable Rate Preferred Securities, or ARPs. Unlike other preferred stocks or bonds, ARPs are not really fixed-income securities. Instead, their dividends are adjusted on a quarterly basis to reflect changes in interest rates.

The adjustment is set by a complex formula determined by changes in short-, intermediate-, and long-term interest rates. Most ARPs have a designated *collar,* essentially an upward and a lower limit on where yields can go. The result is a security with a remarkably steady price, thanks to a dividend that rises and falls to match changes in interest rates.

The most interesting thing about ARPs is that, unlike most bonds and preferred securities, they tend to do best when interest rates (and their yields) are rising. The best time to buy an ARP is after interest rates have dropped for a time, and the yield is near the bottom of its designated collar. In that case, yields will have nowhere to go but up, and the ARPs will only become more attractive.

Next up on the risk-reward spectrum is the new breed of preferred stock that combines high yields with the ability to convert into common stock. Old-style convertibles offer investors two ways to win. If interest rates fall, the value of their dividends rises; if the underlying stock rises, so will the price of the convertible preferred or bond. The investor has the right to convert into common stock at any time until the converts either mature or are called by the issuer. At that point, he or she can take either stock or cash.

Sporting such acronyms as PEPS and PIES and yielding as much as 10 percent, the new-style convertibles offer a slightly different risk-reward twist. Instead of it being the investor's option to convert into stock, there's a set, future date when the security will be automatically converted into a range of stock.

There's no cash component or fixed dollar value at maturity. Instead, the ultimate return on the securities is entirely linked to the price of the underlying common stock. If the common stock rises, the convert's value will rise. If it falls, so will the convert's value at maturity.

The number of shares in the conversion is determined by the price of the underlying stock and a *target* value set when the securities are issued. If the common stock stays within a certain price range, the converts will be worth the target value at maturity. If the stock is above the range, the converts will be worth more at maturity. If it falls below it, they'll be worth less.

In a best-case scenario, the common stock will rise, pushing up the value of the convertible as it nears the exchange date, even while it continues to dish out high income. That was the case with the KN Energy PEPs that matured in late 2001, though the road there was somewhat bumpy.

After growing rapidly throughout the 1990s, diversified energy company KN Energy hit a snag late in 1999 after it acquired the Mid-Continent natural gas pipeline, processing, and gathering system. It soon became clear that, despite the strong quality of the company's assets, management was incapable of running it effectively. Coupled with low prices for natural gas liquids, KN suffered several quarters of abysmal earnings, ending with the collapse of its planned merger with California-based Sempra Energy.

KN Energy stock fell from the 30s into the low teens. KN Energy PEPs—which were convertible into a range of from 1.25 to 1.50 shares of KN Energy common with a target value of $43—sank from the low 40s into the high 20s.

Then came the announcement of the company's merger with energy investment powerhouse Kinder Morgan. Though technically a buyout of Kinder, the deal was structured to leave Kinder's CEO Richard Kinder—a man held in deep respect by the energy industry from his days at Enron—in charge of the combined company. Since KN Energy was always considered an asset-rich outfit in need of strong management, the deal immediately triggered a sharp rise in the common stock, renamed Kinder Morgan.

Within a year, the stock had soared into the 50s. The PEPs followed suit, moving as high as the 70s. Investors nearly doubled their money from stock price appreciation and the 10 percent–plus semiannual yield they'd garnered along the way.

Not every convertible preferred stock you buy will have spectacular results, but if you like the companies, they do offer a superb way to participate in growth while drawing high income. The key, as with any fixed-income investment, is to buy only the convertibles of companies you won't mind owning after the conversion.

Like bonds, most preferred stocks are callable. As with bonds, the key is to buy below the call prices, except when the call date is well off in the future and the yield-to-call is high enough to justify the purchase.

UNCOMMON COMMON STOCKS

No income investment generates growth like solid, dividend-paying common stocks. In the 1950s and 60s, utilities were the ultimate safe growth stocks, as urbanization and electrification spurred strong increases in sales and earnings. In the late 1990s, opportunities from deregulation, merger mania, and global expansion have again transformed utilities into powerful profit engines.

Growth has all but severed the link between utilities and interest rate swings. In 1999, for example, utility stocks barely budged while long-term bond yields soared from 4.7 percent to over 6 percent in a matter of months. In contrast, the average utility stock lost nearly 30 percent of its value in 1994, almost identical to the bond market's horrendous losses of that year.

The tradeoff is that most companies are now shepherding capital, so dividend growth has slowed. In addition, even first-rate common stocks aren't nearly as safe as bonds, preferreds, or even convertibles. Because their inflation-beating potential is unmatched, stocks are still an integral part of income portfolios.

Most common stocks, because of the risks, belong in the aggressive rather than the conservative portion of an income portfolio. The uncommon exceptions are companies involved in mergers with locked-in takeover values.

Unlike mergers in other industries, utility deals involve winning numerous regulatory approvals, a process that can take months or even years to complete. The overwhelming majority of utility mergers, however, are ultimately approved and completed. Investors who buy into deals in progress can reap big gains, in addition to steady dividends.

For mergers with a fixed value—either all-cash or a set-dollar value of stock—the payoff is locked in, no matter what happens to the economy and markets. Investors who buy will gain the difference between takeover value and their purchase price, plus dividends paid. In some cases, that amounts to an effective double-digit yield in a few months.

Getting the most of these deals depends on the price you pay, which is very time-sensitive. For best results, keep careful tabs on the math. If you can get more than 10 percent simply from buying and holding on, and the merger has a reasonable chance of being completed within six to nine months, you've got a rare bargain. This little-known road to maximizing income will continue to offer compelling returns with relatively little risk for some time to come.

I use a simple rule for other income stocks: If a yield looks too good to be true, you can bet it is. Most common stocks paying out double-digit yields, for example, aren't worth the paper they're printed on.

Exceptions include limited partnerships, especially those backed by major energy companies. In the past few years, several giants—including El Paso Energy, Enron, and Williams Companies—have spun off some of their biggest cash-generating assets into partnerships. The companies continue to manage the assets for a fee and they can shelter more of the cash flow from taxes. For investors, the key advantage is a substantial yield.

The biggest risk of owning a limited partnership is trouble with the general partner. Transparency—the ability to get in-depth financial information—can be somewhat limited, but if a good company backs your investment, the actual risk is fairly low.

Another myth about dividends is that you should always pick the utilities that have the highest historical dividend growth rates. A growing payout is definitely a sign of strength for a company, but is the current rate of increase sustainable?

It wasn't in the case of Tucson Electric, now UniSource. That company had the highest 10- and 5-year rates of dividend growth in the industry almost up to the moment it was forced to eliminate its dividend completely in the late 1980s. A decade later, despite struggling toward recovery, the stock was still about 90 percent off its 1989 high.

The best gauge for a sustainable dividend and future growth is how a company matches up against the ratings criteria pinpointed in the last chapter. The rule remains: Companies meeting six or more criteria are best for income investors, who should generally avoid high-yielding companies meeting fewer than four criteria.

THE IDEAL INCOME PORTFOLIO

So what is the ideal income portfolio? The answer depends on your own tolerance for risk and reward.

The rule should be don't risk what you can't afford. That doesn't mean hiding it all in a mattress or, only slightly better, U.S. Treasury bills. It does mean that those living off their investments should build a strong base in the investments on the conservative side of the continuum before venturing too far out on the aggressive end.

If you depend on investment income, don't put it all in limited partnerships and convertibles. Have some MIPs and bonds as well. A fairly timeless mix, slanted toward the conservative, should hold up well in any economic environment, as well as beat the ravages of inflation.

INDUSTRY PROFILE: GÖRAN MÖRNHED

Growing up in environmentally aware Sweden, Göran Mörnhed began his career in the early 1980s with a keen interest in distributed and renewable energy. Two decades later, he's building one of North America's leading companies in both areas as president and chief operating officer of up-and-coming U.S. Energy Systems.

As a systems engineer fresh out of school with Stockholm-based AF Group, Mörnhed participated in a range of energy projects in Europe involving renewables, like biomass, then left for Canada in 1986 to become president of the international district energy department of AF Energi Konsult. In 1990, he joined Trigen Energy, a unit of giant French conglomerate Suez Lyonnaise des Eaux (now Suez) dedicated to small-scale power projects, as manager of business development. Promoted to president and CEO of the company's alliance with U.S. energy utility Cinergy in 1997, Göran oversaw the development of some 13 different combined heat and power projects, primarily for large industrials.

When Suez liquidated Trigen's venture with Cinergy in May 2000, Göran Mörnhed created U.S. Energy in its image, bringing many of his former colleagues with him, as well as the focus on small-scale, customer-tailored power. Resurrecting the alliance with Cinergy, he's already launched several new projects, moving the company to a profit in less than a year of operation. In addition he's completed U.S. Energy's first major merger, buying Connecticut-based biomass producer ZAPCO, with its 27 landfill-to-energy projects in five states.

Q: WHAT'S THE BIGGEST CHANGE YOU'VE SEEN IN THE ENERGY INDUSTRY OVER YOUR CAREER?

A: Market segmentation. Before, every user of energy had to buy from the same sources—mostly regulated monopoly utilities—and had their energy delivered in the same way at roughly the same price. The system was basically a conduit for energy producers to sell their output. That was extremely inefficient, since users have such different needs and preferences.

Today, deregulation and the opening of markets has made it possible for users to assert their individual preferences. That's opened a tremendous opportunity for companies to customize energy services to meet the needs of specific customers. We at U.S. Energy interact with customers, find out what they need, and construct energy systems to meet those needs.

Q: WHAT ADDED VALUE DO YOU PROVIDE FOR YOUR CUSTOMERS?

A: We can dramatically increase value in several ways. First, we can reduce costs by better tailoring customers' energy use to their needs. Generating on-site as we do also boosts reliability, particularly in areas where the grid-generated power has become somewhat unreliable. This is especially important for large industry, which simply can't afford to have their power shut off.

We can also help companies become less dependent on volatile-priced fuels by bringing in such sources as biomass. And we can increase their financial flexibility and ability to expand by forging a relationship with them to boost efficiency and/or reduce energy costs.

Most important, by converting a customer to cogeneration, we automatically double their fuel efficiency. That's because, unlike conventional generation, cogen uses the heat and steam produced by a power plant to generate even more electricity.

Most of our prospective clients are large companies, in many cases very big users of power, such as industry. That's where these advantages count the most, but the principle of tailoring a generation system to individual clients theoretically applies all the way down the value chain to smaller users as well.

Q: HOW DOES U.S. ENERGY USE GREEN ENERGY TO MEET ITS GOALS?

A: One of the biggest misconceptions about green energy is that it's somehow more costly or inefficient than conventional sources of generating electricity. What we've found is it can allow us to take power production inside a large user's operations, which is much more efficient because of reduced line losses and the elimination of transmission and distribution costs.

With our acquisition of ZAPCO, for example, we can now do a lot of things with biomass. One of these is the use of gas generated from waste dumps. ZAPCO gives us the ability to literally mine this gas, created by the decomposition of all sorts of things, to generate power.

Q: HOW DO YOU COPE WITH BEING A SMALL COMPANY IN AN INCREASINGLY COMPETITIVE INDUSTRY DOMINATED BY GIANTS?

A: First by focusing on individual customers. This keeps us competing in areas where we actually have the advantage over giants. Second, we've consciously set out to ally ourselves with our competitors, the utilities, for mutual gain.

Our alliance with Cinergy, for example, joins our technical and customer expertise with their deep pockets and marketing reach. It also gives us credibility in the financial markets, which we need to access in order to finance growth. Plus it gives them an additional growth vehicle.

As part of our alliance, Cinergy has taken an equity stake in U.S. Energy, and may buy more of our stock in coming years as our financing needs grow. We're also looking for other partners to help us sell our services and to increase our credibility in other markets, including Europe.

We now have the management team to literally tackle any market that's open and where customer segmentation is occurring. We know how to take advantage of deregulation in a cost-effective, clean, and environmentally responsible way, and we've got the pipeline of products under development to prove it.

....

CHAPTER 12

The Consumer's Guide
to Utility Deregulation

Every investor is also a utility customer. No matter where you live, the changes now transforming energy, communications, and water will affect your quality of life.

Unfortunately, what's happened thus far hasn't been good for most consumers. Most Americans haven't yet experienced the widespread blackouts that have hit California over the past couple of years. Power rates across the country have been volatile, though, especially in the West where the Golden State's growing energy shortage has dramatically tightened supplies from Idaho to Arizona. In the Northeast, rates have skyrocketed since the late 1990s as rising wholesale power costs have flowed directly through to consumer rates under deregulation plans.

Natural gas prices have fluctuated wildly in both winter and summer, as more gas-fired power plants have come on line. In 2000 and 2001, they averaged more than three times their levels of a couple of years ago, and the difference has gone straight into consumers' bills. The winter of 2000–2001 was a shocker for many, who saw their gas bills triple from the year before.

In communications, long-distance rates continue to decline for high-volume users, but, for everyone else, particularly low-volume users, they've soared. Cable television offers its high-end users more options than ever before, and basic cable rates on average have risen 33 percent since the Telecommunications Act of 1996.

Rates for basic as well as high-speed Internet service are starting to move higher, for both direct subscriber line (DSL) and
cable modem service. Fees imposed by regulators and the Bell
companies are sending local phone bills higher as well.

At the same time, phone service problems have mounted.
Orders for DSL service are sometimes filled months, not days,
later. According to the Federal Communications Commission,
the percentage of Americans dissatisfied with the quality of their
local phone service rose from 10.5 percent in 1997 to 17 percent
in 2000. The instances of slamming—customers involuntarily
switched from one service provider to another—are rising.

The problems are even worse for the poorest Americans and
those living in harder-to-serve, rural areas. Under the doctrine of
universal service, energy, communications, and water monopolies were required to provide a high level of service to everyone in
their service territory at reasonable rates. For the poorest of the
poor, that meant an effective subsidy paid for monthly by the federal government and pushing the costs to wealthier users. In general, large industrial users, and commercial users in particular,
paid more than they would otherwise have, given their buying
power. Small users paid less.

The rules of utility deregulation continue to pay lip service to
universal service, but the social compact has become badly frayed.
Energy and communications companies have focused on keeping
and broadening their business with their largest and most-
profitable customers. In contrast, less-profitable customers, especially low- to middle-income consumers, have been ignored.

Utilities' focus on their big customers was originally a defensive
action. Almost every new entrant in both energy and communications after deregulation has tried to cherry-pick the utilities'
most-profitable customers as the easiest way to make money, but
utility companies have also learned they can increase profits most
effectively by selling new services to their top customers. Because
the upstarts have ignored small consumers, they've discovered
they can afford to do so, as well.

In the days before the first utility investment boom, utility services existed only for a wealthy few. The rest of the world made do
with candles and lanterns for light, local water supplies, and, on

rare occasions, telegraph messages. The price of utility services was hardly relevant to the quality of life. Today, most of us live in or around big cities where power, communications, and clean water services are critical.

The effect of this quantum shift in utility service buying power therefore amounts to a colossal transfer of wealth from the average citizen to the heaviest users of services. As with the utility companies themselves, those who don't find a way to get big fast are going to be at an increasing disadvantage. Some may drop out of the emerging new economy all together.

BUYER POWER

The consumer movement of the 1970s was founded on the premise of buyer power. No longer did consumers have to be helpless victims of a corporate America focused more on the immediate bottom line than quality and customer service. In case after case, the movement proved ordinary citizens could take on and beat entrenched power in their demand to get their money's worth.

Sometimes the weapons were the courts, but the most effective were those focused on buying power: individuals voting with their checkbooks and credit cards to shun inferior merchandise and service, rewarding companies that did the job right.

The best example was in the auto industry, where the Big Three oligopoly of GM, Ford, and Chrysler had grown used to being able to sell anything to the public, including vehicles shown to be dangerous. Using the popular Corvair as an example of a car that was "unsafe at any speed," a young Ralph Nader led a charge that dramatically increased awareness of the inferior products being pushed by the Big Three.

The Big Three were also way behind the curve when the energy crisis hit, driving up gas prices. Rather than immediately shifting to gas-saving cars, they kept pumping out the big guzzlers, almost oblivious to the public's changing attitudes and needs.

As a result, consumers voted with their money and began to buy Japanese and European cars that did meet their needs for gas savings, as well as superior quality and safety standards. Eventually American car companies—despite their immense influence on the U.S. government—were forced to respond, making safer cars that burned less gasoline. Also, despite their original protestations about how much the changes would wind up costing consumers, prices were reasonable.

Since the 1970s, savvy consumers have continued to impose the discipline of the market on corporate America with their buying power. *Consumer Reports* today has become a mainstream publication, helping anyone who wants to shop smart for anything from appliances to insurance policies.

The changes going on in the energy, water, and communications industries today have already hurt consumers. Some could wind up being a greater threat to public health than the Corvair and other faulty products of the 1970s. Figure 12.1 illustrates the growing number of complaints from Bell customers.

But utility deregulation is also one of the best opportunities for consumers and businesses alike to exercise their buying power. No longer are Americans forced to buy the same level of service at the same price. Even in areas of little competition like local phone service, there are options as well as opportunities to band together to demand better.

The key is recognizing what's going on in these industries: consolidation accompanied by a major investment boom that's needed to take the world into the emerging economy of the

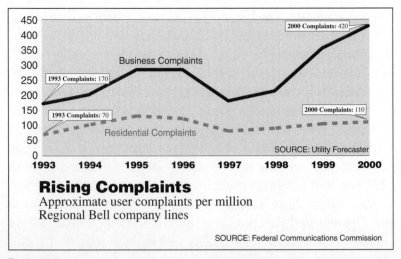

Rising Complaints
Approximate user complaints per million
Regional Bell company lines

SOURCE: Federal Communications Commission

Figure 12.1

twenty-first century. Knowledge is the key to taking advantage of change, rather than being taken advantage of.

VILLAINS AND VICTIMS

Unfortunately, many of today's most vocal consumer advocates—including some who led the buyer-power revolution of the 1970s—are not focused on the possibilities for deregulation. For many, fighting energy and communications deregulation is part of a crusade to expunge 20 years of unbridled corporate greed.

Viewed in this light, deregulation is actually a fairly simple story. Like any fairy tale, there's a readily identifiable villain—utilities—who have fallen prey to capitalism's inevitable temptation of corporate greed. The clear victims are the American public, the less fortunate in particular, who are being forced to pay unreasonable rates.

In this story, government action is the only way out. Deregulation must be reversed. The utility villains must give up all their ill-gotten gains and the American public will live happily ever after, as we return to the good old days of cost-based regulation.

This story has not been a difficult sell, particularly in California. Governor Gray Davis himself has picked up the ball and run with it, excoriating owners of the state's power plants as "out-of-state pirates" who are creating misery in the name of boosting profits, even as he negotiates with them. A referendum making its way to the state's 2002 ballot, which threatens state expropriation of utility systems, is gaining popularity.

The tragedy is the threats and finger-pointing can only make a bad situation worse. Simply, if you need investment, the worst thing you can do is to scare it away by threatening to confiscate property. That's the hard lesson learned by developing world government officials and policymakers in the 1960s and 70s. They had the power to nationalize foreign-owned assets in everything from utilities to mining; once they did, they had to come up with the capital to keep them going. Many were set back decades in their efforts to modernize.

The critics are clearly right that there's a lot wrong with the way the transition to deregulation has been handled. One reason is that many of the regulators and politicians—most of whom were otherwise very intelligent people—had little understanding of what they were doing.

Alarmingly, that remains true. In early 2001, a survey conducted by credit-rater Standard & Poor's found that many of the regulators who crafted deregulation legislation were unfamiliar even with the concept of demand elasticity. In other words, their plans took no account of how changes in electricity rates would influence consumers' use. In addition, many felt overwhelmed by the issues related to industry restructuring.

Far-reaching legislation was enacted in an almost religious leap of faith that opening markets would increase competition, bringing down utility rates and improving service. Those from the old monopoly systems who raised concerns were treated with scorn as the "just say no" crowd. Examples of huge rate cuts in Argentina and Britain were held up as shining examples of what would happen here, if those in authority just had the courage to act.

As the momentum for change increased, even those who knew better threw in their lot with the deregulators. Utilities such as John Bryson's Edison International stopped trying to block change and instead focused on getting the best deal for themselves during the transition.

Throughout the entire process, everyone forgot their Economics 101: When you change the pricing on a fixed-price service to a commodity, you open it up to the laws of supply and demand. Prices can come down, but they can also rise.

In their rush to try to bring down rates by any means possible, regulators, politicians, consumers, and their advocates forgot that there had been virtually no new investment in energy supply for nearly 20 years. In their blind faith in the magic of markets, they forgot what markets do. A commodity's price will rise sharply if a big boost in demand occurs—in this case from e-commerce—when supplies are tight.

As for finger-pointing, everyone can take a piece of the blame for what's gone wrong since. In California, former Governor Pete Wilson, his staff, and all who advised him are at fault for crafting a plan that had no basis in sound economics. His successor, Gray Davis, has been unwilling to pay the political price needed to defuse the crisis. Instead, he delayed until both Edison and PG&E were on the brink of bankruptcy. Then he enacted an alphabet soup of measures that only angered everyone, even while searching feverishly for scapegoats.

Even the consumer advocates are to blame. They, as well as big industrial companies, were swayed by promises of lower rates and are now paying the price of their folly. So are the state's utilities, which were sucked into a deal when they knew better. Environmental advocates who choked off new power plant and gas pipeline construction throughout the 1990s must wear a hair shirt as well.

The generating companies can't entirely be faulted for shutting down plants for maintenance or to comply with emissions limits. In the extremely volatile environment of 2000, there was almost certainly some gaming going on to tweak prices and profits higher. Now they're paying the price by having to write off hundreds of millions of dollars due to PG&E's early 2001 bankruptcy, and they face a real threat from California's attempt to shake them down for billions of dollars.

This is a story where everyone is a villain and a victim at the same time. What lies at the root of the problem is 20 years of underinvestment in America's energy, communications, and water infrastructure. There's no Blofeldt tucked away on some volcanic island, plotting world domination and waiting for a real-life James Bond to take him down. Only a sustained wave of investment will bring down prices and restore service quality.

In fairness, there's little that consumer advocates can do to boost the investment wave, though they can discourage it by fighting to turn the clock back on change. Despite the cherished arguments of public power advocates, state governments—at least outside of California—will not foot the bill by nationalizing systems. Neither will the federal government, which has already committed whatever surplus will emerge in the next 10 years to tax cuts, social spending, and a defense buildup.

What consumer groups can do is use the turmoil of the transition to reassert the principles of consumer buying power, but that won't keep electricity, natural gas, communications, and water rates from rising in coming years. In fact, the higher prices go in the near-term, the more money will flow into these industries, and the faster the investment deficit will be wiped out. Consumer groups can make a huge difference whether average consumers get hit with the whole tab, or just their fair share.

The other key consumer issue is the environment. Technological advances and rising natural gas prices have brought us closer than ever to generating cost-competitive renewable energy. Again, it's a matter of spending the money to further bring down costs in wind, biomass, geothermal, and solar power. If not, the historically cheaper route of building plants run on natural gas, clean coal, and possibly nuclear energy has plenty of advocates, particularly in the Bush administration.

Whether groups like Consumers Union or Public Citizen's Critical Mass will seize this opportunity remains to be seen, but there are several things that individual consumers can do to tilt the odds of deregulation in their favor. Note that the consumer movement does recommend most of the following four tips.

TIP #1: TAKE CONTROL OF WHAT YOU'RE PAYING FOR AND WHOM YOU'RE PAYING

Most people know the name of their power company, but not one in a thousand can say where or how the electricity they use is generated.

In the old days of monopolies, that hardly mattered. In the postderegulation era, your power company might simply be a T&D company that buys its electricity from one of the major generating companies. The ultimate rate you wind up paying will depend on the generator's costs and, more important, what it can charge its wholesale customers like your T&D company.

If you live in a state that hasn't opened its doors to competition, you have little choice of where your power comes from or what you pay for it. If you're in one of the two dozen states that has opened its market, it's critical to know the hows, whats, and wheres.

The best source of information is your bill. In the monopoly era, power and natural gas bills were summed up by a single figure, which included the cost of generating electricity, purchasing gas, and sending them over wires and pipes to your home, as well as network maintenance. The postderegulation bill breaks that down into several separate charges. In most states, there are now separate items for taxes and fees; the distribution charge, which includes the cost of running the network; and the cost of the energy itself, which may be provided by the utility or an outside marketer.

You can't avoid the distribution charge and taxes, which are generally fixed to all customers, but you may be able to have an impact on the energy cost, depending on whom you buy from. Consequently, you owe it to yourself to shop the alternatives, principally retail marketers.

One of the largest of these is New Power Corporation (customer service 877-901-7059). As a subsidiary of energy giant Enron, the company has access to its parent's power-trading portfolio, which should help it to hold down costs. Enron's financial power is another key strength, as are the company's strategic alliances with IBM and America On Line. Another major marketer is Green Mountain Energy, which is backed by oil giant BP.

In the past few years, several unregulated marketers in California, Georgia, and New England have gone out of business, leaving their customers high and dry. There are many ways a marketer can go belly-up. Hooking up with a creditworthy marketer who has the backing of a major energy company can save you a lot of grief.

Note that conservation, making your home more energy-efficient, is the surest way to take control of your energy bill. Buying more energy-efficient lights and appliances are two of the most time-tested ways to be green without changing your lifestyle.

In communications, knowing what you're buying and whom you're buying from can be considerably more complicated. For one thing, there are many more items to a bill. Keeping up with spending can be especially complex for those who use wireless phones, cable television, and the Internet, as well as basic local and long-distance telephone service. The wealthiest 24 percent of the American population tend to be the largest communications spenders, as shown in Figure 12.2.

As with power and gas, every bill includes taxes and fees that are unavoidable. Everything else, however, can be controlled at least to some extent by smart shopping. For services like wireless,

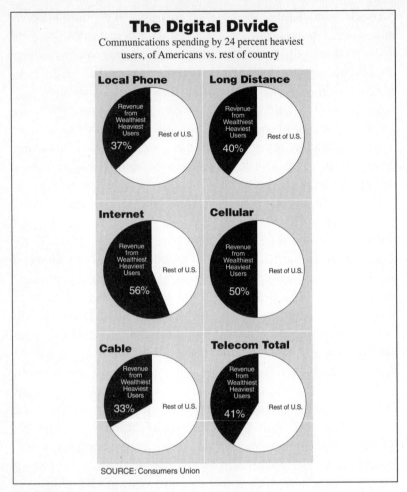

Figure 12.2

long distance, and the Internet, there are now several major competitors. Even a call to your current provider can cut your cost considerably, if you do nothing else but have the representative find a plan that better suits your lifestyle.

Cable television remains a monopoly, but it too has competition, notably from satellite providers. A cable bill will include taxes and other fees, but the bulk of your bill is what service you have chosen. Compare the channels and services you're getting with what a satellite-based carrier would provide. If it's a better deal, take it.

Local phone monopolies have controlled 95 percent–plus of their market since deregulation, and given the demise of their competitors, they're likely to stay in control in the years ahead. That doesn't mean, however, that you need to pay for everything they want to sell you. You can cut your bill by subscribing to the following only if you really use them: call waiting, call forwarding, call return, caller ID, call tracing, priority ringing, repeat dialing, speed calling, three-way calling, and inside wire maintenance service.

Slamming is the questionable practice of switching a consumer to a new long-distance phone company without permission. The victims are almost always placed on the slammer's highest-priced plans. To avoid this, The Utility Reform Network (TURN) advises consumers to request a separate bill for long-distance service. Alternatively, in some states, as in California, you can ask your local phone company to give you primary interexchange carrier protection.

In either case, there's no substitute for at least scanning your communications bill before you pay it. That's also the only way to avoid cramming, that is, being charged for services you haven't ordered.

TIP #2: ORGANIZE WHENEVER POSSIBLE

Size means strength in the deregulated utility industry. That goes for consumers as well. Basically, the more you buy, the greater your buying power. Just as utility companies are merging to get stronger, consumers who join forces will boost their buying power in the marketplace.

The evidence that size is critical is everywhere. Residential consumers in California, for example, paid prices several times higher for natural gas in 2000 than did industrial consumers. The reason: Big industrial consumers use a lot more gas, making them far cheaper and therefore more profitable to serve. A similar price disparity exists between big and small users' electricity and water rates, for the same reason.

In communications, a 2001 study by Consumers Union points to a growing digital divide between high-volume users of services, who are mostly well-heeled, and low-volume users, who are not. In the study, high-volume or premier users make about 60 percent of long-distance phone calls, but they pay far less per call than lower-volume customers. The reason: As valued, high-volume customers, the phone companies offered them a better rate to keep their business and to encourage more volume.

Most of the 76 percent of the public that are not high-volume customers of the communications companies can't afford to become high-volume users on their own, and residential and small business customers by themselves will never consume the kilowatts sucked down by large industrial and commercial concerns. By banding together with others in the same boat, however, even the poorest and lowest-volume user can become a virtual giant in terms of buying power.

With the help of TURN, citizens of the Almaden Valley of San Jose, California, recently took matters into their own hands to improve energy and telephone utility service. Rebuffed by local providers PG&E and PacBell in efforts to replace overloaded power and phone lines, they formed a neighborhood group—Almaden Valley Citizens for Responsible Utilities (AVCRUT)—to increase public awareness of the problem, and held a news conference that drew the attention of local media and politicians. In the end, utilities acted to improve service to save face in the community.

Not everybody can be Erin Brockovich, and not every community has the means to organize the way Almaden Valley did, but, in an era where regulators are increasingly scrutinizing service at distribution utilities, communities that do unite to act are more likely than ever to get action. AVCRUT suggests the following steps:

- *Document the problem.* Define what's wrong and what the cause is, as clearly as possible. State the damage to the community and what can be done to fix it.

- *Create an organization.* Assign key people to gather information to report back to the committee on the different elements of the problem, and meet regularly.

- *Consider several approaches to fixing the problem.* These should include developing statements and petitions to forward to government agencies, gaining the support of local politicians, contacting consumer groups like TURN, holding public meetings, and engaging the press.

- *Regularly assess your plan's progress with weekly meetings.* Develop open lines of communications with the utilities to demonstrate a willingness to work cooperatively, but maintain the momentum of your plan to maximize leverage.

Any large agglomeration of people—whether it be a condominium organization, an apartment building, an office building, or a cooperative—should consider organizing to buy utility services together. In some cases, this won't be practical, but those who make it work will at a minimum dramatically increase their bargaining power with their current provider. Citizens of several Ohio towns, for example, were able to gain lower rates and clean energy by aggregating and signing a deal with Green Mountain Energy, and New Power Corp. is also launching a product to encourage aggregating.

Industrial companies may find themselves large enough to contract a company like U.S. Energy Systems, which is in the business of meeting the energy needs of large, individual clients with specialized solutions. Such an arrangement can save a lot of money, and it gives the user control over where the energy comes from.

At some point, Congress is certain to act to help consumers increase their buying power in postderegulation markets. In 1999, seven Democrats in the U.S. House of Representatives introduced the Community Choice bill, designed to make it easier for consumers and small businesses to form aggregating units by working with municipalities to gain buying power for utility services. Similar legislation is likely to pass in coming years as deregulation unfolds.

TIP #3: IF YOU BELIEVE IN RENEWABLE ENERGIES, BUY GREEN

Four years ago, the consensus on both Wall Street and Main Street was that organic food was a passing fad, something health-conscious consumers would buy for awhile and then switch back to lower-cost traditional foods. Businesses like Fresh Fields were given little chance of ever competing with the Safeways and Giants of the supermarket world.

Today, the organic food movement is one of the fastest-growing sectors in American business. Many people, it seems, do care about what they eat. Now that they have the option to buy something grown without potentially dangerous pesticides, they're taking advantage, even if it means paying more.

Nonpolluting or green energy has had to climb a similar wall of worry. A majority of Americans agree there is a pollution problem that must be dealt with, but many still doubt there's a market for high-priced, renewable energy sources, especially when cheaper electricity is available, generated from conventional fuels like natural gas or coal (see Figure 12.3).

Enter the green electricity movement, which is using deregulated markets to sell renewable energy directly to consumers. Consumers in California and several northeastern states now have the opportunity to buy energy generated from wind, biomass, geothermal, solar, and other renewable sources, though at a premium price.

The actual electrons used by green consumers aren't necessarily from any of these sources, but buying from green marketers does create demand for renewable energy on the power grid. As the demand increases, so will the available green capacity to meet it.

The biggest problem renewable resources have had historically is cost, and despite great strides made in efficiency in the past two decades—particularly in Europe—that's still true. What's needed

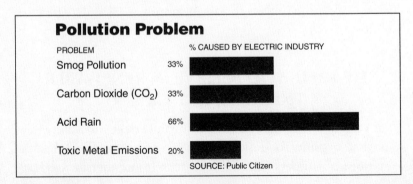

Figure 12.3

is investment in the technology, which will occur if there's a demonstrated demand for the product.

The time is ripe: Rising natural gas prices have made sources like wind power more competitive than ever on a standalone basis. Companies like FPL, Scottish Power, UtiliCorp, and others are building giant wind farms based on advanced technology in several states. These plants will only become more competitive in coming years. In addition, several states have mandated the use of renewable fuels on their power grids, a move that was originally treated as a burden but which marketers are beginning to embrace wholeheartedly as gas prices move higher.

Green marketers have drawn a great deal of criticism, with some of the harshest words coming from environmentalists. Public Citizen's Critical Mass points out that there's no direct relationship between boosting green marketing sales and increasing the output of renewable energies. That's because most sales now come from existing plants owned by utilities rather than new facilities constructed to meet the green demand. California's largest green marketer Green Mountain Energy, for example, gets 90 percent of its renewable power from Scottish Power subsidiary PacifiCorp and only 10 percent from its own sources.

Other complaints about green marketing include the cost of selling itself, which subtracts from funds that could be spent to develop more renewable energy. In addition, there's no national tracking system to verify green product claims, that is, that marketers actually do draw on wind or solar, and many marketers' promises are based on projections of future capacity. Also, plans for green plants nationwide are lagging well behind those for gas plants.

The point, however, is not the failure of green marketing to have an immediate impact on renewable energy output, but that over time a demonstrated demand for green energy on the part of the public—combined with enforcement to ensure renewables are truly being sold—will boost growth in renewable energy use. That in turn will reduce dependence on fossil fuels and other polluting energy sources.

Merchant energy companies are in business to make money. If they can sell renewable energy at a premium price, they'll do it, especially if it limits exposure to increasingly volatile fossil fuel prices. Companies like Enron are interested in wind because it is becoming more price-competitive and will be even more so as natural gas prices continue to rise in coming years.

Signing up for green energy programs is the one sure way to send a signal that there's money to be made in the sector. Despite the Bush administration's preference for fossil fuels, the merchant generators will make it happen. It's also worth noting that big oil companies like BP and Royal Dutch Shell are becoming some of the world's biggest investors in renewables. That's a clear sign the energy industry's biggest players view them as the future in a coming era when global competition for fossil fuels intensifies with emerging countries like China.

Scrutinize a green marketer just as thoroughly as you would any other energy seller in a deregulated market place. Again, the best bets are companies that are tied to large industry players, such as New Power Holdings and Green Mountain Energy. Enron is also one of the leading players in wind power in the United States, giving its unit strong technical and financial backing, and Green Mountain is backed by oil giant BP. The only drawback with New Power is it operates mostly in the Northeast. Enron itself withdrew its retail marketing effort from California several years ago.

The bigger the market for clean energy is perceived to be, the more money will be invested in research to cut the cost. Government has historically filled this role, but given the current state of affairs in Washington, it's not likely to take the lead this time around. Instead, the best hope for alternate energies to be developed in this country—instead of Europe, Japan, or China—lies in the private sector.

You don't have to chain yourself to the fence outside of Exxon-Mobil's corporate headquarters, but if you own stock and want to promote green energy, vote for the shareholder initiatives that appear on the ballots of big energy companies every year to encourage their development. These initiatives almost always lose. Coupled with a demonstrated growing market in green energy, however, they do send a signal to management that their owners are greening and that there's a market out there to be won.

TIP #4: USE THE INTERNET FOR INFORMATION

Deregulation has occurred at the same time the Internet has exploded as a communications medium. As a result, anyone with a computer can access a mountain of consumer-based information about changes in the communications and energy industry.

All the major consumer advocates are making use of the Internet. The bad news is much of their effort is still focused on how to stop deregulation, rather than how to shape it, but they're also compiling a great deal of information on the various pitfalls awaiting consumers in the marketplace.

Public Citizen (www.citizen.org), for example, has published a range of reports on the practices of California's green marketers. Despite the overall negative tone, there is some good information for those looking for a marketer. TURN (www.turn.org) offers Californians advice on how to interpret their phone and power bills.

Both organizations and Consumers Union (www.consumers union.org) are excellent sources for keeping abreast of utility legislation that will affect consumers. They offer contact points for getting involved on issues of concern, and can also be valuable sources of information for those attempting to organize for size.

The best use of the Internet in coming years is likely to be for pricing utility services. Just as Enron has pioneered cyberspace for high-volume trading in everything from energy to communications bandwidth, so has it become possible for consumers in deregulated markets to price their energy options on the Web.

One such service is www.wattagemonitor.com. Consumers log on by zip code and receive information on the energy options in their region, as well as on how available rates compare with the local utility. It's an excellent starting point for researching a retail energy marketer.

....

INDUSTRY PROFILE: TYSON SLOCUM

Since its inception in 1971, Public Citizen—founded by Ralph Nader—has built a reputation as the nation's foremost champion of consumer rights, fighting for everything from safe automobiles to affordable insurance rates. Forged from a series of meetings of anti–nuclear power activists in the early 1980s, Public Citizen's Critical Mass Energy & Environment Program has brought that passion to the energy industry and today is a major advocate for consumers' rights under deregulation.

As Critical Mass's senior researcher on energy issues, Tyson Slocum brings a resume that includes advocacy for a wide range of tax policy and consumer issues. He and his team are charged with compiling the data and analysis needed to articulate the organization's positions. Slocum is also the organization's chief spokesperson on electricity and natural gas deregulation, as well as on oil and nuclear policy.

Q: WHAT ARE THE KEY CONSUMER ISSUES WITH
    ENERGY DEREGULATION?

A: The clearest problem is a lack of public accountability on the part of the corporations. The fact that Governor Davis has had to ask President Bush to help out California is a dead giveaway that deregulation is anti–states' rights. Essentially, once a state elects to break up its utility monopolies, it's voluntarily giving up control over its wholesale power market to the Federal Energy Regulatory Commission (FERC). As a result, California and the other deregulating states are now powerless to control wholesale markets, barring the seizure of power plants. They've literally handed over the keys to the system to a handful of corporations who decide how much power to sell for how much and to whom.

California is suffering rolling blackouts because the state can no longer force power plant owners to sell electricity to consumers. The biggest risk is there's no longer any control over pricing of a critical commodity, in an industry that's not very conducive to competitive markets. That's because consumers simply don't have a choice about whether to use a core amount of electricity for their primary needs throughout the day.

Q: HOW CAN CONSUMERS INCREASE THEIR CONTROL OVER THE MARKET WITH BUYING POWER?

A: The problem is, after the industry consolidation we've seen, consumers don't really have a lot of choices. That's why my first advice to the consumer is to take back their government from the corporate special interests. The antitrust regime has been tilted to corporations at consumers' expense since the 1980s. There may be some benefits from deregulation, particularly in telecom, but there have also clearly been problems. That's why it's extremely important that consumer protection be carried out on a government level.

The one way some consumers have been able to exercise control is by municipal aggregation. This is basically when consumers pool their buying power into a single, huge, purchasing unit, which gives them the leverage to get better deals. The only successful model thus far is in Ohio, a state which has community choice.

Over 100 cities and towns in the Cleveland area voted in 1999 to form a municipal aggregation. They recently signed a deal with energy marketer Green Mountain Energy that provides slightly lower electric rates, as well as environmental benefits. These consist of a commitment to build eight windmill farms within the aggregation unit, a plan to produce pilot solar programs, and a switch to natural gas from coal, all under a long-term contract to control the price consumers will pay.

Aggregation has the potential to become a model for consumers nationwide. The main obstacle to its success is a lack of competing sellers of power in a truly competitive wholesale market. Without real competition, aggregation won't help consumers.

Q: HOW CAN ENERGY CONSUMERS GO GREEN?

A: The easiest and most effective way is to aggregate like the Ohio municipalities did. This depends on the state-by-state status of retail competition, as well as on the availability of green energy suppliers. One reason why only 1 percent of consumers are eligible to switch energy providers is that there are so few viable options.

Distributed generation based on renewable energy also has considerable potential and may wind up being more practical. One positive effect of the California crisis is that it has increased the awareness of consumers, cities, and businesses of the benefits of reducing dependence on grid-generated power. That's increased use of distributed generation from sources such as solar and wind, particularly for peak-demand uses.

Q: WHICH CONSUMER PROTECTIONS IS PUBLIC CITIZEN ADVOCATING NOW?

A: First, we want to see a moratorium on deregulation, because we do not have competitive wholesale power markets. Second, we want FERC to start exercising its enormous power to ensure open markets. As California shows, electricity markets are vulnerable to gaming, price gouging, and collusion. Third, we want an end to market pricing and a return to cost-based rates, in which producers can charge only what it costs to generate power, plus a modest return of 10 percent on capital. That's basically what we had before this out-of-control experiment was launched.

Incidentally, the natural gas industry is going through the same kind of thing now. The fact that gas pipeline and transportation companies have such control over what supplies get to market is what's behind the lawsuits in California, Missouri, and other places. Again, states are powerless to prevent the use of market power by corporations, and FERC is not doing its job in policing these markets. Public Citizen is a strong believer in the ability of markets to bring benefits to society. But we believe that government is necessary to ensure that those markets are fair and competitive. Government has a duty to make sure we've got adequate competition.

Q: ARE WE HEADED FOR GRIDLOCK IN FEDERAL ENERGY POLICY?

A: That's tough to predict, but one thing I will forecast is this crisis will get worse. The president's energy policy is very irresponsible and won't be that successful. I do think the proposal to drill in the Alaska National Wildlife Refuge is a distraction and will be used as leverage to open up other public lands to drilling.

Bush's plan does contain some fairly radical proposals regarding the federalization of energy markets. Basically, FERC would gain the power of eminent domain to locate power plants and power lines, taking the whole issue out of local hands. That would be the biggest step yet toward deregulation's biggest goal, which is states ceding control of wholesale markets to FERC. It's ironic that the Republicans—who made states' rights their policy centerpiece during the 1990s—are now taking such an anti–states' rights stance on energy.

Nuclear power is another area where the administration seems determined to push forward. There's a very sophisticated lobbying campaign and a lot of money involved here. The industry still hasn't overcome either the long- or short-term problem of dealing with nuclear waste, or how to cite new plants, but it's certainly not out of the realm of possibility to see new units built. Four companies have already applied for new plant permits, and the Nuclear Regulatory Commission's entire permitting process could be altered to shut out public concerns altogether. We have to also remember that nuclear power is prohibitively expensive. It costs $2,080 per kilowatt/hour to generate electricity with nuclear, compared to $1,200 per kilowatt/hour with coal and $500 per kilowatt/hour with natural gas.

....

Making Change Your Friend

Politics is the art of compromise. In our American democracy, the ultimate resolution of any problem or issue boils down to a working agreement between the warring parties, no matter how strident and intractable positions may seem to be or how powerful the players.

Because they're especially high-profile and essential to modern life, energy, communications, and water utilities have always been especially dependent on politics to maintain peace between the parties. When a clearly stated set of rules has prevailed, the system has worked well. Consumers and businesses have enjoyed solid service and reasonable rates. Utilities have enjoyed the certitude that a job well done will be rewarded with a fair return.

On the other hand, when the rules have broken down, nothing works well. In a worst case, systems are thrown into chaos until a new compact is agreed to.

At this crucial juncture, the country is engaged in a hot debate over the future of utility deregulation. On one side are most industry players anxious to reap the profits from the newly opened market, backed most visibly by the Bush administration and its allies in Congress. On the other are a growing array of deregulation critics including environmentalists, consumer advocates, and even some utilities, backed most visibly by Congressional Democrats and California Governor Gray Davis.

Proponents—particularly the aggressive new breed of utility managers that have taken over in the past five years—include some of the most capable and knowledgeable people the industry has ever seen. They see clearly the possibilities of ongoing changes.

Today's bigger, stronger utilities increasingly have the ability to respond to supply/demand crises by marshaling and deploying resources on a scale that would have been impossible under the old monopoly system. Companies are free to meet the unique needs of customers, who have the ability to pick and choose the services they want and how they want them delivered. Particularly in communications, consumers also have the ability to seek the best price, rather than one set by regulators.

Under the old system, even the most incompetent utility management could draw multimillion-dollar salaries, simply by keeping all-powerful local regulators happy. The most skillful were restricted by often-intrusive bureaucracy, which in many cases actually discouraged or prohibited them from making needed changes.

Under deregulation, the market punishes poor performance. Wrong decisions have consequences for companies and their shareholders, just as great moves are richly rewarded. The industry is no longer a haven for company men who just want to collect a rising paycheck until retirement. Instead, it's attracting some of the best and brightest men and women.

Ultimately, that means better service for all Americans. That's been the experience of the nearly two dozen nations who have deregulated their energy and communications and opened their water systems to private investment.

Deregulation's critics see the shortcomings of recent changes: rising rates for basic services; declining service quality, particularly for those further down the socioeconomic ladder; the concentration of industry power in the hands of a few very powerful companies; the lack of oversight from local authorities; and, most recently, the wave of blackouts, bankruptcies, and spiking prices for electricity and natural gas that's plagued California.

Some advocate turning back the clock to the old monopoly era, when regulators, not the market, decided what the price of electricity, natural gas, and other essential services should be. Some favor a direct public takeover of utility property along the lines of developing-world nationalizations in the 1960s and 70s.

Others prescribe more moderate measures, such as capping the commodity element of services—that is, wholesale electricity prices—or intervening in the market itself to tilt the playing field to encourage more competition, leaving the essence of deregulation intact.

In many ways, the battle over deregulation is part of a wider struggle over the future of the world economy. To resolve it, we have to answer the question of how far market forces should be allowed to shape events without some government intervention in the interest of the general public.

Is there a right amount of regulation, or are we better off as a society with as few rules as possible constraining investment? The resolution will determine everything from the future of economic globalization to the shape of our future health care system. And nothing is more important to the future than the fate of the energy, communications and, water industries.

PROBABILITIES

Few foresaw how bad the power crisis in California would become. Forecasting how the debate over utility deregulation will be resolved is even more of a guessing game.

One reason is because politics is shaped by personalities. Will Gray Davis survive the California gubernatorial election in November 2002 to continue his battle against the utilities? Will the Democratic Senate Majority Leader Tom Daschle block the president's agenda, or will Mr. Bush and his allies find a way to retake Congress' upper chamber?

Proderegulation FCC Chairman Michael Powell will likely be a major force shaping communications over the next three years, but his chief adversary, the wily and skeptical Senator Ernest Hollings (D-SC), may prove to be more than a match. Similarly, the battle over environmental regulation between proenvironment members of Congress and EPA chief Christine Whitman could speed or slow the shift in power to private water utilities from the muni monopoly.

In energy, much of the future may be written by something as mundane as the weather. Cool summers may allow industry the time it needs to build enough power plant capacity to prevent a repeat of the dramatic price spikes of 2000. A cool spell in California in summer 2001, for example, triggered a dramatic dip in the state's electricity prices, far below levels thought possible only weeks before.

Several aspects of this debate, however, are relatively certain. First, a compromise is the only real way anything is going to happen. Both sides are capable of blocking action by the other, at least until the November 2002 congressional elections, and very likely until the 2004 presidential election.

Second, there's a clear incentive to do something. The unprecedented terrorist attacks on Wall Street and the Pentagon on September 11, 2001, have increased public awareness about the inadequacy of America's energy, water, and even communications infrastructure. In its immediate aftermath, politicians in both parties seem determined to take a wide range of actions to encourage investment, ranging from removing regulations to tax incentives.

Parts of Bush's original 2001 energy plan—particularly the more controversial aspects such as promoting nuclear energy and drilling in the Alaska National Wildlife Refuge (ANWR)—will probably be bottled up in Congress. Neither will deregulation critics be able to roll back deregulation on a wide scale across the country. Even price caps on electricity prices are likely to be muted by FERC, given the president's recent proderegulation appointees. Sweeping legislation further deregulating telecommunications will also have a tough time getting to the floor, just as proregulation bills are certain to be vetoed by the president.

The battle between Davis and the merchant energy companies in his state will almost certainly continue. Other states will closely watch the action in California for clues on whether to open their markets. The regulation and deregulation of the nation's dilapidated power transmission systems meanwhile will accelerate as the FERC forces consolidation of the grid and attempts to wield ever-greater enforcement powers.

In this book, I've presented the problems brought by deregulation, and how they originated in a lack of understanding about what it really means: Opening markets doesn't automatically cut rates or improve service. It simply ensures investment will flow where it's needed most. The money flows the easiest through big powerful companies and benefits mostly those with the greatest buying power.

I've also espoused my own belief that, if allowed to flower, new investment brought by utility industry deregulation will bring immense benefits for consumers as well as for investors. And it's the best way to ensure our essential services against the threat of terrorism as well. Conversely, it's also my view that reregulation would cripple the energy, communications, and water sectors, drying up badly needed investment and ultimately triggering far worse shortages, higher prices, and declining service quality. I also believe there are numerous opportunities for consumers to profit from deregulation, from aggregating to increased buying power to simply shopping smarter for services.

My reason for writing *Power Hungry*, however, is not to be an advocate for a particular policy or industry. It's to help investors and consumers navigate this new and increasingly uncertain era. That means looking at what's likely to happen, rather than my opinion of what should.

For investors, the key point is—regardless of what the politicians do—there's a critical need for investment in energy, water, and communications. As a result, the utility industry is in the beginning stages of an investment boom that has a long way to run. The almost certain winners are the largest, best-positioned, well-heeled, and most aggressively managed players. There will also be more takeovers, as price competition forces energy, communications, and water companies to become ever more efficient, and executives strive to maximize returns.

Government action or inaction could theoretically slow down any of these trends. For example, we could see legislation designed to make it a lot tougher for utilities to merge. Caps on utility rates, lawsuits, and even confiscation of utility property are possible. Equally, the Bush administration is likely to promote deregulation wherever it can, both administratively and by utilizing its own influence with the public, industry, and Congress to shape events.

Ultimately, one of three things will happen. Most likely, the seriousness of the situation will overwhelm the politics leading to a compromise that incorporates the best ideas from each side. It's also possible proderegulation forces could take back the U.S. Senate, either in the 2002 election or before, through a party switch, or that antideregulation forces will succeed in whipping up enough popular sentiment to gain power over energy policy.

Even if there's no consensus, nothing is likely to happen to slow the pace of change, at least for the next few years. As long as that's the case, the investment strategies in this book should be extremely profitable. So will the strategies for consumers detailed in Chapter 12.

There's no doubt we live in interesting times. For three generations, Americans enjoyed the stability—some would say stagnation—of regulated utility stock returns and service. Today, things are no longer certain. Volatile markets present dangers to both consumer and investor that were never dreamed of during the monopoly era.

This is also a time, however, of unmatched opportunity for consumers to shape the way we get our energy, communications, and water. For the first time ever, we can use our paycheck power to ensure development of renewable resources in the free market. It's also a time when investors can cash in on the new decade's most promising investment opportunity in perhaps the most secure industries of all.

The key to making change your friend is knowledge. This book doesn't have all the answers. Rather, this is an unfolding story whose lines are constantly being rewritten. My only hope is this book has provided some enlightenment on these critical issues, and perhaps a gateway to further exploration. Ultimately, that's the only way we'll all become better essential-service investors and consumers.

APPENDIX 1
Utility Data Bank

Diversified Energy Utilities

STOCK (SYMBOL)	CO/DRIP PHONE	WORLD WIDE WEB SITE	ASSETS (BILLIONS)	PAYOUT	REGS/RELS/ DEREGULATED	TOP EXEC (AGE, SERVICE)	RATING (BUS POS, CFC, OUTLOOK)	CRITERIA MET	DRIP/ PURCHASE	APPROX DIV DATES
AES Corp (AES)	703-522-1315	aes.com	$31.00	0.0%	IL, FERC/good/all	Bakke (55, 14)	BB (none, no, positive)	4	no, no	none
Allegheny Energy (AYE)	800-648-8389	alleghenyenergy.com	7.70	60.6	MD, FERC/good/all	Noia (53, 6)	A (5, no, stable)	7	yes^, yes	M, J, S, D—1
Allete (ALE)	800-535-3056	allete.com	2.91	64.1	MN/good/none	Russell (56, 5)	BBB+ (7, yes, stable)	4	yes^, yes#* ($250)	M, J, S, D—1
Alliant Energy (LNT)	800-356-5343	alliant-energy.com	6.73	81.3	WI, IA/average/partly	Davis (56, 11)	A+ (5, no, negative)	5	yes^, yes#* ($250)	F, M, A, N—15
American Elec Power (AEP)	800-551-1237	aep.com	54.55	88.9	TX, OH/average/partly	Draper (59, 9)	A— (4, yes, stable)	4	yes^, yes* ($250)	M, J, S, D—8
Ameren Corp (AEE)	800-255-2237	ameren.com	9.70	73.8	IL, MO/tough/partly	Mueller (63, 7)	A+ (5, yes, stable)	5	yes^, yes*	M, J, S, D—29
Black Hills Corp (BKH)	800-468-9716	bh-corp.com	1.32	47.3	SD, WY/good/none	Landguth (54, 10)	A (6, no, stable)	6	yes, yes#	M, J, S, D—1
CINergy Corp (CIN)	800-325-2945	cinergy.com	12.30	69.0	OH, IND/average/partly	Rogers (60, 6)	BBB+ (5, yes, negative)	6	yes^, yes	F, M, A, N—15
CLECO (CNL)	800-253-2652	cleco.com	1.85	58.4	LA/good/none	Eppler (50, 2)	BBB+ (6, no, negative)	6	yes^, yes#	F, M, A, N—15
CMS Energy (CMS)	517-788-1868	cmsenergy.com	16.00	57.7	MI/average/all	McCormick (56, 16)	BB (7, no, stable)	4	yes^, yes#* ($500)	F, M, A, N—22
Conectiv (CIV)	800-365-6495	conectiv.com	6.48	41.9	NJ, DE, MD/average/all	Cosgrove (57, 15)	BBB+ (7, no, developing)	5	yes^, yes#* ($500)	J, A, J, O—31
Constellation Energy (CEG)	800-258-0499	constellation.com	12.40	73.0	MD/average/all	Poindexter (62, 4)	A (5, yes, negative)	5	yes^, yes#	J, A, J, O—2
Dominion Resources (D)	800-552-4034	domres.com	29.40	77.5	VA, OH/good/all	Capps (65, 6)	BBB+ (5, yes, stable)	6	yes^, yes#* ($250)	M, J, S, D—20

Company	Phone	Website			State/Regulation	Contact (age, yrs)	Rating (score, dividend, outlook)		Proxy	Board mtg months
DP&L (DPL)	800-322-9244	dplinc.com	4.44	60.3	OH/good/all	Hill (55, 4)	BBB+ (5, no, developing)	7	yes^, yes	M, J, S, D—1
DTE Energy (DTE)	800-551-5009	dteenergy.com	1.27	58.2	MI/average/all	Earley (51, 6)	BBB (6, yes, stable)	4	yes^, yes* ($100)	J, A, J, O—15
Duke Energy (DUK)	800-488-3853	duke-energy.com	58.20	52.3	NC, SC/good/partly	Priory (54, 9)	A+ (6, no, negative)	6	yes^, yes#* ($250)	M, J, S, D—16
Dynegy (DYN)	713-507-6400	dynegy.com	21.42	21.0	FERC, IL/avg/all	Watson (51, 5)	BBB+ (7, no, stable)	4	yes^, yes#* ($250)	M, J, S, D—15
Edison Int'l (EIX)	800-347-8625	edisonx.com	36.23	0.0	CA/tough/all	Bryson (57, 10)	CC (6, no, negative)	0	yes^, yes#	none
El Paso Elec (EE+)	800-592-1634	epelectric.com	1.63	0.0	TX, NM/avg/partly	Haines (54, 5)	BBB— (6, yes, stable)	3	no, no	none
El Paso Energy (EPG)	713-757-2131	epenergy.com	27.45	31.6	FERC/average/all	Wise (55, 11)	BBB+ (5, no, stable)	6	yes, yes#	J, A, J, O—2
Empire District (EDE)	888-261-6784	empiredistrict.com	0.83	93.4	MO, ARK/average/none	McKinney (56, 10)	A— (5, no, negative)	3	yes^, yes#* ($250)	M, J, S, D—15
Enron Corp (ENE)	800-662-7662	enron.com	65.50	34.0	FERC/good/all	Lay (58, 15)	BBB+ (6, no, stable)	6	yes^, yes# ($250)	M, J, S, D—20
Entergy Corp (ETR)	888-368-3749	entergy.com	24.10	42.4	LA, TX/average/partly	Leonard (50, 3)	BBB (7, yes, positive)	5	yes^, yes* ($250)	M, J, S, D—1
Exelon Energy (EXC)	800-626-8729	exeloncorp.com	35.00	59.1	PA, IL/average/all	McNeil (61, 10)	A— (6, yes, stable)	5	yes^, yes# ($1000)	M, J, S, D—20
First Energy (FE)	800-736-3402	firstenergycorp.com	17.94	55.8	OH, PA/average/all	Burg (54, 2)	BB+ (8, yes, positive)	3	yes*, yes* ($250)	M, J, S, D—1
FPL Group (FPL)	888-375-1329	fplgroup.com	15.30	51.1	FL/good/none	Broadhead (65, 11)	AA— (5, no, negative)	6	yes^, yes# ($250)	M, J, S, D—15
Hawaiian Elec (HE)	808-532-5841	hei.com	8.47	175.9	HI/average/none	Clarke (58, 11)	BBB+ (7, yes, negative)	3	yes^, yes* ($250)	M, J, S, D—11
IdaCorp (IDA)	208-388-2200	idacorp.com	4.30	50.0	IDA, WA/good/none	Packwood (57, 2)	A+ (4, yes, stable)	6	yes^, yes# ($10)	F, M, A, N—30
Kansas City P&L (KLT)	800-245-5275	kcpl.com	3.40	71.9	MO/tough/none	Beaudoin (60, 1)	A— (6, yes, stable)	6	yes^, yes# ($500)	M, J, S, D—20

Diversified Energy Utilities (*Continued*)

STOCK (SYMBOL)	CO/DRIP PHONE	WORLD WIDE WEB SITE	ASSETS (BILLIONS)	PAYOUT	REGS/RELS/ DEREGULATED	TOP EXEC (AGE, SERVICE)	RATING (BUS POS, CFC, OUTLOOK)	CRITERIA MET	DRIP/ PURCHASE	APPROX DIV DATES
KeySpan Energy (KSE)	718-403-2000	keyspanenergy.com	11.55	73.9	NY, MA, NH/good/all	Catell (63, 14)	A (3, no, stable)	6	yes^, yes#* ($250)	F, M, A, N—1
Kinder Morgan (KMI)	303-989-1740	kindermorgan.com	8.42	12.4	FERC/average/all	Kinder (56, 2)	BBB— (5, yes, stable)	4	yes^, yes#	F, M, A, N—14
Madison G&E (MDSN)	800-356-6423	mge.com	0.57	79.2	WI/avg/none	Mebane (67, 19)	AA (5, no, stable)	5	yes^, yes#* ($50)	M, J, S, D—15
MDU Resources (MDU)	800-437-8000	mdures.com	2.31	48.9	Dakotas/good/none	White (59, 8)	A (5, no, stable)	7	yes^, yes#* ($50)	J, A, J, O—1
NiSource (NI)	800-348-6466	nisource.com	19.70	65.2	IND, MA/good/all	Neale (61, 9)	BBB (4, no, stable)	6	yes, yes#	F, M, A, N—20
Northwestern Corp (NOR)	800-677-6716	northwestern.com	2.54	65.0	SD, NEB/average/none	Lewis (53, 7)	A+ (6, no, negative)	5	yes^, yes#* ($500)	M, J, S, D—1
OG&E Energy (OGE)	800-842-7629	oge.com	4.15	70.4	OK/tough/none	Moore (54, 6)	A+ (5, no, stable)	5	yes^, yes#* ($250)	J, A, J, O—30
Otter Tail Corp (OTTR)	800-664-1259	otpco.com	0.72	65.0	MN/average/none	MacFarlane (61, 10)	AA— (5, no, negative)	5	yes, yes#	M, J, S, D—9
Peoples Energy (PGL)	800-228-6888	peoplesenergy.com	2.50	70.1	IL/tough/all	Terry (63, 16)	A+ (4, no, stable)	6	yes^, yes#* ($250)	J, A, J, O—15
PG&E Corp (PCG)	800-367-7731	pge-corp.com	29.72	0.0	CA/tough/all	Glynn (59, 4)	D (6, no, developing)	0	yes, no#	none
Pinnacle West (PNW)	800-457-2983	pinnaclewest.com	7.18	42.1	AZ/average/all	Post (50, 18)	BBB+ (6, yes, stable)	5	yes^, yes#* ($50)	M, J, S, D—1
PP&L Resources (PPL)	800-345-3085	papl.com	12.37	32.3	PA/average/all	Hecht (57, 10)	BBB+ (7, no, stable)	5	yes^, yes#	J, A, J, O—1
Progress Energy (PGN)	800-662-7232	progress-energy.com	20.09	69.7	NC, SC, FL/good/none	Cavanaugh (62, 7)	BBB+ (5, no, stable)	7	yes^, yes#* ($20)	F, M, A, N—1

Company	Phone	Website								
P.S. Enterprise Group (PEG)	800-242-0813	pseg.com	19.63	60.9	NJ/average/all	Ferland (58, 14)	BBB (8, no, stable)	3	yes^, yes#* ($250)	M, J, S, D—29
P.S. of New Mexico (PNM)	800-545-4425	pnm.com	2.89	31.6	NM/tough/partly	Montoya (65, 8)	BBB– (6, yes, negative)	4	yes^, yes#* ($50)	E, M, A, N—16
Reliant Energy (REI)	888-468-3020	reliantenergy.com	7.52	51.0	TX, MN/avg/partly	Letbetter (52, 2)	BBB+ (6, no, stable)	5	yes^, yes#* ($250)	M, J, S, D—9
SCANA (SCG)	800-763-5891	scana.com	7.42	47.9	SC, NC, GA/good/partly	Timmerman (54, 9)	A (4, no, negative)	7	yes^, yes#* ($250)	J, A, J, O—1
Sempra Energy (SRE)	877-773-6772	sempra.com	15.61	48.5	CA/tough/all	Baum (59, 1)	A (4, no, negative)	2	yes^, yes* ($500)	J, A, J, O—15
Southern Co (SO)	800-554-7626	southernco.com	20.30	62.9	GA, AL/good/none	Dahlberg (60, 15)	A (4, yes, stable)	7	yes^, yes* ($250)	M, J, S, D—6
TECO Energy (TE)	888-540-7094	tecoenergy.com	5.68	67.3	FL/good/none	Fagan (56, 2)	A (5, no, negative)	7	yes^, yes# ($250)	E, M, A, N—15
TXU Corp (TXU)	800-828-0812	txu.com	44.99	70.0	TX, UK/average/all	Nye (63, 18)	BBB+ (5, yes, negative)	4	yes^, yes* ($500)	J, A, J, O—2
UniSource (UNS)	888-269-8845	unisourceenergy.com	2.60	30.1	AZ/average/all	Pignatelli (57, 6)	BB (6, yes, stable)	3	yes^, yes#* ($250)	M, J, S, D—8
UtiliCorp (UCU)	800-884-5426	utilicorp.com	14.72	54.3	MO, NZ/average/partly	Green (46, 18)	BBB (6, no, stable)	6	yes^, yes#* ($250)	E, M, A, N—12
Vectren Corp (VVC)	812-465-5300	vectren.com	2.91	57.3	IND, OH/good/all	Ellerbrook (52, 2)	A (4, no, negative)	8	yes^, yes	M, J, S, D—1
Western Resources (WR)	800-527-2495	wstnres.com	7.98	75.0	KS/tough/none	Wittig (45, 4)	BB+ (6, yes, positive)	1	yes^, yes#* ($250)	J, A, J, O—2
Williams Cos (WMB)	918-573-2000	williams.com	41.00	30.8	FERC/average/all	Janzen (47, 7)	BBB (5, no, positive)	4	no, no	M, J, S, D—25
Wisconsin Energy (WEC)	800-881-5882	wisenergy.com	8.61	53.0	WI, MI/average/partly	Abdoo (56, 11)	A+ (4, no, negative)	5	yes^, yes#* ($50)	M, J, S, D—1
WPS Resources (WPS)	800-236-1551	wpsr.com	2.82	81.4	WI, MI/average/partly	Weyers (55, 4)	AA (5, no, stable)	5	yes^, yes#* ($100)	M, J, S, D—20
Xcel Energy (XEL)	877-778-6786	xcelenergy.com	21.77	70.8	MN, CO, TX/avg/partly	Howard (65, 13)	A– (5, no, stable)	6	yes^, yes#* ($100)	J, A, J, O—20

Energy Distribution Utilities

STOCK (SYMBOL)	CO/DRIP PHONE	WORLD WIDE WEB SITE	ASSETS (BILLIONS)	PAYOUT	REGS/RELS/ DEREGULATED	TOP EXEC (AGE, SERVICE)	RATING (BUS POS, CFC, OUTLOOK)	CRITERIA MET	DRIP/STK PURCHASE	APPROX DIV DATES
AGL Resources (ATG)	800-633-4236	aglr.com	$2.02	80.0%	GA, TN, VA/good/ partly	Rosput (44, 1)	A− (3, no, stable)	7	yes^, yes#* ($250)	M, J, S, D—1
Amerigas (APU)	610-337-7000	amerigas.com	1.26	NMF	nationwide/good/all	n/a	BB+ (5, no, stable)	4	no, no	n/a
Atmos Energy (ATO)	800-382-8667	atmosenergy.com	1.60	84.1	TX, TN/average/ partly	Best (54, 4)	A− (3, yes, negative)	6	yes^, yes#* ($200)	M, J, S, D—11
Avista Energy (AVA)	800-642-7365	avistacorp.com	12.56	32.7	WA/tough/none	Ely (53, 1)	BBB (6, yes, negative)	2	yes^, yes	M, J, S, D—15
Buckeye Partners (BPL)	610-254-4600	buckeye.com	0.67	77.0	FERC/good/all	Shea (n/a, n/a)	A− (4, yes, stable)	6	no, no	F, M, A, N—30
Cascade Natural Gas (CGC)	800-524-4458	n/a	0.33	65.8	WA/tough/none	Matsuyama (55, 12)	BBB+ (3, yes, positive)	5	yes^, yes#* ($250)	F, M, A, N—15
Central Vermont P.S. (CV)	800-354-2877	cvps.com	0.54	111.4	VT, NH/tough/all	Young (53, 6)	BBB− (7, no, negative)	3	yes, yes#* (250)	F, M, A, N—15
Chesapeake Utilities (CPK)	888-742-5275	chpk.com	0.18	68.4	MD/good/all	Adkins (58, 11)	none (none, no, none)	5	yes^, yes#	J, A, J, O—5
CH Energy (CHG)	800-428-9578	cenhud.com	1.53	69.9	NY/tough/all	Ganci (62, 3)	A (5, yes, stable)	3	yes^, yes#* ($100)	F, M, A, N—1
Consolidated Edison (ED)	800-522-5522	conedison.com	16.77	77.7	NY, NJ/tough/all	McGrath (59, 11)	A (5, no, negative)	4	yes^, yes	M, J, S, D—15
Delta Gas (DGAS)	859-744-6171	deltagas.com	0.13	83.8	KY/average/none	Jennings (50, n/a)	none (none, yes, none)	6	yes^, yes#* ($250)	M, J, S, D—15
DQE Inc. (DQE)	888-247-0400	dqe.com	3.87	58.7	PA/good/all	Marshall (48, 9)	BBB+ (6, yes, developing)	5	yes^, yes* (#105)	J, A, J, O—1
El Paso Energy Part (EPN)	713-420-2131	epenergy.com	0.58	243.8	FERC/average/all	Wise (55, 3)	BB+ (6, no, stable)	5	no, no	F, M, A, N—15
Energy East (EAS)	800-225-5643	nyseg.com	7.00	43.6	NY, CT, ME/ average/mod	VonSchack (57, 5)	A− (3, yes, negative)	6	yes^, yes	F, M, A, N—15

Company	Phone	Website			Region/regulation	Contact	Rating			Codes
EnergySouth (ENSI)	334-450-4638	mobile-gas.com	0.17	56.2	AL/good/none	Davis (58, 6)	none (none, yes, none)	6	yes^, yes#	J, A, J, O—1
Energy West (EWST)	406-791-7500	ewst.com	0.07	68.5	MT/tough/all	Geska (62, 21)	none (none, yes, none)	4	yes^, yes#	J, A, J, O—5
EOTT Energy Part (EOT)	713-993-5200	eott.com	1.56	NMF	nationwide/good/all	n/a	none (none, yes, none)	3	no, no	n/a
Florida Pub Utils (FPU+)	561-838-1729	fpuc.com	0.10	63.7	FL/good/none	English (57, 6)	none (none, yes, none)	6	yes^, yes#	J, A, J, O—2
Green Mtn Power (GMP)	800-851-9677	gmpvt.com	0.30	loss	VT/tough/all	Dutton (52, 4)	BBB— (7, yes, developing)	1	yes^, yes	M, J, S, D—29
Kinder Morg En Part (KMP)	303-989-1740	kindermorgan.com	4.63	101.9	FERC/average/all	Kinder (56, 5)	A— (4, no, stable)	5	no, no	F, M, A, N—14
Laclede Gas (LG)	800-884-4225	lacledegas.com	1.10	72.8	MO/tough/none	Yaeger (51, 2)	AA— (3, no, negative)	4	yes, yes#	J, A, J, O—2
Maine Pub Serv (MAP+)	207-768-5811	mainepub@mfx.net	0.15	38.6	ME/average/all	Cariani (60, 8)	none (none, yes, none)	3	no, no	J, A, J, O—1
New Jersey Resources (NJR)	908-938-1230	njng.com	1.09	61.1	NJ/average/all	Downes (44, 16)	A (2, yes, positive)	6	yes^, yes#* ($25)	J, A, J, O—2
New Power Corp (NPW)	203-531-0400	newpower.com	0.11	0.0	nationwide/good/all	Pai (53, 1)	none (none, yes, none)	1	no, no	none
NICOR Inc (GAS)	630-305-9500	nicor.com	2.56	56.5	IL/tough/all	Fisher (56, 12)	AA (2, yes, stable)	6	yes, yes#	E, M, A, N—1
Northeast Utils (NU)	800-286-5000	nu.com	9.69	25.8	CT, MA, NH/tough/all	Morris (54, 4)	BBB— (5, yes, developing)	4	yes^, yes	M, J, S, D—29
Northern Border Part (NBP)	713-853-6161	northernborderpartners.com	2.09	112.0	FERC/good/all	DeRoijo (58, 1)	A— (3, no, negative)	6	no, no	F, M, A, N—14
Northwest Nat Gas (NWN)	800-422-4012	nwnatural.com	1.28	69.7	OR/tough/none	Reiten (61, 5)	A (3, no, stable)	4	yes^, yes#	F, M, A, N—15
NSTAR (NST)	617-424-3562	nstaronline.com	5.57	64.6	MA/good/all	May (53, 9)	A— (4, no, stable)	5	yes^, yes#	F, M, A, N—1
NUI Corp (NUI)	908-781-0500	nui.com	0.92	49.2	NJ, FL/avg/partly	Kean (72, 32)	BBB (3, yes, stable)	4	yes^, yes#* ($125)	M, J, S, D—15
Piedmont Nat Gas (PNY)	800-693-9917	piedmontng.com	1.45	72.6	NC, SC, TN/ good/none	Maxheim (66, 16)	A (3, no, stable)	8	yes^, yes#* ($250)	J, A, J, O—12
Potomac Elec (POM)	800-527-3726	pepco.com	7.03	92.2	MD, DC/tough/all	Derrick (61, 8)	A (5, yes, negative)	4	yes#	M, J, S, D—29
Puget Sound Energy (PSD)	800-997-8438	psechoice.com	5.23	85.2	WA/tough/none	Weaver (56, 9)	BBB+ (4, no, negative)	4	yes^, yes#* ($25)	F, M, A, N—15
RGC Energy (RGCO)	800-829-8432	roanokegas.com	0.11	59.6	VA, WVA/good/none	Williamson (46, 8)	A— (5, yes, stable)	5	yes, yes#	F, M, A, N—1
RGS Energy (RGS)	800-724-8833	rge.com	2.57	69.0	NY/tough/all	Richards (57, 8)	A— (5, yes, negative)	5	yes^, yes#	J, A, J, O—25

Energy Distribution Utilities (*Continued*)

STOCK (SYMBOL)	CO/DRIP PHONE	WORLD WIDE WEB SITE	ASSETS (BILLIONS)	PAYOUT	REGS/RELS/ DEREGULATED	TOP EXEC (AGE, SERVICE)	RATING (BUS POS, CFC, OUTLOOK)	CRITERIA MET	DRIP/STK PURCHASE	APPROX DIV DATES
SEMCO Energy (SEN)	810-987-2200	semcoenergy.com	0.82	73.0	MI, AK/average/ partly	Johnson (58, 5)	BBB (3, no, developing)	4	yes^, yes#* ($250)	F, M, A, N—15
Sierra Pacific (SRP)	800-662-7575	sierrapacific.com	2.15	loss	NV, CA, OR/ tough/partly	Higgins (56, 1)	BBB+ (5, no, negative)	2	yes, yes#* ($250)	F, M, A, N—1
So Jersey Industries (SJI)	609-561-9000	sjindustries.com	0.87	68.5	NJ/good/all	Biscieglia (56, 2)	BBB+ (3, yes, stable)	5	yes^, yes#* ($100)	J, A, J, O—4
Southern Union (SUG)	800-736-3001	southernunion.com	2.02	stk	RI, MO, PA, TX/ avg/part	Lindemann (64, 11)	BBB+ (3, no, stable)	5	yes, yes* ($250)	June—30
Southwest Gas (SWX)	702-876-7237	swgas.com	1.96	73.9	AZ, NV, CA/ tough/partly	Maffie (53, 12)	BBB– (4, no, stable)	3	yes, yes#* ($100)	M, J, S, D—1
Suburban Propane (SPH)	973-887-5300	suburbanpropane.com	0.77	117.5	FERC/average/all	Alexander (42, n/a)	none (none, yes, none)	4	no, no	F, M, A, N—13
UGI Corp (UGI)	800-UGI-9453	ugicorp.com	2.28	81.2	PA/average/partly	Greenberg (51, 6)	A– (4, no, stable)	5	yes^, yes#	J, A, J, O—1
UIL Holdings (UIL)	800-722-5584	uil.com	1.87	67.6	CT/average/all	Woodson (59, 3)	BBB+ (5, yes, stable)	4	yes^, yes#	J, A, J, O—1
UNITIL (UTL+)	800-999-6501	unitil.com	0.37	93.9	NH, MA/average/all	Schoenberger (50, 5)	none (none, yes, none)	4	yes^, yes#	F, M, A, N—15
Washington Gas (WGL)	800-221-9427	washgas.com	2.24	60.8	MD, DC, VA/good/all	DeGraffenreidt (47, 13)	AA– (2, no, stable)	7	yes^, yes#	F, M, A, N—1
Williams Energy Part (WEG)	918-573-2000	williams.com	0.32	NMF	nationwide/good/all	n/a	none (none, no, none)	5	no, no	n/a

Natural Resource Utilities

STOCK (SYMBOL)	CO/DRIP PHONE	WORLD WIDE WEB SITE	ASSETS (BILLIONS)	PAYOUT	REGS/RELS/ DEREGULATED	TOP EXEC (AGE, SERVICE)	RATING (BUS POS, CFC, OUTLOOK)	CRITERIA MET	DRIP/STK PURCHASE	APPROX DIV DATES
Aquila Energy (ILA)	800-884-5426	utilicorp.com	n/a	0.0%	nationwide/good/all	Green (46, 18)	n/a (none, no, stable)	4	none	none
BP Amoco (BP)	877-272-2723	bp.com	$143.94	32.0	UK, EPA/average/all	Browne (n/a, n/a)	AA— (none, no, stable)	5	yes^, yes#* ($250)	M, J, S, D—11
Burlington Resources (BR)	800-262-3456	br-inc.com	7.51	17.6	EPA, Canada/avg/all	Shackouls (50, 6)	A— (none, yes, stable)	4	no, no	J, A, J, O—3
Calpine Corp (CPN)	408-995-5115	calpine.com	9.74	0.0	CA, FERC/good/all	Cartwright (71, 17)	BB+ (none, no, stable)	1	no, no	none
ChevronTexaco (CHV)	415-894-7700	chevron.com	41.26	31.1	EPA/average/all	O'Reilly (54, 2)	AA (none, yes, stable)	5	yes, yes* ($250)	M, J, S, D—11
Energen Corp (EGN)	800-946-4316	energen.com	1.23	35.2	AL/good/none	Warren (53, 17)	A+ (6, yes, negative)	6	yes^, yes#* ($250)	M, J, S, D—1
EOG Resources (EOG)	713-651-7000	n/a	3.00	0.0	nationwide/good/all	n/a	BB (8, no, stable)	3	no, no	none
Equitable Resources (EQT)	412-261-3000	eqt.com	2.46	34.3	PA/average/partly	Gerber (47, 2)	A (6, no, negative)	5	yes, yes#	M, J, S, D—1
ExxonMobil (XOM)	800-252-1800	exxonmobil.com	149.00	36.6	EPA/tough/all	Raymond (62, 16)	AAA (none, yes, stable)	5	yes^, yes#* ($250)	M, J, S, D—11
Mirant Energy (MIR)	770-379-7000	southernco.com	24.14	0.0	FERC/good/all	Fuller (40, 4)	BBB— (7, no, stable)	3	no, yes* ($250)	none
National Fuel Gas (NFG)	800-648-8166	natfuel.com	3.23	55.7	NY, PA/tough/partly	Kennedy (69, 22)	A— (5, no, negative)	5	yes, yes# ($1000)	J, A, J, O—15

Natural Resource Utilities (*Continued*)

STOCK (SYMBOL)	CO/DRIP PHONE	WORLD WIDE WEB SITE	ASSETS (BILLIONS)	PAYOUT	REGS/RELS/ DEREGULATED	TOP EXEC (AGE, SERVICE)	RATING (BUS POS, CFC, OUTLOOK)	CRITERIA MET	DRIP/STK PURCHASE	APPROX DIV DATES
NRG Energy (NRG)	612-373-5300	nrgenergy.com	5.97	0.0	FERC/good/all	Peterson (58, 2)	BBB− (none, no, stable)	3	no, no	none
ONEOK (OKE)	800-653-8083	oneok.com	7.36	42.6	OK, KS/tough/partly	Kyle (47, 1)	A (5, no, stable)	5	yes^, yes# ($250)	F, M, A, N—15
Orion Holdings (ORN)	410-230-3500	n/a	3.87	0.0	nationwide/average/all	n/a	BB (7, no, stable)	3	no, no	none
Phillips Pete (P)	918-661-6600	phillips66.com	20.51	18.1	EPA/average/all	Mulva (53, n/a)	BBB (none, no, positive)	5	yes, yes* ($500)	M, J, S, D—1
Questar Corp (STR)	801-324-5000	qstr.com	2.24	35.9	UT, WY/average/partly	Cash (58, 23)	A+ (2, no, negative)	6	yes^, yes* ($250)	M, J, S, D—11
Reliant Resources (RRI)	888-468-3020	reliantenergy.com	n/a	0.0	nationwide/average/all	n/a	n/a (none, no, stable)	4	none	none
Royal Dutch Shell (RD)	3170-3774540	n/a	57.09	31.3	EPA/average/all	Wachem (n/a, n/a)	AAA (none, yes, stable)	5	yes, yes* ($250)	n/a
Southwestern Energy (SWN)	501-521-1141	swn.com	0.67	0.0	EPA/average/all	Korell (56, 3)	BBB (5, no, negative)	3	no, yes* ($250)	none

Communications Utilities

STOCK (SYMBOL)	CO/DRIP PHONE	WORLD WIDE WEB SITE	ASSETS (BILLIONS)	PAYOUT	REGS/RELS/ DEREGULATED	TOP EXEC (AGE, SERVICE)	RATING (BUS POS, CFC, OUTLOOK)	CRITERIA MET	DRIP/STK PURCHASE	APPROX DIV DATES
Adelphia Comm (ADLAC)	814-274-9830	adelphia.net	$21.50	0.0%	FCC/average/partly	Rigas (75, 16)	B+ (stable, no)	3	no, no	none
ALLTEL (AT)	888-824-9786	alltel.com	12.18	48.2	FCC/average/all	Ford (63, 40)	A (stable, no)	6	yes, yes#	J, A, J, O—3
America On-Line (AOL)	703-265-1000	aol.com	10.87	0.0	Net entertainment	Case (42, 8)	BBB (stable, yes)	4	no, no	none
AT&T (T)	212-387-5400	att.com	242.22	9.2	FCC/average/all	Armstrong (62, 4)	A (negative, no)	2	yes, yes	F, M, A, N—1
AT&T Wireless (AWE)	212-387-5400	att.com	35.30	0.0	FCC/average/all	Zeglis (52, 1)	none (none, no)	2	no, no	none
BellSouth (BLS)	800-631-6001	bellsouthcorp.com	50.96	34.1	FL, FCC/tough/partly	Ackerman (58, 11)	AA— (negative, no)	6	yes^, yes* ($500)	F, M, A, N—1
Broadwing Inc (BRW)	800-345-6301	broadwinginc.com	6.47	0.0	OH, FCC/avg/partly	Ellenberger (48, 2)	BB+ (stable, no)	4	no, yes#* ($250)	none
Cablevision (CVC+)	516-364-8450	cablevision.com	8.08	0.0	NY/average/partly	Dolan (73, 16)	BB+ (stable, no)	3	no, no	none
Century Telephone (CTL)	800-969-6718	centurytel.com	6.39	11.5	FCC/average/partly	Post (48, 15)	BBB+ (negative, no)	5	yes^, yes#	M, J, S, D—15
Citizens Utilities (CZN)	203-614-5600	czn.com	6.96	0.0	NY, FCC/average/partly	Tow (72, 11)	A— (negative, no)	3	no, no	none
Comcast (CMCSA)	215-665-1700	comcast.com	35.74	0.0	FCC/average/partly	Roberts (81, 6)	BBB (stable, no)	3	no, no	none
Covad (COVD)	408-844-7500	covad.com	1.15	0.0	FCC/good/all	McMinn (48, n/a)	B— (negative, no)	0	no, no	none
Cox Comm. (COX)	404-843-5000	cox.com	24.72	0.0	FCC/average/partly	Robbins (53, 3)	BBB (stable, no)	4	no, no	none
Global Crossing (GX)	800-836-0342	globalcrossing.com	30.19	0.0	FCC, EU/average/partly	Winnick (52, 1)	BB+ (stable, yes)	1	no, no	none

Communications Utilities (*Continued*)

STOCK (SYMBOL)	CO/DRIP PHONE	WORLD WIDE WEB SITE	ASSETS (BILLIONS)	PAYOUT	REGS/RELS/ DEREGULATED	TOP EXEC (AGE, SERVICE)	RATING (BUS POS, CFC, OUTLOOK)	CRITERIA MET	DRIP/STK PURCHASE	APPROX DIV DATES
Level3 Comm. (LVLT)	720-888-1000	n/a	14.92	0.0	FCC/average/all	n/a	B (stable, no)	2	no, no	none
Nextel Comm. (NXTL)	703-394-3500	nextel.com	0.98	0.0	FCC/average/all	Akerson (51, 5)	B (stable, no)	1	no, no	none
Qwest Comm. (Q)	303-291-1400	qwest.com	73.50	0.0	FCC, WA, AZ/avg/partly	Nacchio (51, 5)	BBB+ (stable, no)	6	no, no	none
RCN Corp (RCNC)	609-734-3700	rcn.com	4.78	0.0	NY, MA, CA/avg/all	McCourt (43, 1)	B− (stable, no)	0	no, no	none
SBC Corp (SBC)	800-351-7221	sbc.com	98.65	43.8	FCC, CA, TX/avg/partly	Whitacre (59, 11)	AA− (stable, no)	6	yes^, yes* ($500)	F, M, A, N—1
Sprint (FON)	800-259-3755	sprint.com	40.85	22.6	FCC/average/partly	Esrey (61, 16)	BBB+ (negative, no)	4	yes^, yes#	M, J, S, D—28
Sprint PCS (PCS)	800-259-3755	sprint.com	19.76	0.0	FCC/average/all	Esrey (61, 16)	none (none, no)	3	no, no	none
Telephone & Data Syst (TDS+)	312-630-1900	teldta.com	9.07	14.9	FCC/average/all	Carlson (54, 8)	A− (stable, yes)	4	yes^, yes#	M, J, S, D—29
TouchAmerica (MTP)	800-245-6767	mtpower.com	2.63	0.0	MT, FCC/avg/partly	Gannon (56, 8)	BBB+ (developing, yes)	2	no, yes# ($100)	none
Verizon Comm. (VZ)	800-BEL-5595	verizon.com	164.74	52.9	NY, NJ, FCC/avg/partly	Lee (60, 1)	A+ (stable, no)	6	yes^, yes* ($1000)	F, M, A, N—1
Williams Comm (WCG)	918-588-2000	williams.com	7.41	0.0	FCC/average/all	Janzen (47, 7)	BB (negative, no)	2	no, no	none
WorldCom (WCOM)	601-360-8600	wcom.com	98.90	0.0	FCC, EU/average/all	Ebbers (59, 16)	BBB+ (stable, yes)	5	no, no	none

UTE Tech

STOCK (SYMBOL)	CO/DRIP PHONE	WORLD WIDE WEB SITE	ASSETS (BILLIONS)	PAYOUT	KEY TO GROWTH	TOP EXEC (AGE, SERVICE)	RATING (OUTLOOK, CFC)	CRITERIA MET	DRIP/STK PURCHASE	APPROX DIV DATES
American Superconductor (AMSC)	508-836-4200	amsuper.com	$0.25	0.0%	Reliable power	Yurek (53, n/a)	none (none, yes)	2	no, no	none
Astropower (APWR)	302-366-0400	astropower.com	0.06	0.0	Clean energy	Basnelt (59, n/a)	none (none, yes)	2	no, no	none
Capstone Turbine (CPST)	818-734-5300	capstoneturbine.com	0.30	0.0	Reliable power	Almgren (53, n/a)	none (none, no)	2	no, no	none
Convergys (CVG)	513-723-7000	convergys.com	1.78	0.0	Ute cost cutting	Orr (55, 3)	BBB (stable, yes)	4	no, no	none
Ericsson (ERICY)	212-685-4030	ericsson.com	24.68	75.2	Asia econ growth	Ramquist (n/a, n/a)	A (negative, no)	2	yes, yes* ($250)	May, Nov—11
Exodus (EXDS)	408-346-2200	exodus.net	3.89	0.0	Internet growth	Hancock (58, 3)	B (stable, no)	0	no, no	none
Lucent Technologies (LU)	908-582-8500	lucent.com	48.79	11.1	Management focus	Schacht (66, 1)	BBB— (negative, no)	0	no, no	none
Plug Power (PLUG)	518-782-7700	plugpower.com	0.15	0.0	Management focus	Saillant (57, 1)	none (none, no)	0	no, no	none
Power-One (PWER)	805-987-8741	power-one.com	0.78	0.0	Reliable power	Goldman (42, n/a)	none (none, no)	2	no, no	none
US Energy (USEY)	914-993-6443	usenergy.com	0.02	0.0	Clean energy	Schneider (63, 1)	none (none, no)	2	no, no	none

Water

STOCK (SYMBOL)	CO/DRIP PHONE	WORLD WIDE WEB SITE	ASSETS (BILLIONS)	PAYOUT	REGS/RELS/ DEREGULATED	TOP EXEC (AGE, SERVICE)	RATING (BUS POS, CFC, OUTLOOK)	CRITERIA MET	DRIP/STK PURCHASE	APPROX DIV DATES
American States Wtr (AWR)	909-394-3600	aswater.com	$0.62	68.4%	CA, WA, AZ/tough/none	Wicks (57, 9)	A+ (3, yes, stable)	4	yes, yes* ($500)	M, J, S, D—1
American Water Works (AWK)	877-987-9757	amwater.com	6.07	58.4	CA, PA, NJ/avg/none	Barr (59, 3)	A (3, yes, stable)	7	yes^, yes#	F, M, A, N—15
Artesian Water (ARTNA)	800-368-5948	artesianwater.com	0.15	92.4	DE/tough/none	Taylor (55, 8)	none (none, no, none)	3	yes, yes#	F, M, A, N—20
California Water Svc (CWT)	800-750-8200	calwater.com	0.67	85.1	CA, WA, NM/tough/none	Foy (64, 23)	AA– (3, yes, stable)	5	yes^, yes* ($500)	F, M, A, N—15
Connecticut Water (CTWS)	800-428-3985	ctwater.com	0.22	73.6	CT, MA/good/none	Chiaraluce (58, 9)	none (none, yes, none)	6	yes^, yes* ($100)	M, J, S, D—15
Middlesex Water (MSEX)	908-634-1500	middlesexwater.com	0.22	120.8	NJ, DE/tough/none	Tomkins (62, 19)	A (3, yes, stable)	3	yes^, yes#	M, J, S, D—1
Pennichuck Corp (PNNW)	603-882-5191	pennichuck.com	0.08	116.3	NH/tough/partly	Arel (63, 16)	none (none, yes, none)	3	yes, yes* ($500)	F, M, A, N—15
Philadelphia Suburban (PSC)	800-205-8314	suburbanwater.com	1.41	63.3	PA, NC, OH/good/none	DeBenedictus (55, 8)	A+ (2, no, stable)	7	yes^, yes#* ($500)	M, J, S, D—1
SJW Corp (SJW+)	800-736-3001	sjwater.com	0.39	70.3	CA/tough/none	Roth (48, 5)	none (none, yes, none)	4	no, no	M, J, S, D—1
Southwest Water (SWWC)	800-356-2017	southwestwater.com	0.14	36.1	CA, NM/average/partly	Garnier (60, 33)	none (none, no, none)	4	yes^, yes#	J, A, J, O—19

Foreign Communications

STOCK (SYMBOL)	PHONE	WORLD WIDE WEB SITE	ASSETS (BILLIONS)	PAYOUT	REGS/RELS/ DEREGULATED	TOP EXEC (AGE, SERVICE)	RATING (OUTLOOK, CFC)	CRITERIA MET	DRIP/STK PURCHASE	APPROX DIV DATES
BCE Inc (BCE)	800-561-0934	bce.ca	$32.92	66.3%	Canada/good/partly	Monty (n/a)	A+ (stable, no)	6	yes, yes	J, A, J, O—15
British Telecom (BTY)	800-331-4568	bt.com	54.07	199.5	UK/tough/partly	Vallance (57)	A (negative, no)	2	yes, yes* ($250)	Feb, Sep—20
Cable and Wireless (CWP)	800-989-0297	cwplc.com	30.56	loss	UK, US/avg/partly	Wallace (51)	A (stable, yes)	4	no, no	Mar, Sep—11
CANTV (VNT)	582-500-6800	cantv.com.ve	4.64	141.5	Venez/tough/partly	Roosen (n/a)	B (stable, yes)	1	no, no	Apr, Dec—28
Compania Tel de Chile (CTC)	562-696-6840	ctc.cl	5.00	0.0	Chile/tough/partly	Aguirre (49)	BBB+ (stable, no)	2	no, no	none
Deutsche Telekom (DT)	800-808-8010	telekom.de	43.18	50.4	Germany/tough/partly	Sommer (50)	A− (negative, no)	2	yes, yes* ($250)	Jun—5
Embratel (EMT)	5521-519-6474	embratel.net.br	5.46	28.5	Brazil/avg/partly	Crawford (60)	none (none, yes)	3	yes, yes* ($200)	J, A, J, O—5
France Telecom (FTE)	800-BNY-ADRS	francetelecom.fr	48.25	66.6	France/avg/partly	Bon (67)	A (negative, no)	4	yes, yes* ($200)	Jul—27
Nippon T&T (NTT)	800-749-1687	ntt.com.jp	50.00	81.0	Japan/avg/partly	Miyazu (n/a)	AA (stable, yes)	4	yes, yes* ($250)	Sept—26
Philippine Long Distance (PHI)	632-816-8024	pldt.com	6.59	13.3	Philipns/tough/partly	Cojuanco (n/a)	BB+ (stable, no)	1	no, no	J, A, J, O—22
Portugal Telecom (PT)	888-BNY-ADRS	telecom.pt	11.67	43.9	Prtgl/avg/partly	Nabo (60)	A (stable, no)	4	yes, yes* ($200)	M, J, S, D—28
Singapore Telecom (SGTJY)	65-838-3388	n/a	7.71	86.7	Singap/good/partly	n/a (n/a)	none (none, yes)	2	no, no	Jan-5, Oct-23
Telecom Italia (TI)	800-749-1687	telecomitalia.it	58.35	118.8	Italy/average/partly	Colaninno (56)	BBB+ (positive, no)	4	yes, yes* ($250)	F, M, A, N—13
Telecom of New Zealand (NZT)	888-BNY-ADRS	telecom.co.nz	3.26	86.2	NZ, Aust/tough/partly	Deane (n/a)	A− (stable, no)	2	yes, yes* ($200)	M, J, S, D—22
TeleDanmark (TLD)	4533-42-7681	teledanmark.dk	8.93	32.1	Denmark/avg/partly	Dyresmose (54)	A (stable, no)	5	no, no	May-1
Telefonica (TEF)	341-584-4700	telefonica.es	50.00	0.0	Spn, LatAm/avg/partly	Vega (44)	A+ (stable, no)	5	no, no	none
Telefonos de Mexico (TMX)	800-749-1687	telmex.com.mx	16.87	25.5	Mexico/tough/partly	Pardo (n/a)	BB+ (stable, no)	4	yes, yes* ($250)	M, J, S, D—29
Telesp Cellular (TCP)	5511-30597590	telespcelular.com	1.96	61.2	Brazil/avg/all	Costa (50)	none (none, yes)	3	no, yes* ($200)	none
Vivendi (V)	3317171-1000	vivendi.com	73.88	30.0	EU/average/partly	Messier (42)	BBB (negative, no)	4	yes, yes* ($200)	M, J, S, D—11
Vodafone Airtouch (VOD)	888-BNY-ADRS	vodafone.co.uk	220.75	32.7	EU, FCC/avg/all	Gent (51)	A (stable, yes)	4	yes, yes* ($200)	F, M, A, N—19

Foreign Utilities

STOCK (SYMBOL)	PHONE	WORLD WIDE WEB SITE	ASSETS (BILLIONS)	PAYOUT	REGS/RELS/ DEREGULATED	TOP EXEC (COUNTRY)	RATING (BUS POS, CFC, OUTLOOK)	CRITERIA MET	DRIP/STK PURCHASE	APPROX DIV DATES
CLP Holdings (CLPHY)	800-749-1687	clpgroup.com	$5.86	60.0%	China/avg/partly	Kadoorie (58)	A+ (4, no, stable)	5	yes, yes* ($250)	M, J, S, D—22
Consolidated Water (CWCO)	345-945-4277	n/a	0.02	52.6	Caymans/avg/none	Parker (55)	none (none, no, none)	5	no, no	J, A, J, O—31
Endesa (ELE)	212-750-7200	endesa.es	43.99	46.4	Spn, LatAm/avg/partly	Villa (n/a)	A+ (5, no, stable)	4	yes, yes* ($250)	Jul, Dec—27
Enersis (ENI)	56-2-638-0840	enersis.cl	18.61	0.0	Lat Am/avg/partly	Garcia (55)	A— (6, no, stable)	3	no, no	none
E.ON (EON)	49211-4579367	eon.com	48.47	25.5	Germany/avg/partly	Hartman (62)	AA (none, no, none)	4	no, no	June—5
Kelda Group (KELGF)	44113-2343234	n/a	5.01	76.6	UK, CT/tough/none	Napier (n/a)	A+ (none, no, negative)	3	no, no	Mar-1, Oct-9
Lattice Group (LICEF)	212-921-1060	bg-group.com	18.26	0.0	UK/tough/partly	Giordano (n/a)	A (2, no, stable)	3	no, no	none
National Grid (NGG)	441203-537777	nationalgrid.com	12.62	57.3	UK, MA/tough/partly	Ross (61)	A+ (2, no, negative)	4	no, no	Jan, Aug—25
Powergen (PWG)	44171-8262826	pgen.com	10.38	54.0	UK, KY/tough/partly	Wallis (60)	BBB+ (6, yes, negative)	4	yes, yes* ($200)	May, Nov—13
RWE (RWE)	49201-1200	n/a	29.66	65.1	Germany/avg/partly	n/a (n/a)	AA— (4, no, stable)	4	no, no	Nov—24
Scottish Power (SPI)	888-BNY-ADRS	scottishpower.plc.uk	17.85	82.3	UK, US/rough/partly	Robinson (58)	A (4, no, negative)	4	yes, yes* ($200)	M, J, S, D—15
Transalta Utilities (TSE:TA.TO)	403-267-7110	transalta.com	4.77	76.3	Canada/tough/all	Snyder (n/a)	A— (none, no, stable)	4	yes, yes#	J, A, J, O—1
TransCanada Pipelines (TRP)	403-267-6555	transcanada.com	16.37	60.0	Canada/tough/partly	Haskayne (n/a)	A— (2, yes, stable)	4	yes, yes#	J, A, J, O—31
Vivendi Environment (VIVEF)	0171-711000	vivendi.com	35.31	0.0	EU, US/avg/partly	Messier (42)	BBB+ (none, no, negative)	5	no, no	none
Westcoast Energy (WE)	604-488-8000	westcoastenergy.com	9.69	55.1	Canada/tough/partly	Phelps (n/a)	A— (none, yes, stable)	4	yes^, yes#	M, J, S, D—31

APPENDIX 2

Mergers

2001 COMPANY	1991 COMPANIES
AES Corp	AES, Cilcorp, Ipalco
AGL Resources	Atlanta Gas Light, Virginia Natural Gas
Alliant Energy	WPL Holdings, Interstate Energy, IES Industries
Alltel	Alltel, Lincoln Telecom
Ameren Corp	Union Electric, CIPSCO
American Electric Power	American Electric Power, CSW Energy
American Water Works	American Water Works, National Enterprises
AOL Time Warner	America On-Line, Time Warner Inc, Turner Broadcasting
Atmos Energy	Atmos Energy, United Cities Gas
AT&T	AT&T, Tele-Communications Inc, MediaOne Inc
BP Amoco	British Petroleum, Amoco, Atlantic Richfield
Broadwing	Cincinnati Bell, IXC Communications
Chevron Texaco	Chevron Corp, Texaco
Cinergy Corp	PSI Energy, Cincinnati G&E
Conectiv	Atlantic Energy, Delmarva P&L
Consolidated Edison	Consolidated Edison, Orange & Rockland Utilities
Cox Communications	Cox Communications, TCA Cable

Deutsche Telekom	Deutsche Telekom, Aerial Telecom, Powertel
Dominion Resources	Dominion Resources, Consolidated Natural Gas
DTE Energy	Detroit Edison, MCN Energy
Duke Energy	Duke Power, Panenergy
Dynegy	Dynegy, Illinois Power
El Paso Energy	El Paso Energy, Coastal Corp, Sonat
Endesa	Endesa, Enersis, Endesa Chile
EnergyEast	NYSEG, CTG Resources, Central Maine P.S., Connecticut Energy, RGS
Enron Corp	Enron Corp, Portland General
Entergy Corp	Middle South Utilities, Gulf States Utilities
E.ON	E.ON, Powergen, Kentucky Utilities, LG&E Energy
Exelon Corp	Philadelphia Electric, Commonwealth Edison
ExxonMobil	Exxon Corp, Mobil Corp
FirstEnergy	Ohio Power, Centerior Energy, GPU Inc
Global Crossing	Global Crossing, Rochester Telephone
KeySpan Energy	Brooklyn Union Gas, Lilco, Eastern Enterprises, EnergyNorth
Kinder Morgan	Kinder Morgan, KN Energy
National Grid	National Grid, New England Electric, Eastern Utilities, Niagara Mohawk
NiSource	Northern Indiana Pub Serv, Bay State Gas, Columbia Energy
Northeast Utilities	Northeast Utilities, Public Service of New Hampshire
NSTAR	Boston Edison, Commonwealth Energy
Philadelphia Suburban	Philadelphia Suburban, Consumers Water
Progress Energy	Carolina Power & Light, Florida Progress, North Carolina Natural Gas
Qwest Communications	Qwest Communications, U S West
Reliant Energy	Houston P&L, NorAm Energy

RWE	RWE, Thames Water, E-Town Water
SBC Communications	Southwestern Bell, Pacific Telesis, Ameritech, Southern New England Telecom
SCANA	South Carolina Elec & Gas, Pub Serv of North Carolina
Scottish Power	Scottish Power, PacifiCorp
Sempra Energy	San Diego G&E, Southern California Natural Gas
Sierra Pacific Resources	Sierra Pacific, Nevada Power
Telefonica	Telefonica de Espana, Telef Argentina, Telef Peru, Lycos, Telesp Cellular
TXU Corp	Texas Utilities, Enserch, The Energy Group
UtiliCorp United	UtiliCorp, St. Joseph L&P
Vectren Corp	SIDGECO, Indiana Energy
Verizon Communications	Bell Atlantic, GTE, NYNEX
Vodafone	Vodafone, Mannesmann, Airtouch Communications
Western Resources	Kansas P&L, Kansas G&E
WorldCom	LDDS, UUNet, MCI Communications, MFS Communications
WPS Resources	Wisconsin Public Serv, Upper Peninsula Energy
Xcel Energy	Northern States Power, Southwestern P.S., Pub Serv Colorado

Glossary

AC   Alternating current, the form of electricity currently used on the nation's power grid. Highly flexible but somewhat volatile.

Arbs   Professional arbitrageurs who make money from the spreads between merger premiums and market prices of takeover targets.

Baby Bells   The original seven regional, local phone monopolies spun off from AT&T as part of the 1984 divestiture: Ameritech, Bell Atlantic, BellSouth, NYNEX, Pacific Telesis, SBC Communications, and U.S. West.

California Department of Water and Power   Entity that purchased power for California's defaulted utilities in 2000 and 2001 using state bond issues.

Call price/date   The price and date at which a preferred stock or bond may be forcibly redeemed by its issuer.

Capital preferred stocks   New breed of preferred stocks, issued by subsidiaries of companies set up solely for that purpose, that allow issuer to treat dividends as interest payments for tax-reduction purposes. This allows higher yields to be paid to investors.

Clean Air Act of 1990   Set air pollution control standards for automobile, industrial, and power plant industries. For the latter, it controlled emissions of sulfur oxides (SOX) and nitrogen oxides (NOX) blamed for the creation of acid rain.

CLECs   Competitive local exchange carriers, a product of the years immediately following the Telecommunications Act of 1996. CLECs built high-speed fiber networks to compete with the Baby Bells, but most were ultimately undone by the debt needed for the task.

Cusip number   A trading system used primarily for bonds and preferred stocks when a listed exchange symbol is either nonexistent or too obscure.

DC   Direct current, Thomas Edison's favored form of electricity, currently used in most sensitive electronics, such as computers.

Deregulation   The process of industry change from regulated, local monopolies to global competition.

Distributed generation   Term given to microgenerators, fuel cells, photovoltaics, and other isolated plants that reduce or eliminate a user's dependence on the power grid.

DJUA   Dow Jones Utility Average, the most commonly used measure of utility stock performance. Contains most of the biggest blue-chip utilities.

DOE   U.S. Department of Energy is responsible for setting energy policy in United States. Also collects data and oversees the U.S. Nuclear Regulatory Commission.

DRIPs   Dividend reinvestment plans allow investors to buy additional shares of stock by automatically reinvesting their dividends. Most plans also allow buying of additional shares.

DSL   Direct subscriber line is high-speed Internet access carried over phone company networks. Competes directly with cable modems.

E-business   Businesses involving high-speed data and the Internet, blamed for much of the quantum leap in electricity demand during the late 1990s and early 2000s.

Edison Electric Institute   Principal lobbying group of the electric utility industry, based in Washington, D.C.

Electric Power Research Institute (EPRI)   One of the primary research arms of the electric power industry.

EMFs   Electromagnetic fields allegedly created by high-voltage power lines, with tremendously harmful effects on human health. The spur for landmark lawsuits against utilities in the early 1990s that proved unsuccessful.

Energy Act of 1992   The Act which opened wholesale power markets to competition along the lines of the late 1980s natural gas deregulation. Also delegated considerable powers to the Federal Energy Regulatory Commission.

Energy Information Administration   Branch of the U.S. Department of Energy that compiles energy statistics and forecasts. Information is available to the public.

Energy marketing   The business of lining up consumers and producers, primarily of electricity and natural gas, on unregulated wholesale markets. Also referred to as merchant energy.

EPA   Environmental Protection Agency was set up in 1972, primarily to monitor the degradation of the nation's water supply and its potential health effects. Now involved in all aspects of environmental regulation.

Federal Communications Commission (FCC)   The federal agency charged with overseeing the nation's communications network, particularly when it comes to the rules of competition and approving mergers. A branch of the U.S. Department of Energy, members are appointed by the U.S. president.

FERC   The Federal Energy Regulatory Commission has ultimate authority over the nation's power and gas grid, sets rates on transmission, and has veto power over industry mergers. Members are appointed by the U.S. president.

The Grid   The nation's network of power plants, power lines, natural gas pipelines, and storage and other energy infrastructure.

Internet protocol (IP)   The communications system that relies on sending packets of information over large networks, as opposed to circuit communications used in traditional communications, that relies on opening a channel on each end. IP's currently most popular applications are e-mail and instant messaging.

IPO   Initial public offering is a company's first attempt to sell shares directly to investors, generally handled by investment banks.

IPPs   Independent power producers created from the Public Utility Regulatory Power Act (PURPA) of 1978. Utilities were forced to buy power from them under an escalating rate schedule to encourage their development.

ISO   Independent system operator, the entity blamed in California for creating an inefficient market during the state's power crisis. It was originally set up to ensure a nonbiased market for power.

ISPs   Internet service providers are companies set up to provide access to Web users. The most successful now are subsidiaries of larger communications companies.

Maturity   Date by which bonds and preferred stocks are to be redeemed by their issuers at par value.

Megawatt   Standard measurement of electricity, estimated as the amount of power needed to light 1,000 homes. A megawatt is

1,000 kilowatts; 1,000 megawatts is a gigawatt. Power is typically priced in kilowatt hours.

Merger premium   The percentage a takeover offer for a company exceeds its current market price. Wider premiums are attractive but may indicate a greater degree of risk.

Microturbines   Small plants in the tradition of the isolated plants that proliferated in the early days of electricity. Designed to help users insulate against power grid disruptions, primarily run on natural gas.

Moody's   Another, larger rater of companies' credit. Ratings are assigned from Aaa (highest degree of safety equal to AAA from Standard & Poor's) to D (default).

OPEC   Organization of Petroleum Exporting Countries attempts to control the price of oil to keep demand steady by altering supply, sometimes successfully, sometimes not.

PCS   Personal Communications Systems is a term given to the first generation of digital cellular systems. 3G and 4G are the next scheduled upgrades and will allow for greater wireless Internet use.

Powerchips   Technology that allows users to smooth out fluctuations in grid power to run highly sensitive electronics.

PUHCA   The Public Utility Holding Company Act of 1935 that ended the era of energy holding company dominance and ushered in a 60-year era of regulation of regional monopolies that lasted until the mid-1990s.

PURPA   The Public Utility Regulatory Power Act of 1978 attempted to create incentives to develop non–fossil fuel energy supplies. Utilities were obliged to purchase energy from these sources on an escalating price scale.

Regulators   Federal, state, and local officials who oversee utilities' operations and set policies on industry change (deregulation) and other matters. In transmission and distribution, they set customer rates. They also have veto power over utility mergers.

RTOs   Regional Transmission Operator is the most common form of organizing high-voltage electric transmission systems in the early 2000s. It involves utilities pooling their transmission assets and giving up direct control to ensure a competitive market and promote investment.

Safe Drinking Water Act of 1974 (SDWA)   The Act which set up the nation's rules for water pollution. It was amended in 1986 and again in 1996. The Act authorizes the EPA to set and enforce standards.

S&P 500   Standard & Poor's index of the 500 biggest blue-chip companies in America. The most commonly used benchmark of stock market performance.

Standard & Poor's   The nation's foremost rater of companies' credit. Ratings are assigned from AAA (highest degree of safety) to D (default).

Superconductors   Technology that allows operators of power lines to dramatically limit wasted power by storing it and regulating its flow.

Telecommunications Act of 1996   The act that opened local phone companies to competition and set the rules for their entry into the long-distance telephone and high-speed data business.

Tennessee Valley Authority (TVA)   Government-backed entity set up by the Franklin D. Roosevelt administration to sell power in the economically destitute Southeast. Started by building dams on Tennessee River, now a major power producer.

Transmission and Distribution (T&D)   The business of transporting energy over power lines and gas pipelines for a fee, optimally with no commodity price risk.

Turbines   The component of a power plant that turns energy into electricity.

Washington Water Power Authority   Government-backed entity set up to control rivers and produce water power in the northwestern United States.

Yield to maturity   The annual return to the investor in a fixed-income investment taking into account its current price, par value, and time to maturity.

APPENDIX 4

....

Model Portfolios

Growth and Income Objective

CORE HOLDINGS (85%) SECURITY (SYMBOL)	TYPE UTILITY	OBJECTIVE
Alltel Comm (AT)	telecom	takeover
American Water Works (AWK)	water	emerging giant
CLECO (CNL)	energy	takeover
CMS Energy (CMS)	energy	asset rich
Dominion Resources (D)	energy	emerging giant
Duke Energy (DUK)	energy	emerging giant
Energen Corp (EGN)	oil/gas	asset rich
Entergy Corp (ETR)	energy	asset rich
KeySpan Energy (KSE)	energy	asset rich
MDU Resources (MDU)	oil/gas	asset rich
NiSource (NI)	energy	takeover
Philadelphia Suburban (PSC)	water	emerging giant
SBC Communications (SBC)	telecom	emerging giant
Scottish Power (SPI)	foreign	asset rich
TECO Energy (TE)	energy	takeover
UtiliCorp United (UCU)	energy	asset rich
Verizon Communications (VZ)	telecom	emerging giant
Vodafone (VOD)	telecom	asset rich
WorldCom (WCOM)	telecom	takeover

Growth and Income Objective *(Continued)*

AGGRESSIVE HOLDINGS (15%)	TYPE UTILITY	OBJECTIVE
AES Corp (AES)	energy	emerging giant
AT&T Wireless (AWE)	telecom	asset rich
Cox Communications (COX)	telecom	asset rich
Edison Int'l (EIX)	energy	asset rich
Mirant Corp (MIR)	energy	takeover
Southwest Water (SWWC)	water	asset rich
Telefonica (TEF)	telecom	emerging giant

Income Objective

CONSERVATIVE HOLDINGS (65%) SECURITY AND TYPE (EXCHANGE: SYMBOL)	RISK LEVEL	GROWTH POTENTIAL
Broadwing 6.75% Conv Pf (NYSE: BRW B)	low	moderate
Dominion Res 8.125% of 6/15/2010	low	low
Mid-American En 7.23% of 9/15/2005	low	low
Mission Cap 8.5% MIPS B (NYSE: ME B)	moderate	moderate
Niagara Mohawk Holdings (NYSE: NMK)	moderate	moderate
No Ind P.S. 6% ARPS (NYSE: NI A)	very low	low
Southern Co 6.875% QUIPS (NYSE: SO C)	low	low
Texaco Cap ARPS (NYSE: TXC B)	very low	low
AGGRESSIVE HOLDINGS (35%) SECURITY AND TYPE (EXCHANGE: SYMBOL)	RISK LEVEL	GROWTH POTENTIAL
AES 6.75% Conv Pref (AES C)	moderate	high
Cox Comm PRIDES (NYSE: COX I)	moderate	high
El Paso Energy Part (NYSE: EPN)	moderate	moderate
EnergyEast (NYSE: EAS)	moderate	moderate
Kansas City P&L (NYSE: KLT)	moderate	moderate
Southern Company (NYSE: SO)	moderate	moderate
Xcel Energy (NYSE: XEL)	moderate	moderate

For Your Information

INVESTOR INFORMATION

Utility Forecaster—12 monthly issues, 12 pages. Regularly follows more than 200 energy, communications, and water companies, with specific buy/hold/sell advice. Provides wide range of company- and industry-specific information. Regular features include a table of information on all companies covered, portfolios for income and growth, spotlighted stocks for purchase, a dividend watch list, and more.

Utility Forecaster was named Best Investment Advisory by the Newsletter and Electronic Publishers Association in 1997 and 1999 and was cited for excellence in 1992, 2000, and 2001 (800-832-2330, utilityforecaster.com, $99/year).

Personal Finance—24 issues/year, 12 pages. Covers the waterfront of investments, with regular features on utilities and other income investments. Cited for Investment Advisory excellence by the Newsletter and Electronic Publishers Association nine of the 10 years to 2001. (800-832-2330, pfnewsletter.com, $99/year).

Power Plays—Fax/e-mail trading service spotlighting high-potential, short-term trading opportunities in the utility sector, mostly involving betting on the success of mergers (800-832-2330, $599/year).

Value Line—Still useful for sheer volume of information provided on a very wide range of companies. Energy, communications, and water utilities featured every three months. Copies can be found in most libraries, and on-line editions are available (valueline.com).

Yahoo!—Easy-to-follow finance web site offers access to range of information including direct links to company web sites, press releases, and reports on file with the Securities and Exchange Commission (yahoo.com).

CONSUMER INFORMATION

Consumers Reports—The most comprehensive shopping guide with no axe to grind except to pinpoint quality. Wide range of items covered. Energy and water efficiency of appliances is a regular feature. Also available online (consumersreports.com).

Consumers Union—Primary consumer-interest lobbying group with very active presence on Capitol Hill. Active in legislation with consumer angle (consumersunion.org).

Public Citizen—Critical Mass project has researched utility issues since the 1970s and is a valuable source of information on a wide range of topics including nuclear energy and green energy marketers (Citizen.org).

TURN (The Utility Reform Network)—Grassroots organization that regularly lobbies governments on consumer issues. Has been helpful in aiding consumer organizing.

Index